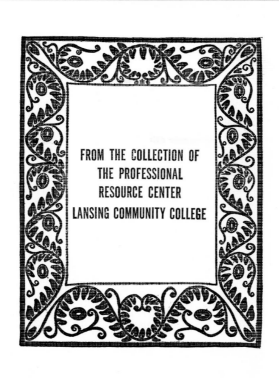

Jerry G. Gaff

General Education Today

A Critical Analysis
of Controversies,
Practices, and Reforms

Jossey-Bass Publishers
San Francisco • Washington • London • 1983

GENERAL EDUCATION TODAY
A Critical Analysis of Controversies,
Practices, and Reforms
    by Jerry G. Gaff

Copyright © 1983 by: Jossey-Bass Inc., Publishers
                     433 California Street
                     San Francisco, California 94104
                              &
                     Jossey-Bass Limited
                     28 Banner Street
                     London EC1Y 8QE

Library of Congress Cataloging in Publication Data

Gaff, Jerry G.
    General education today.

    Bibliography: p. 221
    Includes index.
    1. Universities and colleges—United States—Curricula.
2. Education, Humanistic—United States. 3. Educational
surveys—United States. I. Title.
LB2361.5.G33   1983   378'.199'0973   82-49037
ISBN 0-87589-560-3

Manufactured in the United States of America

The paper in this book meets the guidelines for
permanence and durability of the Committee on
Production Guidelines for Book Longevity of the
Council on Library Resources.

JACKET DESIGN BY WILLI BAUM

FIRST EDITION

Code 8305

*The Jossey-Bass Series
in Higher Education*

Contents

Preface   ix

The Author   xxi

Part One: Scope of the Controversy

1. The Ideal and the Issues   1

2. Voices in the Debate   30

Part Two: Current and Developing Practices

3. Toward a New Philosophy   59

4. Emerging Curricular Patterns   76

5. Rethinking Courses, Teaching, and Faculty
    Development   107

6. Providing Support Through Administration,
    Finance, and Evaluation   135

Part Three: Guidelines for Effective Change

7. Implementing Successful Curricular Reforms   163

8. Epilogue: Assessing Current Progress
    and Future Needs   187

    Appendix A. Association of American
                 Colleges Survey   197

    Appendix B. Directory of Institutions
                 Reviewing General Education   207

    References   221

    Index   235

Preface

General education is an idea whose time has come—again. Conferences have been held to discuss issues; books and articles have been written to expound analyses and to make proposals; projects have been initiated to stimulate improvements; associations have mounted programs to assist reform; and foundations have set up funding programs to support curricular change. Above all, hundreds of individual colleges and universities have taken concrete steps to strengthen their general education offerings.

  This is the first time since the years immediately following World War II that sustained national attention has been focused on general education. The publication in 1945 of the Harvard "Redbook," *General Education in a Free Society,* launched a wave of new programs. But circumstances have changed since then; rather than turning the clock back to those earlier concepts and practices, fresh approaches are needed today, and fortunately, as this volume indicates, they are starting

to emerge. For instance, private colleges and universities at the
earlier time were numerically and influentially dominant, and
the recommendations of the Harvard report were adopted widely. Now the system of postsecondary education is much more
differentiated, with the increase of community colleges, state
colleges and universities, and special purpose schools. The result
is that a single model of effective general education no longer
exists (if indeed it ever did); the recent curriculum proposals at
Harvard have been more controversial and less emulated at
other institutions than those three decades earlier. Second,
Western civilization, the heart of earlier integrated programs of
study, is no longer the only important tradition; larger global
perspectives are necessary in contemporary curriculums, reflecting the rise of the non-Western world in such areas as the Middle East, Africa, and Asia. Third, the increase in the diversity of
students is a fundamental change with increasing numbers of
women, adults, ethnic minority, part-time, poorly skilled, and
foreign students enrolled. Programs today must be designed to
realize the traditional values of general education for growing
numbers of nontraditional students. In short, any reformulation
of general education must be undertaken in light of contemporary realities.

The major task facing colleges and universities is not simply to reaffirm the values of general, or liberal, education but
also to fashion a new working consensus about a sound contemporary curriculum. The curriculum is, in the final analysis, a
social contract. It brings together the various purposes, alternative concepts, and multiple interests found on any campus into
an institution's statement about the meaning of a proper education. The earlier consensus has broken down, especially about
that portion of the curriculum outside a student's major field of
specialization; most colleges and universities must now renew
the social contract about the purposes of general education as
well as the means to achieve them.

This book analyzes the current attempts to reformulate
the general curriculum and discusses how campus leaders can
generate a meaningful consensus about the core of the undergraduate curriculum. Part One stresses the ideal of general edu-

cation and examines why its practice leaves so much to be desired. It also discusses the multiple voices and views about reformulating the general education portion of the curriculum. Because developing an educational philosophy shared by all segments of the college community and finding the means to carry that philosophy out in practice is an aspiration realized only infrequently, with great difficulty, and after long struggle, results of curriculum reviews conducted at many colleges are just beginning to appear. Part Two describes the educational philosophies, curricular structures and content, and the pedagogy that are emerging. It also deals with supports needed for general education—administering, financing, and evaluating new programs. Part Three considers effective strategies for curriculum change, summarizes the progress to date, and points out challenges that remain if the current revival is to realize its full potential.

What comes out of all the ferment concerning general education, in the end, is determined by what happens on individual campuses, not by recommendations of commissions, no matter how prestigious, nor by calls for particular actions by individuals, no matter how brilliant. My approach in this volume, therefore, is institutional. That is, the primary source of information derives from individual campuses; it is found largely in "fugitive literature," such as "idea papers" by faculty members or administrators, committee reports, resolutions drawn and debated in academic senates, funded project proposals and reports, and other unpublished campus materials. Similarly, the primary audiences are members of the campus community—faculty members, administrators, students, and trustees—as well as all those interested in developments in higher education, such as state officials, journalists, and public school educators.

The institutional focus implies other aspects of my approach. For instance, it is also eclectic, since few examples of conceptually "pure" curriculums can be found in colleges and universities; most general education programs in practice embrace many different concepts and components. Further, it is practical, since what matters most are not the views of individ-

uals about what a program should be but practices that actually become part of the curriculum. And it is action-oriented,
since this analysis derives from actions at a large number of colleges, and since I hope it might spark further changes in institutions of higher learning.

In presenting a comprehensive analysis of today's revival
of general education, this volume differs significantly from
other recent works. It differs from the three volumes prepared
by the Carnegie Foundation for the Advancement of Teaching
under the leadership of Clark Kerr (Carnegie Foundation, 1977;
Rudolph, 1977; Levine, 1978) in that the focus is on general
education rather than the entire curriculum and the stress is on
what large numbers of institutions are actually doing to reformulate this part of the curriculum. It differs from the publications of the subsequent incarnation of the Carnegie Foundation
under the egis of Ernest Boyer (Boyer and Levine, 1981; Boyer
and Hechinger, 1981) as well as the writings of individual scholars (Bailey, 1976; Conrad and Weyer, 1980) by dealing more extensively with concrete institutional realities, practical problems, and specific program alternatives. It differs from the
various institutional reports that are available, such as those
from Harvard, Amherst, and Columbia, by drawing on many
more contexts than a single setting. It differs from reports of
funded projects, such as National Project IV: Examining the
Varieties of Liberal Education, sponsored by the Fund for the
Improvement of Postsecondary Education, and the Project on
General Education Models (Wee, 1981), by reaching beyond the
borders of any single project to deal with the entire national
scene. It differs from handbooks and resource guides, such as
those of Chickering and Associates (1981) and the Project on
General Education Models (1980), by providing a more coherent and integrated treatment of general education. In fact, it is
the kind of book I wanted to give to key participants of the
Project on General Education Models when I began to direct
that enterprise, but nothing like it was then available. It is largely because of what I learned from that experience that the present volume exists—and that it might serve to fill that gap for
others seeking to restore coherence and integrity to the undergraduate curriculum.

The Project on General Education Models (GEM) was sponsored by the Society for Values in Higher Education as a three-year (1978-1981) collaboration of twelve different colleges and universities taking concrete steps to strengthen their general education programs. It was supported by grants from the Exxon Education Foundation and the Fund for the Improvement of Postsecondary Education (FIPSE). The institutions were selected purposefully to be diverse so that different "models" of operational programs could emerge and we could learn about general education as it was conducted in various contexts. The institutions included Bucknell University, Carroll College (Wisconsin), Catonsville Community College (Maryland), Community College of Denver, Florida A & M University, Indiana University at South Bend, Northeastern Illinois University, Oregon State University, Rochester Institute of Technology (both the College of General Studies and the National Technical Institute for the Deaf), State University of New York College at Brockport, University of the Pacific, and Valparaiso University.

The design of the project called for each institution to establish a task force consisting of faculty members, an academic administrator, and students. The task force reviewed the general education program and provided leadership for making revisions. Since the applications to participate in Project GEM were submitted by the president and contained a letter of support from a key faculty body, the task forces were established squarely within the authority structure of each institution. The provision of institutional support was required as a condition of participation, including some reassigned time for at least the leader(s) of the task forces, travel funds for members to attend project-wide meetings, and small amounts of funds to support their work. The upshot of these arrangements was that each task force was supported by its school while it worked to fashion improvements in general education.

The project was administered by a small staff and governed by a blue-ribbon advisory board. The staff, board, and consultants provided assistance to the task forces. At the outset, Project GEM published a resource book, *General Education: Issues and Resources*; conducted a student survey across the several institutions; and developed a faculty interview for use where appropriate. On an on-going basis, the project held meetings for representatives to share experiences, learn about progress at other institutions, and discuss substantive issues; held week-long summer conferences during which task force members worked on their own agendas with the assistance of consultants; published a newsletter to share information and air issues among member institutions as well as to communicate with the larger academic world; provided occasional consultation to the campuses; and arranged for dissemination activities to assist colleagues at other institutions with the review process.

When Project GEM terminated, I joined the staff of the Association of American Colleges (AAC), where, with the assistance of a grant from the Exxon Education Foundation, I continued to work on curricular matters, especially general education. In addition to conducting workshops, organizing a national conference, and operating a clearinghouse of information and materials, I was able to conduct a survey to determine the curriculums that are beginning to emerge from this era of reform. Thomas Klein, a National Fellow at AAC and a faculty member from Bowling Green University, worked with me to conduct the survey; largely because of his efforts we obtained reliable data about the nature of the curriculum changes that are taking place at many colleges and universities around the country. A summary of these results is in Appendix A.

I have been fortunate during these jobs with Project GEM and AAC to come into contact with many institutions actively reviewing and revising their programs. A directory of hundreds of institutions conducting formal reviews has been compiled and is in Appendix B; descriptive materials have been collected from the majority. Further, I have learned a great deal from serving on the staff of workshops and conferences, consulting with a number of campuses, participating in special curriculum projects, and discussing issues with research scholars and leaders of various national and regional organizations. In short, this manuscript rests on an extensive range of experience and data, which collectively provides a broad and solid basis for making sense of the current revival.

The writings of a person necessarily reflect his own personal perspectives and predilections, and a little confession may help the readers identify some of my biases. First, I deeply believe in the ideal of general education, and I have pursued it as a student, teacher, researcher, and director of national projects. It is gratifying that, after many years of neglect, we are at last resurrecting this ideal and revising the curriculum to achieve it. Revitalizing undergraduate education requires not just a change of mind among the "infidels" who do not share this ideal but also among the "true believers" who have failed to adapt the purposes of liberal learning to the needs of today's students and modern circumstances. Hence, the proper step, I believe, is not the simplistic and political one of imposing more requirements in the liberal arts and sciences but for both those with beliefs and those with doubts to reformulate the core of the undergraduate curriculum appropriate to our times.

Second, after working in the area of faculty development, I am convinced that the problem with general education is basically a problem with the faculty. Faculty specialization has fostered a narrowness of vision; academic disciplines have worked against serious intellectual discussion among experts in different fields; the emphasis on cognitive rationality has all but purged values and feelings from our professional concern; the focus on academic respectability has turned faculty away from the fundamental, if messy, social and political problems facing our society, indeed, all of humanity; and the current period of retrenchment has pitted faculty against their colleagues and reduced much of the debate about the curriculum to self-serving statements and protective posturing. Yet these trends seem to have reached a watershed. The solution, just as much as the problem, rests with the faculty and now is within their grasp. Many faculty on every campus I visit are eager to pitch in to reformulate the curriculum; several are broadening their own understanding and renewing themselves even as they provide general education for their students.

Before getting involved with faculty development, I taught in one experimental cluster college and studied others. We need to learn the lessons from those innovations of the 1960s, as well as from more recent experiments with women's studies, ethnic studies, and adult education, so that our current reforms may be more effective and longer lasting. One of the key lessons is that most of these earlier efforts were radical alternatives that often were tacked onto the periphery of an institution. What is happening today is that the general education program is being redefined on an institution-wide basis and is emerging as the centerpiece of the undergraduate curriculum for all students. My interest is that we preserve both nontraditional curriculum features, which have brought new students into higher education and validated alternative practices, as well as traditional features of liberal learning as we reshape mainstream general education for all students.

I have developed an interest in the interplay of ideas and action as a result of conducting research and directing improvement projects. I have observed that much of the rhetoric about general and liberal education is vacuous and little more than petty pieties—ideas that lack connectedness to actions. The fact of the matter is that, despite proclamations about the virtues of liberal education, many students pass through the curriculum without becoming liberated in thought, emotion, or behavior. On the other hand, many well-meaning people are seeking to vitalize general education without reference to the vast amount of scholarship and published literature on the topic. Faculty members tinker with their courses, administrators add patches to a shabby curriculum, and curriculum committees adopt little more than an autobiographical approach to curriculum change. These are mindless actions that are inadequate to the task. At their best, ideas and action, scholarship and reforms, are joined to produce changes that yield truly liberal learning among students. This requires what Robert Merton called "theories of the middle range," not global philosophical statements that are too amorphous to relate to specific actions or discrete empirical findings that, even in aggregate, fail to produce useful generalizations or principles. This volume concentrates on middle-level statements that connect ideas about general education with concrete actions taken by a number of colleges and universities to strengthen their programs.

Having worked in several academic environments and

most recently in the nation's capital, I have come to see the curriculum as a mirror, albeit a far from perfect reflection, of larger cultural circumstances. The disappearance of community, the rise of special interest politics, the recognition of limits to growth, the prevalence of "do your own thing," the rise of the non-Western world—these and many other social trends have their counterparts in the academy and in curriculum reformulation. For instance, it is folly to expect that a college curriculum can have coherence when the culture surrounding the college itself has little unity. Yet, the effort to seek commonalities and design an effective general education program is one way to help renew a college or university, one step toward reestablishing confidence in social institutions, and another measure to cope with the myriad of problems that confront us as a society and as a species.

The current interest in general education signals a renewed concern for undergraduate rather than graduate education, for the liberal arts rather than career preparation, and for general competence rather than technical specialization. Although some critics dismiss this revival as a mere fad, I see these as substantive rather than superficial issues; the reorientation in values that are involved will take years to complete. From my perspective, the "movement" of general education is just beginning and will occupy center stage in our colleges and universities for a long time. This judgment is based not on wishful thinking but on hardheaded realism that such basic shifts are necessary for the survival of many institutions of higher learning. So many institutions are giving attention to general education today precisely because they are gearing up to face the even leaner years ahead by strengthening the heart of their undergraduate programs. It is my hope that this volume will contribute in some small way to their success.

Acknowledgments

Although my name appears as the author of this volume, it would prove to be a tangled web, indeed, were one to attempt to trace the origins of the ideas, analyses, judgments, and even

certain phrases that are found herein. Proper professional recognition, of course, is given for specific contributions throughout these pages, but that is an inadequate mechanism to recognize the large number of significant, yet more subtle, influences
that shaped my writing. Here a more complete acknowledgment
of the many people who contributed to my understanding of
general education and who played a role in preparing this manuscript is appropriate.

Because the most formative experience in my understanding of this topic occurred when I directed the Project on General Education Models, my greatest indebtedness is to individuals associated with that enterprise. Foremost among them are
members of the project committee, under the very able chair-
manship of Susan Wittig, who provided policy leadership—Her-
man Blake, Patricia Cross, Joseph Katz, Patricia Kendall, Charles
Reynolds, Gresham Riley, Donald Stewart, and David Wee. All
these individuals were generous with their time and energy, and
every one provided intellectual insights, sound counsel, and personal support at various stages of our work. John Maguire, president, and David Smith, executive director, of the Society for
Values in Higher Education made especially important contributions in gaining funding and administering the effort. Rebecca
Yount and Barbara Franck, each of whom served as my assistant,
contributed far more than they know. Their hard work, common sense, and uncommon good spirits made it possible for all
the various pieces of the puzzle to come together in the project
and therefore in this volume. Many consultants were helpful,
but Arthur Levine and Jack Lindquist deserve to be singled out
for their special assistance; they taught all the rest of us much
about the substance and process of curriculum change.

The troops on the front line, the ones who were faced
with the obligation to make demonstrable progress in revising
the curriculum, were faculty members, administrators, and students serving on the task forces at Project GEM's member colleges
and universities. Although there are too many to name individu-
ally, even in this format, those persons who provided liaison
between the campuses and the project office were a continuous
source of information, ideas, wisdom, and even much-valued wit
—Richard Clinton, Barry Culhane, Michael Davis, Reynold Feld-

man, William Frascella, Clifford Hand, Judith Peters, Marcus Reidel, Pamela Phillips Riley, Donna Skane, Robert Strayer, Mary Sullivan, Roger Sweeney, Glen Van Haitsma, Eva Wanton, and Wilson Watson. These individuals, and through them their colleagues too, taught me a great deal about the subtlety, complexity, and practicality of reforming general education.

At the Exxon Education Foundation, Richard Johnson and Robert Payton were extremely helpful. At the Fund for the Improvement of Postsecondary Education, Ernest Bartell, Charles Bunting, and Hilda Moskowitz provided welcomed assistance.

My involvement with the Association of American Colleges, six years as a tenant while directing projects for the Society for Values in Higher Education and one as a staff member, has been valuable in many ways. During my tenant days, I was able to stay abreast of developments in liberal learning and the curriculum around the country. When I became a member of the staff, Mark Curtis, president, and William O'Connell, vice-president, provided me opportunities to work on a number of significant curriculum activities, primarily in connection with the Project on Redefining the Meaning and Purpose of Baccalaureate Degrees. They also allowed me time, amid other pressing needs, to complete this manuscript.

The sheer mechanics of preparing a manuscript such as this are formidable, and many people assisted with the task. Margaret Foster prepared an early draft of Chapter Two as an internship in her doctoral program at the University of Maryland. David Gaff worked as a research assistant. Phyllis Meyers, Carole Johnson, Margaret Brown, and Ernestine Harrison typed various portions of the manuscript. An earlier draft was reviewed by Clifton Conrad, JB Hefferlin, and Arthur Levine, each of whom offered suggestions that have made this final version better than it would otherwise have been.

If any "single-authored" book ever was a group effort, it is this one. Even though I am fully responsible for the treatment of the topic, this volume, very simply, could not have been written without the assistance of these persons.

Washington, D.C.   Jerry G. Gaff
January 1983

The Author

Jerry G. Gaff is director of curriculum development at the Association of American Colleges. A native of Fort Wayne, Indiana, he received his A.B. degree from DePauw University in 1958. He pursued interdisciplinary studies before earning the Ph.D. degree in social psychology at Syracuse University in 1965. He has held faculty positions at Hobart College, University of the Pacific, the University of California, Berkeley, and California State College, Sonoma.

During his appointment at Berkeley's Center for Research and Development in Higher Education, he conducted studies of the attitudes, values, and behavior of faculty members, and particularly the impact of faculty members on students. This work resulted in several articles and led to further research as well as to national action projects and work with colleges and universities to improve the quality of teaching, learning, and the curriculum.

Through his studies, projects, and related professional activities, Gaff has contributed to three different movements to improve undergraduate education. During the 1960s, while a teacher at Raymond College, an experimental cluster college at the University of the Pacific, he conducted a study of the consequences of several innovations. Subsequently he wrote and compiled *The Cluster College* (1970), which was the first systematic analysis and assessment of this form of experimental college.

During the 1970s Gaff helped define the terms of the faculty development movement with his book *Toward Faculty Renewal* (1975), outlining the basic premises and alternative ways of carrying out faculty development programs to emphasize excellence in teaching as well as in scholarship. He established the Center for Professional Development within the California State University and Colleges system and directed the Project on Institutional Renewal Through the Improvement of Teaching for the Society for Values in Higher Education. These efforts gave him an opportunity to help establish operational programs, translating his ideas into practical campus activities.

Since 1978 he has been working in the area of general education, primarily through directing the project on General Education Models, another activity of the Society for Values in Higher Education. Since 1981 he has continued to work on the curriculum at the Association of American Colleges, where he was a chief staff member of the Project on Redefining the Meaning and Purposes of Baccalaureate Degrees. This volume reflects his wide experience with several colleges and universities intent on strengthening their curriculum offerings.

Gaff has written, lectured, and consulted on such topics as faculty evaluation, institutional change strategies, college structures, institutional vitality, as well as a range of concerns about teaching, learning, and the curriculum.

General Education Today

A Critical Analysis
of Controversies,
Practices, and Reforms

Chapter One

The Ideal
and the Issues

One of the most encouraging and important developments now taking place in American higher education is the reformulation of general education programs. The current national effort to restructure and redefine undergraduate general education was touched off by three separate events in 1977. That year the Carnegie Foundation for the Advancement of Teaching published the first of its volumes on the curriculum and labeled general education "a disaster area." At Harvard University the Task Force on the Core Curriculum issued its long-awaited report, and the faculty began to discuss proposals to strengthen undergraduate education. In addition, U.S. Commissioner of Education Ernest L. Boyer and his assistant Martin Kaplan called for the creation of a core curriculum that would emphasize our common needs and thereby increase the chances of survival for the human species (Boyer and Kaplan, 1977).

Other prestigious persons and interest groups have joined the chorus calling for reform. The President's Commission on

1

Foreign Language and International Studies (1979) lamented
the neglect of foreign language and international studies, while a
foundation commission (Commission on the Humanities, 1980)
declared that the humanities are fragmented, poorly supported,
and losing ground. A government report prepared by the National Science Foundation and the U.S. Department of Education decried the fact that large numbers of students graduate
with "the most rudimentary notions of science, mathematics,
and technology [that] portends trouble in the decades ahead"
(1980, p. 3). In their various ways, each of these reports con-
demned the quality of vital components of undergraduate general education and documented detrimental results both for
college students and for the welfare of the nation.

     These reports reinforced the concern for quality in high-
er education all across the country. A host of conferences have
been held to discuss issues; articles and books written to expound analyses and make proposals; projects initiated to solve
problems; programs mounted by associations to assist reforms;
and funding programs established by private and public agencies
to support improvements. Above all, hundreds of individual colleges and universities have taken concrete steps to strengthen
their general education programs. Included are schools of all
types—two year and four year, private and public, coed and single sex, liberal arts and professional—located in all sections of
the country. Together, these events indicate that a veritable
movement to reformulate general education is taking place on
the nation's campuses.

The Ideal

     A broad general education is an ideal that has guided
American colleges since their inception. Indeed, the earliest colleges offered a broad but uniform classical education for all students. With the rise of science, the growth and subdivision of
knowledge into academic disciplines, and the need for specialization, depth of study in a specialized field took its place alongside the earlier ideal. Together, breadth and depth have since
been regarded as the cornerstone of a quality baccalaureate education.

Despite its apparent simplicity and common currency, the phrase *general education* remains ambiguous, and its various interpreters each propose different standards of practice and directions for reform. Four distinctive philosophical approaches to general education are at the heart of the current debate—idealism, progressivism, essentialism, and pragmatism.

Idealism is well defined by John Henry (Cardinal) Newman ([1873], 1947), who saw the university serving simply as a setting for teaching and learning. Newman would not have considered research an appropriate function, and he would have been appalled at recent proposals to use the university as a remedy for social ills, whether for liberal or conservative purposes. Ideally, teaching and learning are to occur in a community of scholars; current practices—such as commuter-students and credit for prior experience—preclude participation in an academic community and are anathema to Newman's vision. The goal is a liberal education, without specific practical or vocational applications, but one that prepares students for all of life. Humanistic study, especially of religion and literature, is deemed the best means to this end.

Newman's ideas have become conventional wisdom within many liberal arts circles. Contemporary idealism is perhaps best illustrated by Leon Botstein, who, as president of Bard College, author, lecturer, and commentator, is a forceful spokesman for general education. Botstein (1979a, 1979b) believes that recent changes in liberal arts curriculums often lack vision and that expressions of idealism cleverly mask self-interest. He argues that reforms must stress substance rather than methods, particularly the "central political and personal questions facing students." Colleges should "disband a narrow departmental structure and stop emulating universities in their thinking, governance, and structure" (1979b, p. 36). Furthermore, he observes that the United States is facing a genuine cultural crisis and that the amelioration of American education requires the revision of aspects of American culture. Though Botstein addresses contemporary issues, his vision, like Newman's, advocates a liberal education consisting of substantive humanistic study, as well as science and technology for non-scientists in teaching-oriented colleges.

The progressivist perspective of Alfred North Whitehead, mathematician and philosopher, characterizes another approach to general education. Whitehead (1929) sees no essential difference between the study of the general culture and specialized knowledge; both are integral parts of a full education. Further, education must offer something useful: effective education presents concepts relevant to life, not inert ideas. He argues that general education should be concerned with the concrete present and that the primary value of the past is to guide the learner's present and future life. Whitehead's views, along with those of John Dewey and others, have contributed to the progressive spirit that inspired so much of higher education's development, including the establishment of experimental colleges during the 1920s and 1930s, such as Bennington and Sarah Lawrence.

Progressivism informs the ideals of those who approach education from the point of view of the student. For example, Stephen Bailey holds that education must serve three basic purposes, helping persons "anticipate and increase their capacity for creative engagements with major predictable changes in their stages of development;... to cope, to work, and to use their free time in ways that minimize neurotic anxiety and boredom and that maximize inner fulfillment and joyful reciprocities; ... learn the arts of affecting the enveloping polity in order to promote justice and to secure the blessings of liberty for others as well as for themselves" (1977, pp. 254-255). Curricular implications of this philosophy are that courses should have utility for the future lives of students and that interdisciplinary approaches should function "as supplements to specialization, as links to connect specializations, as new lenses through which to see the three dimensional character of all specializations" (p. 257).

The person perhaps most identified with general education in the United States is Robert Maynard Hutchins, who represents an essentialist perspective, believing that there is an essential core of knowledge that should be taught. Hutchins (1936) states that the goal of general education is to train the intellect and that the best way to accomplish this is to study great books, "books which have through the centuries attained the dimensions of classics" and are "contemporary in every age" (p. 78). Teaching, he claims, should be done by faculty members with wide-ranging intellectual interests who are devoted to this form of undergraduate instruction. He charges the modern university with being too utilitarian, offering subjects that are vocational, and employing faculty whose interests are in research rather than teaching or whose talents center in narrow, specialized topics rather than broad issues. He accuses universities of undermining education with a mechanical system of quantifying instruction and counting credit units. He also believes that universities' acceptance of an extracurriculum diverts attention from the substance of education. For these reasons, he created a separate college at the University of Chicago to function as an enclave for general education.

Ernest Boyer and two coauthors—Martin Kaplan and Arthur Levine—are contemporary essentialists in that they insist on a particular content of general education. Boyer and Kaplan (1977) call for a common core curriculum with four special qualities: a few clusters of ideas and events that influenced the past, key issues that affect the present, some images and alternatives for the future, and the formulation of values and personal beliefs. Boyer and Levine (1981) remain committed to a core but advise a somewhat different content. They advocate general education programs that stress subjects common to all people: use of symbols, membership in groups and institutions, activities of consumption and production, relationships with nature, sense of time, and values and beliefs. Despite their disclaimer that these ideas are merely suggestions and not a blueprint, they argue strongly for students to become knowledgeable about each of their topics.

Pragmatism, the final philosophical perspective, is personified by Clark Kerr. Kerr has been called "the philosopher of the modern university" mainly because his pragmatism recognizes academic pluralism and complexity. The multiversity, he writes, "is not one community but several—the community of the undergraduate and the community of the graduate; the community of the humanist, the community of the social scientist, and the community of the scientist; the communities of the professional schools; the community of all the nonacademic personnel; the community of the administrators. . . . A community, like the medieval communities of masters and students, should have common interests; in the multiversity, they are quite varied, even conflicting. A community should have a soul, a single animating principle; the multiversity has several" (1966, pp. 18-19).

A multiversity can offer a variety of learning opportunities for both students and faculty, but, like life itself, it is also complex, confusing, and difficult to control. Guided by a strong sense of pragmatism, Kerr suggests modest improvements—not the radical restructuring demanded by Hutchins—for undergraduate education. He advocates rewarding faculty for teaching at the undergraduate level, giving more attention to the preparation of generalists, and individualizing and personalizing large and impersonal universities. As head of the Carnegie Commission and Council of Higher Education, Kerr has effectively generated both scholarship and practical interest in renewing general education at the undergraduate level.

Another pragmatist, a contemporary of Kerr, is David Riesman, who is unmatched as an observer of the academy. He pointed out the snakelike academic procession through which institutions seek to emulate those they take to be the leaders; chronicled the ascendancy of professors and their departments over other contending powers of the university; and described reforms of the 1960s, both telic—those embodying a distinctive set of purposes—and popular—those responding to the demands of minorities and other previously disenfranchised groups. In his latest book (1981, p. xix), Riesman confesses, "I believe in incremental improvements particular to a time and locale, rather than packaged reforms applicable anytime everywhere." In an interview about this work (Scully, 1981, p. 20), he is quoted as saying, "I'm proud to be a tinkerer. That's all one is likely to be able to do." Riesman's is a voice for the pragmatic principle of meliorist change.

The ideas and perspectives of these leaders—historical and contemporary—are integral parts of the current debate, providing useful, though limited, approaches. The idealists' vision is appealing, particularly in small, residential, homogeneous, liberal arts colleges; but it has severe limitations in large, commuter, open-door, comprehensive institutions and in major research universities. Similarly, the progressivists' conception of knowledge as a seamless fabric is attractive, but it does not speak to the modern university, in which knowledge is subdivided into tightly guarded territories called academic disciplines, each with a distinctive language and style. Further, while progressivists advocate student choice, the last decade has shown that many students opt for narrowly specialized, vocationally useful studies rather than for a broad general education. Regarding the essentialists' claim that there are eternal truths revealed in a limited number of great books, many educators might agree in the abstract but they lack consensus about the specific truths or books. Finally, though the politics of general education reform, like politics itself, is the art of the possible, and the modest improvements of pragmatists are better than none at all, piecemeal changes do not satisfy the call for comprehensive reform.

But although idealists, progressivists, essentialists, and pragmatists differ in substantive ways, all strongly favor something that advocates of each view would call general education. Indeed, the term, while large enough to encompass various interpretations, does possess a recognizable configuration of qualities. In its broadest terms, general education:

- is rooted in the liberal tradition and involves study of the basic liberal arts and sciences;
- stresses breadth and provides students with familiarity with various branches of human understanding as well as the methodologies and languages particular to different bodies of knowledge;
- strives to foster integration, synthesis, and connectedness of knowledge rather than discrete bits of specialized information;
- encourages the understanding and appreciation of one's heritage as well as respect for other peoples and cultures;
- includes an examination of values—both those relevant to

current controversial issues and those implicit in a discipline's methodology;
- prizes a common educational experience for at least part of
  the college years;
- requires the mastery of the linguistic, analytic, critical, and
  computational skills necessary for lifelong learning; and
- fosters the development of personal qualities, such as tolerance of ambiguity, empathy for persons with different values, and an expanded view of self.

Although some definitions place greater emphasis on
some of these qualities than on others, this list does constitute
a functional understanding of general education. Despite the absence of a single formal definition, these shared notions express
aspirations that serve as the rallying cry for the current revival
of general education. But, as we shall see, attempting to translate these several qualities into specific curricular proposals is
extremely difficult; educators frequently part company over
ideas for advancing any particular change (Reynolds, 1981).

Tarnishing of the Ideal

An ideal is only as powerful as its corporate expression,
that is, the structure of how concerned people realize their aspiration. Maher (1980) asserts that the ideal of general education is very much alive, as seen in the fondest hopes of teachers
for their students, idealistic rhetoric in professional meetings,
flowery phrases in college catalogues, and constant proposals
for improvements. But, understating the case, he adds that,
"Our corporate expression leaves something to be desired" (p.
6). Indeed, he is so pessimistic about significantly altering prevailing patterns that he calls for the self-empowerment of "free-
lance general educators" who are attuned to the broader objectives of undergraduate education and alert for the "teachable
moment" when they can enrich the lives of students.

What is the corporate expression of general education today? One answer is that the *amount* of general education in the
undergraduate course of study has diminished. A national study

by Robert Blackburn and associates (1976) confirms that in four-year colleges general education constituted 43 percent of the curriculum in 1967 but only 33 percent by 1974; in two-year colleges it declined from 59 to 43 percent in the same period. Fully 72 percent of all four-year institutions reduced the amount of general education in their curriculums. Unpublished data from a Carnegie Foundation restudy of the same institutions in 1980 detect a reversal—requirements were up an average of 5 percent, particularly in natural sciences, social sciences, and English composition; however, this still leaves levels lower than the earlier ones. Furthermore, the character of general education programs has changed. Four-fifths of the four-year institutions and three-fourths of the two-year colleges decreased the proportion of prescribed courses. Blackburn and his coauthors conclude: "There has been a marked move away from specific course requirements toward distribution requirements, for which the student selects from among a more or less specified set of course offerings. Furthermore, free choice has substantially increased in those institutions in which distribution requirements were previously the norm. The general education curriculum today is much less structured than it used to be" (p. 33).

Although these trends are starting to be reversed, several consequences flow from them. First, much more responsibility for structuring general education rests with students; they may choose courses that are of immediate interest or have short-term vocational value rather than courses that have more enduring value. Second, some departments have strengthened their hold over the curriculum, not by increasing the number of hours required for a major but by encouraging students to take cognate courses that buttress the major. Blackburn and his colleagues report that at institutions that greatly increased electives, students tended to choose courses within their major divisions rather than range farther afield. Third, the loosening of liberal arts requirements allowed professional and preprofessional programs to expand. Such programs typically require fewer general education courses than do concentrations in arts and sciences colleges.

A second description of our current corporate expression is derived from our institutions' organization of general education. An analysis of college catalogues from a representative national sample by the Carnegie Council on Policy Studies (cited by Levine, 1978, pp. 9-15) reveals that 85 percent of all institutions have distribution requirements. Some schools have rather strict regulations about which courses are acceptable, while others provide only loose guidelines. Students typically are required to take a certain number of courses in each of the major divisions of study, usually lower-division introductory surveys often taught by the lecture method to large classes. All too often, however, such requirements serve political purposes more than educational ones; they constitute the departments' compromises about how to carve up the curricular pie rather than a belief that certain kinds of learning, subsumed by the phrase general education, are crucial. Departments seldom look at general education as an integrated whole; in the words of Maher, they are more engaged in the fine art of "body snatching" than in educating students.

The second most common form of requirements is a core curriculum, a configuration of courses required of all students. Although the core may be a series of courses in certain academic disciplines, it is more commonly interdisciplinary and organized around a theme or issue, such as the history of Western civilization. According to the Carnegie study, 10 percent of the institutions have a core curriculum, although the number may have increased as a result of recent attention to this form.

This form of requirements is not a panacea. First, a core is most commonly found and is most successful in small colleges with a relatively homogeneous student body. In these settings there can be some consensus about which knowledge is most worth having, and a required core is not considered unduly confining by students or faculty. Few schools, however, fit this description. Second, the half-life of interdisciplinary core curriculums is quite short, because such curriculums cut across the grain of academic disciplinary structure. Bailey, referring to these kinds of courses, observes, "Required general education courses, whatever good they did the first generation of teachers and students who participated, have a long history of progressive disaffection, increased deputization to lower academic ranks, and general faculty antagonism" (1977, p. 253). Third, interdisciplinary core curriculums are quite difficult to execute. Faculty must range outside the comfortable confines and familiar language of their fields; they must master content outside their specialties; and they must negotiate pedagogical and personal styles with colleagues with whom they share teaching responsibility. It is little wonder, then, that the past few years have witnessed reversals in highly touted interdisciplinary core curriculums at such schools as the cluster colleges at the University of California, Santa Cruz, as well as the dismantling of the University College at Michigan State University, one of the leading general education programs among large universities.

The third form of organization, free electives, is employed by only a handful of schools. Individualized curricular contracts based on students' interests and future plans, such as those offered at Empire State College and some of the newer adult education programs, are of this type. The amount of general education coursework students elect depends on the attitudes of the faculty, the quality of advising, and the availability of courses.

Why have we failed to give adequate corporate expression to our ideal? Historical trends have run counter to general education, faculty culture has subverted it, new students have challenged it, institutional differentiation has complicated it, and societal changes have undermined it. These factors are obviously interrelated, and collectively they have led to a weakening of general education to the point where Boyer and Levine declare (1981, p. 3), "General education is the spare room of academia, with no one responsible for its oversight and everyone permitted to use it as he will." Let us examine each of these causes in turn.

Historical Trends. During the last quarter of the nineteenth century, the idea of the university was implanted in American soil, took root, and flourished. Research and the advancement of knowledge, rather than preparation of a leisure class of gentlemen, became higher education's central purpose. New facilities were needed, such as libraries with many current volumes and laboratories with new equipment. Faculty needed to be trained as specialists, and universities organized into separate departments and professional schools to pursue particular branches of knowledge. The elective system, and later the distribution scheme, were natural consequences of specialization, and they replaced the classical curriculum. By the turn of the century the essential forms of the modern university were well on their way to becoming institutionalized. At first they were adopted in leading universities, but gradually they spread to other institutions. As Wegener (1978) points out, the new framework provided a sense of dignity for the new professoriate, worth for their productions, and contempt for the earlier drudgery of schoolmastering, but "it was not always clear why there needed to be students at all, or put the other way around, why there was any intrinsic connection between investigation and education or teaching" (p. 17).

This situation, or more accurately its extreme forms, has provoked two major efforts to revitalize general education during this century, one following each of the world wars. New colleges, programs, and courses were created during these revivals to redress the balance with specialism and attempt to compensate "for the narrowness that made specialization so dehumanizing, divisive, and incapable of providing any common ground or bond among educated people" (Rudolph, 1977, p. 256). Yet these efforts ultimately met with failure: "Dramatic experiments in general education, books and pamphlets explaining the need and extolling a plan, even a widespread wish that something might be done to compensate for the loss of unity and shared learning did not succeed in changing the focus of the curriculum from the special to the general. Where large universities created colleges of general studies, the new colleges did not lead to the transformation of the universities. Where highly publicized general education requirements reshaped the course of study in the 1940s and 1950s, less publicized erosion of those requirements took place in the 1960s and 1970s" (p. 253). "Breadth, distribution, and general education were the hobby horses of new presidents, ambitious deans, and well-meaning humanists of the sort who were elected to curriculum committees by colleagues as a gesture of token support for the idea of liberal learning" (p. 253), but the interests of the department, major, and faculty specialists prevailed.

Despite the pessimism of his historical analysis, Rudolph concludes with a note of optimism, suggesting that the unfavorable job market for college graduates may be good news for general education: "If there are not sufficient jobs available to justify an endless production of proficient technicians, . . . perhaps we can stop making technicians and get back to the business of making human beings. The time may be at hand when a reevaluation of academic purpose and philosophy will encourage the curricular developments that will focus on the lives we lead, their quality, the enjoyment they give us, and the wisdom with which we lead them. . . . And perhaps, once more, the idea of an educated person will have become a usable ideal" (p. 289). Still, the long-term movement has been toward specialization and preparation of knowledgeable experts, with periodic short-lived reactions that have stemmed the tide but not reversed the fundamental character of the academic enterprise.

Faculty Culture. The classic analysis of faculty culture is provided by Jencks and Riesman (1968), who claim that a veritable "academic revolution" has lead to the ascendancy of faculty members and to the widespread adoption of their values in the academy. Within this faculty culture, research and publication are valued more highly than teaching; graduate education more than undergraduate; advanced courses more than introductory ones; and the interests of the department more than those of the institution as a whole. Undergraduate general education for nonmajors is considered the least important of activities.

Faculty also highly value freedom. Of course, they rightfully insist on the academic freedom to pursue truth no matter where it leads and to teach the truth even when it conflicts with the teachings of religion, conventional society, or other institutions. Faculty have also sought, and in most instances gained, authority over the curriculum and instruction; over the recruitment, appointment, promotion, and tenure processes; and, through individual research grants, over the conditions of their work. The academic revolution has affected all types of colleges and universities, particularly the leading research universities and elite liberal arts colleges.

Faculty involvement in hiring has led to the appointment of a large number of highly qualified specialists who lack a broad general education. General education is of relatively little concern to them, and they are not prepared to teach broad interdisciplinary courses. Teaching an introductory survey of their own disciplines is the easiest way to dispense with the task. Indeed, the introductory survey course plays a critical role in faculty culture. It subsidizes the research, graduate, and upper-division interests of the faculty. Since a department's budget depends on student enrollment, large lower-division courses in effect support the advanced intellectual interests of the faculty, although such courses provide students with less-than-stimulating circumstances for learning.

The reduction of general education requirements during the late 1960s and early 1970s was perhaps the last phase of the academic revolution, liberating faculty more than students. No longer did faculty have to toil in required general education courses for nonmajors, many of whom were little interested in their subjects. Just as the lifting of *in loco parentis* regulations freed faculty from enforcing parental rules, the abolition of curricular requirements kept the distractions from undergraduate nonmajors to a minimum. It allowed faculty to advance their departments, their research, their specialties, and the teaching of their majors—at the expense of the interests of the institution as a whole and at the expense of a sound general education for all students. Such a strategy may have served adequately during a time of academic expansion, but it poses serious problems when research funds dry up and a department loses majors. The very academic values advanced by the faculty are threatened when student enrollment declines during a period of retrenchment.

New Students. The predominance of faculty culture during the 1960s was fueled by the ever-increasing number of students in undergraduate, graduate, and professional schools. Increased enrollments permitted bigger budgets, the hiring of more faculty, the proliferation of specialized courses, and the mass production of general education. The student protests of the 1960s did not cause the demise of general education, as many assume, with demands for liberation from the prevailing system. They merely recognized that general education already had been subverted; the requirements were then loosened, and general education was officially dismissed.

A second round of demographic changes further battered general education. Once the post-World War II baby boom ended, it became apparent that new sources of students would be needed to keep enrollments healthy. Driven by the ideal of equality of opportunity, educators fashioned financial aid, special recruitment, and open admissions programs to reach a new clientele. These various policy changes increased not only the number but also the diversity of students. Cross, one of the first to call attention to these new students, defines them as those who score in the bottom third of high school graduates on traditional tests of academic achievement. She declares that institutions of higher learning are not prepared to educate them: "Traditional education has failed [them] in the past; and unless substantial changes are made, it will fail [them] in the future" (1971, p. xii). She thus summarizes her description of these students:

> New Students are positively attracted to careers and prefer to learn things that are tangible and useful. They tend not to value the academic model of higher education that is prized by faculty, preferring instead a vocational model that will teach them what they need to know to make a good living. New Students consistently pick the "nonacademic" activities and competencies from among lists that we present to them. New Students prefer watching television programs to reading; they prefer working with tools to working with numbers; they feel more competent in using a sewing machine than in reciting long passages from memory. New Students prefer to learn what others have said rather than to engage in intellectual questioning. New Students possess a more pragmatic, less questioning, more authoritarian system of values than traditional students [p. 159].

These students are not attracted to study the history of Western civilization or a series of great books. Such familiar models of general education, however appropriate for some students, simply are not suited for these new students. Indeed, their prevalence poses serious challenges to traditional general education.

Other new groups of students are also entering college in greater numbers. Adults, perhaps the largest group, are no longer relegated to the periphery of an institution and enrolled in evening courses. However, traditional practices of general education, most persons agree, are inappropriate for adults. For instance, coherence is central to general education, but what does curricular coherence mean for an adult who takes only one or two courses at a time? Also, adults have a considerable amount of experience with the general culture and have developed their values through making a host of decisions. Traditional general education does not recognize the different needs and abilities of late adolescents, persons in midlife transition, and persons approaching retirement. Lifelong learning is an entirely new way of thinking about higher education as providing knowledge or skills for people of any age (Knox, 1977).

Large numbers of women and minority students, too, now attend colleges and universities. Although special programs meet various specific needs and interests of these groups, little attention has been paid to the roles of women and minorities in general education courses. Most such courses focus on the dominant heritage and history, almost exclusively male, white, and Western. Similarly, students who are handicapped or veterans, as well as those from other countries, also pose a challenge to traditional forms of general education.

Institutional Differentiation. Until recently, private colleges and universities dominated American higher education in number and in influence. But the current system is more differentiated. Vastly increased numbers of students are served by an array of community colleges, state colleges and universities, professional and technical schools, proprietary schools, and off-campus degree programs of various sorts. Today private institutions enroll fewer than one-fourth of all students in postsecondary education. General education, like the liberal tradition that nourished it, has enjoyed the strongest commitment at the private schools, most of which have regarded themselves as liberal arts colleges. But general education programs operated by such leading private institutions as the University of Chicago, Columbia University, and St. John's College are now less useful as guideposts to others than when the system was more homogeneous.

Community colleges, in particular, are largely a post–World War II phenomenon; today they are more numerous than liberal arts colleges, comprehensive colleges or universities, or doctoral-granting universities, and they enroll more students than any other category of institution. Since general education traditionally has been relegated to the first two years of college, the largest portion of general education is now assumed to be provided by community colleges. But these institutions, for the most part, are designed to meet community needs, and their students tend to be vocationally oriented, are likely to attend on a part-time basis, and are interested in practical learning rather than abstract thinking. The faculties of community colleges often work part-time and tend to be drawn from the local community. These colleges are faced with the task of designing general education with practical benefits for most students as well as transfer value for many who will continue their studies.

State universities and land-grant institutions have been with us for some time, but recent decades have witnessed a proliferation of comprehensive state schools and a growth in the size of public four-year institutions. While the liberal tradition is stronger in these schools than in community colleges, the character of general education suffers in several ways. They tend to be large, to incorporate a multitude of purposes and programs, to serve a heterogeneous student body, and to have few, if any, common learning experiences. These institutions need to incorporate the ideals of general education into their variegated undergraduate programs, capitalize on the strengths and interests of their faculty, and foster a variety of promising approaches.

Higher education is now so diverse that no single model of general education is possible, although some hoped that the recent Harvard Plan would provide *the* model for all institutions, just as the earlier Harvard "Redbook," *General Education in a Free Society* (Harvard Committee, 1945), inspired many schools. But, a more useful approach, one that recognizes institutional diversity, is advocated in the resource guide of the Project on General Education Models (1980). This report provides information to help an institution devise a program of general education appropriate to its mission, history, and character; to the needs and interests of its students; and to the talents and interests of its faculty.

Societal Changes. Our society's obligation to maintain this large and differentiated system places postsecondary education squarely in the midst of public policy debates. Three issues are paramount: quality, cost, and character. Public opinion reflects the feeling that the quality of education is declining, citing declining scores on standardized tests and announcements such as one by the University of California, Berkeley, that nearly half its freshman students require classes in remedial writing. The widely publicized practice of grade inflation has led many to question whether high grades represent a reduction of standards rather than an improvement in quality. In addition, both the educational economist and the average person are questioning the value of a college degree. Whereas a college education was once seen as a route to a better life and a better job, the record numbers of degrees and the current corps of unemployed and underemployed college graduates, especially in the liberal arts disciplines, suggest that a college education is no longer worth much.

The fact that the system has grown so large, particularly during an era of high inflation, translates directly into a large drain on the public treasury. The public increasingly is demanding more accountability to assure both efficiency and effectiveness. It is not that faculty members, administrators, or staff are overpaid, that facilities are lavish, or that students are living luxuriously; but the entire enterprise is so large and the number of programs so great that the collective cost is high. Any demand for budget cuts further weakens general education, as institutional budgets allocate faculty positions to those areas with large student enrollment. The result has been a loss of faculty in the arts and sciences and the expansion of professional fields, which further weakens general education potentials.

The liberalization of American culture has also affected general education. Discussing the kinds of topics once reserved for college classrooms, Dowd summarizes twenty years of social change:

> In 1960 we did not talk about religion in the secondary schools. I can remember when communism and socialism were taboo topics in the secondary schools of Connecticut, New York, Michigan, and California. Sex and sexual behavior were truly taboo topics in education prior to college. Race was another topic that was ignored. The role of the introductory humanities course in which I taught for several years was to begin a discussion of these topics that most freshmen even out of sophisticated suburban high schools on Long Island and Chicago had never talked about in school except among their peers. Many faculty members got their kicks out of shaking up a class by introducing topics that had never been discussed openly in an approved setting prior to the freshman year in college. Thus, college often meant the transition to a new world of ideas and concepts where animated and exciting discussion could take place.
>
> By 1970 every one of these topics was discussed in nursery school as far as I can make out. The role of general education which had been a kind of opening up of horizons got preempted by every medium including television. . . . [These changes] preempted a distinctive role that general education had for half a century or more [1980, p. 7].

Yet despite these changes, ideas about and attitudes toward sex and race still are riddled with ignorance, myth, and controversy; equity and justice still are not fully realized; and new controversies over energy, inflation, world hunger, and developing nations demand attention and understanding. General education must now go beyond shock treatment in order to prepare students to be citizens having a sophisticated comprehension of the issues of the day.

Views from the Campuses

The ideal of general education has been tarnished by several forces, but those very same forces have, in the past, generated efforts to correct excesses. The modern university's tendency to neglect the interests of students, to produce technicians, and value research over wisdom periodically calls for corrections. Similarly, the tendency of faculty to focus their attention on specialized issues of limited academic concern or to think narrowly about the curriculum occasionally provoke demands for reform. While new students may not meet traditional standards, their presence requires educators to redefine an educated person, just as the diversity of institutions eventually calls for attention to commonalities, public standards, and procedures that assure quality. Today's reform movement is a means of restoring the balance between general and special education.

Although we have outlined the causes that contributed to the decline of general education, we can fully understand the problem only by examining the actual operation of the programs at individual campuses. An insightful look at the difficulties plaguing programs of general education is provided by an analysis of the applications to participate in the Project on General Education Models. Applicants were asked, among other things, to name the problems in their current programs that they would like to improve through participation in the project. Most applicants responded with amazing candor. Although the applications were prepared for the specific purpose of gaining acceptance into the project, and although the applicants included a wide range of institutional types, the documents afford valuable if partial insights. This discussion of results is limited to those institutions that have some configuration of distribution requirements with a few or no required core courses. Their problems fall into five categories: program operation, philosophy and rationale, students and learning, faculty and teaching, and administration and organization.

Program Operation. The lack of coherence in the general education program was the overriding concern. Programs were referred to as ambiguous, unplanned, and undistinguished; one applicant explained: "Our general education requirements do not constitute a program. There is at best an ambiguous relationship between the requirements and the goals of general education as we have defined them. . . . Our current approach is not an agreed-upon set of experiences; not a program with a sense of identity, unity, and cohesiveness; not a program with its own stature, importance, and legitimacy; not a program of unique character, dimension, and distinction."

A second frequent complaint was lack of depth, with applicants noting that students could satisfy general education requirements simply by taking introductory courses and that departments eclipsed the goal of breadth by stressing narrow departmental concerns. Troublesome to some was the absence of a common core of skills and knowledge, as well as the exclusion of significant developments in current knowledge, such as space exploration, life sciences, and international studies. Traditional methods of teaching were also attacked: "We need to provide more experiential learning activities as opportunities for learners to fulfill general education needs." Lastly, unsatisfactory results were cited as an area of significant concern. Wrote one person, "Only through a combination of unusual maturity, exceptional advising, and high determination could a student acquire a truly liberal education."

Philosophy and Rationale. The absence of clearly identified goals for the required curriculum was frequently cited in the applications as a major concern. Ironically, one school reported that its consciously formed rationale dissolved over time even though the program remained intact. Vagueness and uncertainty about program goals and lack of faculty consensus about the purposes of general education were mentioned often. Expediency was targeted by one individual, who may have been speaking for a multitude of others: "This program as it exists today is the result of historical development, expediency, and political compromise. Any semblance of a unified thread running through the whole program is lacking. . . . Our program parallels the development of English Common Law, which is really nothing more than a series of expedient tinkerings. . . . Clearly, any quality program in general education needs much more than this."

An overemphasis on specialization was another applicant's subject: "In the polarity between diversity and unity, this institution has so attended to diversity and specialization that it has inclined toward the neglect of factors of connectedness and unity." An allied problem is that of outmoded assumptions; many respondents stressed that their programs did not relate to the complexity of contemporary human experience, to its "multiple dimensions, conflicting perspectives, and competing centers of action." Several felt that universities were not responding to new social situations and conflicts over traditional values; "[General education] ought to prepare students to formulate their own versions of integrated being and constructive practice," concluded one.

Technical institutions evidenced a particular unevenness in their rationale for liberal arts in their curriculums. Often neither faculty nor students in technical schools see much value in liberal arts studies; they view the nontechnical courses as contributing nothing essential to the formation of marketable skills or professional practice.

Students and Learning. In the forefront of the minds of many were the new student constituencies and how their institutions should adjust to nontraditional students. One referred to this group as "the dispossessed . . . lacking an allegiance to historical, classical values—and challenging old pieties," and concluded that these students had caused "profound unease among faculty." Many were not as uneasy about the new student clientele but agreed that a definition of general education for this group must be developed.

Some institutions had recruited new students but had not adjusted the programs that those students entered to meet their special circumstances and needs. Said one applicant: "Because the educational level and ethnic distribution of our students has changed significantly since the present core program was adopted, the institution has not addressed effectively the question of how the ideals of the general education program, indeed the ideals of the institution, can be transferred to our new clientele." Although not all new students lack basic skills, some do— as many as two-thirds of the incoming students at one university. This phenomenon is not limited to two-year colleges or to less prestigious four-year schools. Similar deficiencies were cited at a major university: "Whether or not the association can be validated, many believe that a causal link exists between the loosening of distribution requirements, a reduced emphasis on general education, and a perceived decline in basic learning skills, particularly, but not exclusively, in the area of expository writing."

Careerism and the avoidance of courses outside the major area were also frequent concerns. Many institutions are trying to develop a rationale to formulate habits of inquiry and a deeper acquaintance with culture in general. But in some cases, their students were originally attracted to the institution by vocational programs that the institution created to increase enrollment. For example, an individual from a small liberal arts college that had added programs in nursing, business, and other vocational fields wrote: "[The students] are only interested in the training program so that they can advance in their position at work or gain a more lucrative salary."

Applicants often complained that students avoided fields of study that they deemed irrelevant to their careers. While many criticized students in science and vocational fields for neglecting humanities courses, one school provided evidence that students in the humanities consistently avoided the natural sciences, mathematics, and technological fields.

Faculty and Teaching. If the nontraditional students are a source of uneasiness to some, the issues of faculty and teaching are outright promoters of anxiety. Fragmentation and the promulgation of disciplinary specialization, not to mention departmental territoriality, were cited by many; one writer explained: "One cause [of faculty specialization] ironically has been an increasing technical virtuosity fostered within the disciplines, creating specialists whose competency may verge on narrowness, aridity, and pedantry. Further opportunities for cross-disciplinary exchange diminish rapidly as each discipline creates its own language. This Babel-effect filters down into undergraduate programs, causing a sense of fragmentation and even preventing integration of academic purposes—negating, in other words, the basic intention of general education."

Specialization is the modern route to intellectual progress, but it has conversely resulted in profound repercussions that led one applicant to quote C. P. Snow's statement: "We have lost even the pretense of a common culture. Persons educated with the greatest intensity we know can no longer communicate with each other on the plane of their major intellectual and, above all, moral life. It is leading us to interpret the past wrongly, to misjudge the present, and to deny our hopes of the future." But others have been captivated by this race toward specialization; at one university "a paradoxical combination of inferiority feelings prevail among faculty in the arts and letters vis-a-vis the other schools and they resolve to outdo others in such tests of professionalism and narrow specialization."

Other applicants noted the poor quality of instruction in some general education courses. Evaluations at some institutions suggested that lack of structure and poor curricular organization were at least partly related to the mediocre quality of instruction. One institution cited results of a survey in which three-fourths of the students claimed that the general education program had "only moderate or negligible impact on their quantitative thinking or on their moral and ethical standards."

Particularly criticized was the lack of adequate advising for students. One respondent wrote: "Ideally, a skilled and dedicated advisor could assist the student in finding a meaningful combination of courses within the program, but there is little to indicate that such support exists. . . . No wonder, too, that students seem to lack a sense of academic community, the sense of belonging to some significant intellectual enterprise."

Administration and Organization. The lack of clear-cut administrative responsibility is one of the most conspicuous features of general education. At some institutions much of the responsibility for general education is decentralized, falling to several departments, and "no single body [is] responsible for the development, supervision, or evaluation of general education." Many reported this to be a critical problem. Lack of coordination with other programs within the institution was also mentioned. From an institution that had established an impressive work-study program, a respondent wrote: "The general education program has not adequately taken into account the kind of learning which our students acquire on their cooperative work program and how it contributes to their personal development in ways that parallel the traditional purposes of liberal learning. It also has failed to take into account the educational goals of responsible community living which are inherent in the program of this institution." In a similar vein, a spokesman from a technical college observed: "Interrelating of content between general studies and specialized, technical courses is ignored."

Lack of coordination, limited support services, and competing institutional pressures—the combination has caused the impression that "general education is a bummer," in the words of one applicant.

Professional Education

Although the concept of general education—its ideals, deficiencies, and need of reform—has been most closely identified with liberal education, it plays an equally important role in professional and preprofessional programs. However, the basic compatibility of general and professional education is seldom recognized and accepted either by the liberal arts faculty or by those in various professional fields (Vander Meer and Lyons, 1979). Two of the harmful results of this situation are cited in an editorial of the *Journal of Chemical Education*: "[American higher education] has developed far too few well-educated citizens who can participate in and understand public issues with the requisite historical, political, scientific, and ethical awareness, and it has graduated far too many professionals in medicine, law, engineering, science, and teaching who are unable to address themselves to the significant issues underpinning their own activities. Both of these failures speak to a certain shallowness of intellectual substance, resulting no doubt from a schooling preoccupied with specialization and focused on the future work, career, and occupational competence of the individual" ("Why Higher Education Continues to Fail," 1979, p. 69). The editorial calls for faculty in all disciplines to recognize that humanistic perspectives and tough moral choices are part of all human discourse and therefore are as central to the preparation of a professional as the techniques of the field itself.

Hutchins helped implant the conventional split between general and professional education by asserting that general education was oriented to the life of the mind, professional programs to the pragmatic purposes of getting a job and making money; the former stressed ideas, and the latter techniques. Liberal education was held to be a higher intellectual calling and was even accorded a degree of moral superiority. It is in this spirit that Adlai Stevenson reportedly commented that at Harvard they humanized the scientist while down the road at M.I.T. they simonized the humanist (cited in Friedman, 1979). The arts and sciences faculty traditionally have seen themselves as providers of "service courses," usually introductions to their disciplines, to the professional students. It is difficult to tell whether this designation was more demeaning to the students who had to take such courses or to the faculty who had to teach them; both held the courses in low esteem.

But in the last decade professional programs have grown like mushrooms in a spring rain. Whether measured by the number of programs, the number of faculty members, or the interests of students, the growth of professional education has been phenomenal, and it has often been at the expense of traditional arts and science fields.

This change in the relative enrollments in professional and liberal arts programs has been accompanied by a change in the types of students who enroll in professional programs. For example, Coyle (1979) reports that students at the School of Business at Pennsylvania State University had among the highest SAT scores of any school on the campus—a radical difference from just a few years ago when the high scorers majored in academic subjects. During the last five years, the school experienced both an increase in the number of majors and a large increase in the number of liberal arts majors taking business courses to enhance their job prospects. The business school was now expected to play a "service" role for the traditional liberal arts disciplines. Moreover, Coyle expressed concern that the business courses the liberal arts students were electing did not consist of a coherent package, and he advocated developing a series of related courses that could be tied closely with various liberal arts majors. By now the familiar categories that once defined the relationship between professional and liberal education have been shuffled and, in some cases, even reversed.

With the ascendancy of professional education has come renewed attention among some of its leaders to the role of general education in their offerings. These leaders reject the notion that technical proficiency is sufficient for the effective practice of their craft and affirm that a broad general education constitutes essential preparation for any professional practice. While any affirmation of the value of general education is to be welcome, we see that the basic rationale for general education seems to have shifted. Advocates used to claim that general education would make a person well rounded and provide a measure of culture and sophistication that would enhance in crucial, if intangible, ways the quality of his or her life. Increasingly, advocates now claim that general education is an integral part of a professional education; that is, it has vocational value.

Consider a few examples. The University of Minnesota College of Business Administration recently increased the number of required liberal arts courses from ten to nineteen. The changes shift the focus of coursework from one of narrow specialization to a broader interdisciplinary approach. Less emphasis is to be placed on the quantitative and technical aspects of management and more on preparing students for business in its larger context. In the words of Dean David Lilly, the traditional business college program produces "narrow-gauged numbers crunchers. . . . It's the difference between being functionally, overtechnically trained and learning how to think, to analyze critically, to adapt to change" (quoted by Youngblood, 1981, p. A-24). Included in the new business curriculum are courses in communications, mathematics, science, social science, humanities, and international studies.

Similarly, the top administrators of the Massachusetts Institute of Technology's School of Engineering have called for a redirection of engineering education (Seamans and Hansen, 1981). They argue that engineers must be prepared to meet changing circumstances and to approach large social issues. They urge a coherent program in written and oral communications, historical and social perspectives of science and technology, ethics, and government. They believe such subjects can be included in most undergraduate curriculums, although the number of electives available to students may have to be reduced.

Other engineering leaders are also restating the ideal of professional competence in the context of larger vistas and wider areas of human competence. Paul Torgersen, dean at Virginia Polytechnic Institute, concludes an article on the role of general education in engineering with this plea: "As educators and members of a community entrusted with the responsibility for preserving the values of our society, we owe all students, including our engineering students, an appreciation for the 'human condition.' The real issue is that a student will live only one life, in one time frame, in one culture, and probably in one narrowly circumscribed walk through seventy years or so of his own portion of joy and sorrow. Humanistic study, including history, literature, and the arts, expands that experience in manifold ways, ensures that he encounters examples of other lives and other values and other times" (1979, p. 174).

Indeed, the ideal that technical proficiency must be based on a broad general education, with its roots in the liberal tradition, is the only justification for locating professional programs on a college campus. If technical proficiency in itself is a program's sole goal, it belongs at a free-standing business college, technical institute, or similar institution. Contrary to conventional folklore, general education is emphasized in statements published by most accreditation agencies that certify professional programs, and professional accreditation standards support the strengthening and reform of general education.

In summary, the ideal of a generally educated person has

been tarnished in professional as well as in liberal education. The lack of convincing rationale, the assortment of disconnected courses, the prevalence of superficial introductory surveys, the uninspired teaching by junior faculty, the absence of strong advocates and role models among faculty, the pressure to master the latest techniques and larger amounts of specialized knowledge—these failures explain the collapse of the ideal. Given these conditions, it is not surprising that all too often students choose their specialized courses first and search for a convenient liberal arts course as a filler. In the words of Torgersen, "It must fill in the schedule on Monday, Wednesday, and Friday at 2:00 p.m., preferably be taught on this side of the campus, and not require too much reading, because thermodynamics is likely to be quite time consuming" (1979, p. 173). In such a context general education becomes at best an empty slogan and at worst a series of barriers to overcome on the way to acquiring a college degree.

Chapter Two

Voices in the Debate

A new national debate about general education has exploded all across America. Leaders on campuses, in government, and in corporations, writers and editors of scholarly publications and the popular press, and others concerned with the quality of a college education seek to restore integrity to the core of the undergraduate experience. At the heart of the debate is the enduring ideal of a broad general education, one that prepares students for their adult lives whatever their specializations or vocations may be. Many voices are being raised—some quite shrill—contributing very different views on fundamental issues. Concerned parties, both off-campus and on, are determined to correct the drift toward illiteracy; faculty members in the various academic disciplines express both expert views and personal interests; critics argue that larger perspectives than those of disciplinarians are needed to restore coherence to the curriculum; employers and others discuss the usefulness of the liberal arts; academic reformers monitor continued access and special programs for nontraditional students; and students are unusually silent. Although none of these groups adheres to a party line, each offers important and legitimate views about the general curriculum and how the ideal of general education should be realized.

Literacy

The subject of literacy figures prominently in the general education debate. One reads about the "new illiteracy," and illiteracies scientific, technological, cultural, and even geographical. There are demands for computer literacy and greater literacy in foreign languages. An editorial in the *Washington Post* laments: "Professors at major universities have been forced to simplify introductory courses in many fields. The military, while spending huge sums for more and more sophisticated weaponry, has been forced to rewrite its training manuals from the eleventh-grade level or higher to the eighth-grade level or lower. Many are aimed at the sixth-grade level. Evidence of falling achievement is everywhere" (Matthews, 1981, p. A-23).

Circumstances such as these fuel the back-to-basics movement, and certainly college students need to be well skilled in the basics if they are to gain a "higher" education. Although the basics movement has been championed by political conservatives, the issue transcends politics and has adherents among educators of all ideologies. Some dispute the definition of *basic,* and others quarrel with the idea of "going back" rather than "moving ahead," but all agree that students should be able to read, write, and compute. Such basics are clearly prerequisite to the more advanced skills traditionally associated with higher education: critical thinking, problem solving, analysis, synthesis, and the like.

Part of the responsibility for students' literacy rests with the high schools. If the foundation they offer is weak, colleges must devote a great deal of time and effort to shoring it up, leaving them less time to erect any kind of impressive edifice. Earlier general education revivals focused on the high schools as well as colleges and universities; the Harvard "Redbook" (Harvard Committee, 1945), for instance, the bible of the last major revival, discussed the public schools at greater length than the university curriculum. It is a commonplace that our high schools are in trouble; violence, dropouts, drugs, and poor-quality education have been documented time and again. Boyer (1980, p. 9) observes, "Today there is no agreement about what it means to be an educated person. Diversity—not coherence—has become the 'guiding principle' in our academic planning. We seem more confident of the length of a high school education than we do about its substance." He then asks rhetorically: "Do we honestly believe that we can have quality in the 1980s if, during the twelve preceding years of formal education, the teaching is not adequate; the testing confused; and the curriculum lacks both purpose and coherence? And do we honestly believe that our colleges and universities have no responsibility to help solve the crisis in the schools which is, in fact, a problem we helped to create?" (p. 11).

Clearly, the problems in the public schools must be corrected so that once again higher education can educate at the truly higher levels and reduce its enormous expenditure of time and money on remedial measures. But however we address the problem of inadequate high school education, many college students now lack basic skills. Remedial courses have been tacked onto regular offerings, but although an important corrective, they are insufficient. Learning resource centers, writing laboratories, and mathematics clinics, while valuable, still fall short of the mark. A more substantial curricular response is necessary if students are to achieve literacy in its basic and more sophisticated forms. General education is being asked to ensure that all students are literate, if not when they arrive on campus, at least by the time they graduate.

Academic Disciplines

Academic disciplines were organized during the late nineteenth century to facilitate the intellectual work of scholars. Throughout the years, the disciplines have become the dominant organizing structures at colleges and universities, and each of the major divisions of intellectual life stakes a claim to its share of the general curriculum. Since faculty members in the disciplines have primary authority for setting the curriculum and providing instruction, their views are vitally important. Naturally, strong vested interests shape their arguments in support of their disciplines' inclusion in general education programs.

The Humanities. "The humanities are widely undervalued and often poorly understood," declared the Commission on the Humanities (1980, p. 4). The humanities were traditionally regarded as the centerpiece of liberal education, sometimes synonymous with it, but they now share this favored place with the sciences and social sciences as partners in liberal education. During the rapid rise of vocationalism during the 1970s, "liberal education and the humanities, their fates still linked, were willed to the periphery of undergraduate learning" (p. 66). Reasserting their central place, the commission states:

> Efforts to give fresh meaning to liberal education must continue; all such efforts should emphasize the importance of the humanities for developing the mental capacities and historical knowledge needed for
>
> —effective command of written and spoken English;
> —enjoyment and informed judgment of the arts;
> —understanding (preferably based on knowledge of foreign languages) of other cultures;
> —analysis and assessment of ethical problems, issues of public policy, and the questions of value underlying science and technology [p. 69].

Responses within the humanities community to these kinds of recommendations are mixed. On the one hand, they are welcomed because they provide a rallying cry for traditional academic disciplines within the humanities. Emboldened by such recommendations, many humanities faculties claim a larger role for their disciplines in the required core curriculum and greater weight for courses in the substantive fields of literature, philosophy, religion, the arts, and other areas of study. On the other hand, some believe that the humanities and their role in undergraduate education must be redefined within the context of contemporary realities. In a paper entitled "The Unhumanistic Humanities," the late Charles Frankel disavowed the simplistic tendency to equate the quality "humanistic" with any of the departments in the humanities. He notes: "Professors have not created the humanities, any more than lawyers created the idea of justice, or doctors the idea of health" (1979, p. 7). Urging educators to adopt a less bureaucratic point of view, Frankel says, "The 'humanities,' to me, are best defined as a certain orientation toward learning. Not the only respectable orientation, but, for me, an indispensable one; namely, the review of *any* field of human endeavor and human inquiry from the point of view of its place in the experience of the human race—its logical preconceptions, its history, its social and moral connotations and implications" (p. 13). This formulation leads him to conclude that the heart of the humanities is to reflect on significant issues in human life and society, often in conjunction with work in other fields of study.

Bernstein (1980, p. 9) urges humanities faculty to embrace recent changes in the academic world and shape their work accordingly: "This world not only contains more students over the age of twenty-two who work while attending school, but also has more women than men students for the first time in the history of higher education and more bilingual and minority students as well. The presence of these learners at the center of the higher education world, coupled with the liberation movements of the 1960s, has radically altered the traditional conception of the humanities for many academics." She cites with enthusiasm what she calls the "new" humanities— "scholarship and curriculum that attempt to rid traditional humanistic study of its racist and sexist biases."

Others seek to revive the humanities by arguing for their utility as an integral part of preparation for a career. Some reason that skills such as clear and forceful expression, creativity, and critical thinking are useful in all endeavors. Others claim a more direct utility, citing the value of courses on medical or business ethics in the core of professional preparation as an example. Cohen and Brawer call for community colleges to include topics from the humanities in their vocational programs:

"The nursing program faculty who would not require their students to take a cultural anthropology course might welcome a three-week unit on the use of grieving taught by an anthropologist. The teachers of auto mechanics will not send their students to a philosophy course, but they might appreciate having a course module on business ethics prepared by a philosophy instructor. The aesthetics of design could be presented to students in an electronics technology program by a teacher of art. And a classicist could teach Greek and Latin roots of medical terms to medical technology students" (1980, pp. 26-27). Although some humanities faculty scoff at such piecemeal efforts to demonstrate the value of their subjects, others see such units as a practical exposure to the humanities for a variety of students.

Levine offers another approach to the humanities, arguing that their role within the college curriculum should be "the exploration of the enterprise of learning": "The focus within humanities departments should shift from majors (dwindling in numbers every day) to interested nonmajors. . . . The required courses (chosen from a variety with different disciplinary angles) should be about other courses and disciplines, a kind of contrapuntal questioning of the first principles of disciplinary methodologies, and the implications of those principles" (1978, p. 3). In his formulation, the special province of the humanities lies in the clarification of assumptions, values, and methodologies, and of learning itself.

Whether by presenting their subject matter, examining significant human endeavors, removing biases from scholarship, or reflecting on the very process of learning itself, professors agree that the humanities should constitute a significant portion of the educational experience of all students, whatever their majors or vocational goals. Theirs is a compelling argument for the inclusion, in some form, of the humanities in the core of the undergraduate curriculum. Neusner (1979, p. 40) expresses eloquently the view that study of the humanities is needed to make people fully human:

> So there is no common core of facts which
> everyone everywhere must know and which we in

particular teach. Nor is there a distinctive grace of
intellect which is ours alone. All we have to offer is
a particular access: to those moments in history of
significant humaneness; to those powerful minds in
philosophy of transcendent self-awareness; to those
sensibilities in literature; and to those anguished,
searching hearts in religions in which we may perceive not what we are but what we too can be. This
is another kind of classicism: the conviction, which
is the value we espouse and profess, that greatness
inheres in humanity; that it is worth being human.
By the exercise of catholic taste and critical judgment we may make choices among works of human greatness of mind and emotion. Through the
selection of what our frail judgment tells us transcends ourselves and surpasses our former expectation, we too may know and therefore be more than
what we know we are.

The Sciences. The physical and biological sciences, too,
claim an essential role in the general education of all students.
Science is one of the driving forces of modern society, and individuals must make daily choices about scientific questions to
perform effectively on their jobs or take an informed part in
public debates and decisions. Holton (1981, p. 10) notes that
"By a recent estimate, nearly half of the bills before the U.S.
Congress have a substantial science-technology component;
some two-thirds of the District of Columbia Circuit Court's
caseload now involves review of action by federal administrative
agencies; and more and more of such cases relate to matters on
the frontiers of technology." The National Research Council
(1982, p. xv) asserts that the failure to acquaint nonspecialists
with the basics of science is "an educational problem of national proportions." Although much of the council's concern is directed at the public schools, it reports that nonscience majors
at colleges and universities take, on the average, only 7 percent
of their courses in science subjects. Courses in technology are
undoubtedly even less frequently elected.

Further, the adequacy of those offerings is very much

open to question. Specialism has proceeded at such a pace that coherent courses and programs are a rarity. The biological sciences, which used to be a single department, are sometimes divided into three or more departments—biochemistry and molecular and cellular biology, ecology and evolutionary biology, and neurobiology and physiology. With so much material to cover, science courses typically are packed full of factual information that swamps the minds of those students unfamiliar with the languages and methods of the field. Such coursework cannot prepare future citizens to cope with the complexities of modern life.

Devising appropriate science courses for general education programs has always been difficult, and a recent report from Columbia University (n.d., p. 19) acknowledges that "in the sixty-two years since the founding of Columbia's general education program, science has never been successfully integrated into the core curriculum." Robert Pollack, dean and biologist at Columbia, is leading an effort to develop a course to fill this need. He notes, "The stakes are high; a Columbia graduate should be able to distinguish between evolution and creation, astronomy and astrology, legitimate cancer research and medical quackery. The alternative to scientific thought is fundamentalism—passively waiting for a mystical authority to tell you where the truth lies. We have ample reason, in the late twentieth century, to fear the consequences of entrusting our destiny to fools, charlatans, and madmen" (n.d., p. 21).

The primary difficulty is a lack of agreement about the appropriate content and methods of science courses for nonmajors. Like general education itself, it is far easier to affirm the ideal than to give it practical expression in an actual program that enjoys at least a working consensus. One of the most contentious issues is whether to teach science or to teach *about* science. Some argue that students can learn about science only by plunging into its substance, as do prospective science majors. Critics argue that courses intended for majors are inappropriate for those who may never take another step, another course in science; rather, the nonmajor needs to learn about science, its methods, history, values, and place in the social order.

Thus they propose courses on the history or philosophy of science and courses on science and society or public policy. But, the opposition retorts that students cannot understand anything substantive *about* science without basic training in one of the sciences.

Educators also disagree on the appropriate scope of courses for nonmajors. The standard approach is to summarize a particular science by surveying its major achievements. A physics course might move from Galileo and Newton to the laws of thermodynamics, relativity, and quantum mechanics. The sheer magnitude of this task virtually guarantees that students will gain only superficial understanding, according to critics of this approach. They advocate a focus on limited topics, particularly those of concern to the average citizen, such as energy, environmental quality, nuclear armament and disarmament, and ethical issues posed by biological advances. Such courses would allow greater depth and address the kinds of practical concerns faced by nonscientists. The rejoinder, of course, is that these topics are trendy, transcend the particular competence of scientists, and result in a limited range of knowledge.

A third issue is whether courses should stress content or concentrate on methodology and the nature of scientific thought. Arons (1980, p. 87) observes: "The pace and volume of material thrust at students in the majority of liberal education science courses are such as to preclude the exercise of time-consuming operations of thinking, reasoning, and understanding. The majority of students are thus forced into blind memorization, and they eventually come to see all 'knowledge' and 'understanding' as the juxtaposition of memorized names and phrases." If students are to cultivate the habits of scientific thought and develop an appreciation for its power, Arons maintains that more attention must be paid to mental skills than to information.

Lewis Thomas argues from yet another perspective for a radical revision of introductory courses: "Leave the fundamentals, the so-called basics, aside for awhile, and concentrate the attention of all students on the things that are not known. . . . At the outset, before any of the fundamentals, teach the still imponderable puzzles . . ." (1982, p. 92). He refers to the strangeness of the world opened up by quantum theory, the interdependence of a complex and little-understood ecosystem, and the mysteries of the tiny cell as proper subjects. Once students grasp the significance of the puzzles, understand some of the outlines of the unfolding intellectual drama, and possibly see an opportunity for them to contribute to its understanding, then they can study the details. But others question whether students can be taken to the frontiers before learning the basics and whether they will ever learn the fundamentals if they are not covered in a formal course.

These difficult issues are further complicated by the matter of technology. A steadily rising chorus of voices calls for students to learn not only science but also technological applications, patterns of applied thought, and the tools of the trade, including computers. The Sloan Foundation has established a funding program to support the inclusion of applied mathematics and technological studies in the undergraduate curriculum of liberal arts colleges, schools that historically have spurned technology. The call for computer literacy is particularly strong, as the computer is becoming a staple of daily life, both at work and at home. Masat (1981, p. 19) states the bottom line: "Students who are learning how their lives and work are affected by computers clearly have a definite intellectual and economic advantage, in the long run, over those who do not."

Despite the intractability of these conflicting views, many institutions are seeking ways to incorporate science into the general curriculum. Some seek to avoid making either-or choices by combining the best of various approaches. For example, Syracuse University designed a multidisciplinary cluster: All students are required to take a two-semester laboratory course in either biology, chemistry, geology, or physics; a course in the technological applications of that area using microprocessors; and another course on the social issues raised by new developments in technology. The four-course requirement in one scientific field achieves many of the several purposes advanced in the debate. If fewer courses are required, as is more common, then choices must be made among competing views, thereby raising the stakes of the various perspectives.

The Social Sciences. No national report has galvanized

the social scientists, but they, too, are reevaluating the character of their fields, their status, and their role in general education. This discussion is taking place in various forums, including professional meetings, publications, research studies, and commentaries. A series of articles in the *Chronicle of Higher Education* about the discipline of history—a cornerstone of general education programs—conveys the spirit that the field is in trouble and contains proposals for restoring vitality (Winkler, 1980a, 1980b, 1980c).

"Instead of wringing our hands over the decline of interest in history, we historians should examine our own products," Richard Morris told the Organization of American Historians at their annual meeting (quoted in Winkler, 1980a). "We are becoming an incestuous profession," he claims, as too many scholars are writing technical monographs for the benefit of a few peers. Significant issues of concern to the informed public are neglected, and "relatively few works of history possess literary distinction."

Bernard Bailyn, past-president of the American Historical Association, commented in an interview (Winkler, 1980b, p. 3) that "history no longer connects." The field has changed dramatically in recent years with the adoption of new methods and subject areas such as family studies, psychohistory, and demographic analyses. Greater use of statistics and the computer permit more sophisticated analysis of historical data. Bailyn does not disparage the specialists, for "the best history must be technical, taking into account all the nuances and complications." But he adds: "In the final analysis, the best history has to be more than technically skilled; it must be interpretive. . . . This will mean reasserting the value of general, large-scale works. In a period when history has become so much more complicated, we must look for synthesis."

A review (Winkler, 1980c, p. 18) of *The Past Before Us,* a collection of essays on the status of historical study by the American Historical Association, notes that one major point characterizes most of the essays: "Research today—despite, or perhaps because of, the rapid expansion of topics and methodologies—fails to pull together the more specialized work into any kind of general overview or synthesis." In this review, William McNeill is quoted as venturing, "The meaning and value of the entire enterprise becomes less and less apparent to ordinary human beings who do not share professional interests or care about questions that have been defined by the historians' debate, rather than by common life experiences or by the course of public events."

There is little doubt on campuses that a knowledge of history and other social sciences is central to general education. Curricular proposals commonly assert that students should acquire a sense of history, an understanding of the main currents of Western culture and American society, as well as other goals relevant to the social sciences, such as knowledge of human behavior and the ability to work with people of different backgrounds. For general education purposes, Birnbaum (1979) suggests that colleges must foster a "sense of history," a study not so much of the facts as of the range of forces involved in events, of the continuity and ongoingness of the present predicament, and of our place in history. He also suggests that history can and should be taught in as close as possible a relation to the students' major, as in the history of technology or management. Others retort that a sense of history requires the knowledge of events and facts and that, although the history of a given profession is useful, the dominant history of the culture is of more generic and enduring value.

Most institutions' approaches to history in the general curriculum date back to the familiar Western civilization courses popular in the post–World War II revival. A large variety of colleges and universities now again require Western history. Although most claim their offerings differ from the earlier incarnation, such differences are slight. Critics of this approach argue that the rest of the world must occupy a prominent spot in any contemporary curriculum, not only because the study of a radically different culture allows students to see their native culture more clearly, but also because most significant aspects of contemporary life are affected by developments in Asia, the Middle East, Africa, and Latin America. Understanding of non-Western cultures is essential for full participation in cultural life and for many occupations.

Others respond that students should learn about their

heritage but ask, Whose heritage is to be taught? The traditional curriculum is heavily biased toward white, male, and middle-class values. Those concerned with the education of women argue for greater attention to topics such as family history, for the infusion of women's perspectives in traditional subjects, and for the purging of sexist biases in such social sciences as Freudian psychology, which regards penis envy as a primary motivation of women, and economics, which uses employment statistics that exclude housewives and women working at home. Treatment of the accomplishments of racial minorities—blacks, Hispanics, Orientals, and Native Americans—is also urged, not just to benefit these groups but to complete the education of all students.

Beyond the genuine belief that their fields contribute to the general education of students, social scientists want as large a piece of the curricular pie as their counterparts in the humanities and natural sciences. Such jealousies, of course, increase the difficulties of devising a curriculum that in practice expresses the ideal of general education.

Interdisciplinarians

While spokespersons for the various scholarly disciplines are making their cases, others press—with equal intensity—for greater attention to interdisciplinary studies. They claim that the world is not organized according to convenient disciplinary categories and that the resolution of actual problems requires multiple disciplinary perspectives: "Everything really is related to everything else, and the person who plumbs the depth of his or her own specialty finds more and more connections with every other specialty" (Cleveland, 1982, p. 2).

At a time when the fragmentation of the curriculum is a major issue, more attention to the disciplines is not sufficient; some "glue" is needed to hold the various pieces of the curriculum together. The integration of knowledge rests, for some, on metaphysical foundations similar to an earlier faith in the unity of science, which held that the universe operates according to regular principles that science progressively discovers. This heuristic notion once led to a great deal of intellectual advance, including interdisciplinary study; many thought that the physical, biological, and social sciences could be unified and that simpler laws could be derived to explain ever-more complex phenomena. Although this idea persists in another form in systems theory, the forces of specialization and pluralism—aided by the continuing development of technical languages, intellectual subcultures, and social structures that support intellectual work (academic guilds, professional meetings, standards of scholarship and training, journals, career paths)—all conspire to challenge the belief that the intellectual world can be fully integrated. Most intellectuals similarly doubt that a pluralistic culture with many separate interest groups can produce a unified curriculum that does not resemble a Procrustean bed.

Thus current claims for curricular integration tend to be more modest. The *intellectual* argument is that ideas from one field are enriched by ideas from other fields, and that problems demand insights from several disciplines. Further, many note that the most exciting innovations cross traditional disciplines: for example, genetic engineering, cognitive psychology and artificial intelligence, and historical interpretation based on sociological data of demography and mobility. The *social* argument is that each human being shares some traits with all other humans and other traits with at least some other humans. The task is to restore balance by stressing the kinship of all members of the species and their common cultural and social bonds, not simply the principles of diversity and individualism. Finally, the *pedagogical* argument is that students learn better when material is organized into meaningful wholes rather than isolated bits. In addition, common studies serve as a basis for a community of learners. For all these reasons, many educators believe we must transcend the disciplinary structure of general education.

The rejoinder from the disciplinarians is that the knowledge is garnered, organized, and disseminated primarily by means of the disciplines. Interdisciplinary courses are suspect, superficial, and often watered-down offerings; they require faculty either to have superhuman competencies or to teach topics they are not well qualified to teach; and they assume students

can integrate two fields (or more) before they fully understand
either. To which, of course, the rebuttal is that the demands of
the future are different from the intellectual repositories of the
past, and new configurations of knowledge, at least for the purpose of teaching, are both possible and necessary.

In one sense general education is burdened with a heav-
ier load than it can reasonably carry. It is discussed variously in
the context of preparing students to cope with a changing society, to ensure the survival of the species, to resolve a myriad of
social problems, or to secure the continuation of democracy. A
few hours of required study by the relatively small proportion of
citizens who manage to earn a college degree does little to guide
social change, ensure survival, resolve the human predicament,
or ensure freedom for the nation. But educators must address
issues that transcend the internal organization and politics of
colleges and universities. The academic enterprise, particularly
the general education portion, must address such monumental
issues and help prepare men and women to cope with them and
to provide leadership for the rest of us, the interdisciplinarians
assert. Courses must be designed to promote civic purposes and
thereby prepare another generation to take responsibility for
our social institutions. This need is so great as to demand a
place in the general curriculum of colleges and universities, say
proponents of integrative learning.

Utilitarians

Spurred by a stagnant economy, students, faculty, and
others have become more utilitarian in their views of a college
education. For example, compared with the preceding generation, students today are more materialistic, preoccupied with
themselves, and oriented toward success—defined as money,
status, and power (Levine, 1980a). Because general education has
little direct or immediate vocational value, it is widely regarded
as useless. Faculty members in newly created or expanded professional and career fields affirm the worth of some study in the
liberal arts but tend to denigrate its overall value (Vander Meer
and Lyons, 1979). Such views are unwittingly aided and abetted

by those proponents of the liberal arts who argue that these subjects possess intrinsic value and should be studied for their own sake, an argument that is lost on this generation of academics.

The recent stress on narrow job preparation is under attack from a curious source—the business community. C. C. Garvin, chairman of the board of the Exxon Corporation, expresses two concerns: "We have a vested interest in the quality of education. There are some worrisome signs that the quality represented by a college degree may not be as high as it was ten years ago—at least in basic subjects like English and math. . . . A second concern is about students. These days they may be becoming too narrowly focused on their first job, and not enough on their long-term goals" (cited in Association of American Colleges, 1982, pp. 5-6). This notion that vocational studies are helpful in getting the first job, but that a broader education is more useful as preparation for a lifelong career is a common theme.

A survey of the attitudes of top corporate executives reports that they consider a good liberal education as important as a technical or professional education for a career in business (Committee for Corporate Support of Private Universities, 1979). In rating the importance of the various liberal arts for future executives, 98 percent of those surveyed consider oral and written communication skills to be either important or very important; 91 percent rate science and mathematics that highly, with history and social studies following closely with an 83 percent rating. Arts, philosophy, and foreign languages also receive support from a majority. Clearly, American executives regard a broad general education as utilitarian; general education not only makes sense but also dollars and cents, according to this survey.

This conclusion receives empirical support from a study of successful managers in the Bell System (Beck, 1981). A group of young employees were given a comprehensive assessment of their managerial potential as inferred from their administrative skills, interpersonal skills, intellectual ability, and managerial motivation. Larger proportions of those with a liberal arts major than with concentrations in either business or engineering were judged high in managerial potential. A twenty-year follow-up study showed that the liberal arts group, most with preparation in the humanities and social sciences, advanced more rapidly and to higher levels of management than those with professional educations.

What is the utility of the liberal arts? Some point to generic thinking skills, such as analysis, critical thinking, or problem solving. Others cite substantive knowledge of history, the natural world, social organizations, and artistic creations that aid in both tangible and intangible ways in the conduct of practical affairs. These claims augment the traditional beliefs that a liberal education develops an expanded sense of self, which is the basis for getting along with others and living a satisfying life, and promotes civic responsibility and preparation for full participation in a democracy.

Others charge that the liberal arts have sold out to corporate America. They argue that the historic role of higher education is to stand at arm's length from worldly affairs and to serve as a critic of corporate and governmental actions by exposing injustice, providing alternative visions, and promoting the social good. The educational enterprise, they continue, should not cozy up to business or cater to established institutions. Utilitarians retort that, since taxes fund so much of higher education, the public has every right to insist that the educational system serve the interests of social institutions by preparing a sophisticated workforce and a generation of civic-minded citizens.

The middle ground in this debate holds that students can have both a practical education and a broad general one. Indeed, the combination is likely to be of greater utility than either one alone, as Cousins argues:

> The irony of the emphasis being placed on careers is that nothing is more valuable for anyone who has had a professional or vocational education than to be able to deal with abstractions or complexities, or to feel comfortable with subtleties of thought or language, or to think sequentially. The

doctor who knows only disease is at a disadvantage
alongside the doctor who knows at least as much
about people as he does about pathological organ-
isms. The lawyer who argues in court from a narrow legal base is no match for the lawyer who can
connect legal precedents to historical experience
and who employs wide-ranging intellectual resources. The business executive whose competence
in general management is bolstered by an artistic
ability to deal with people is of prime value to his
company. For the technologist, the engineering of
consent can be just as important as the engineering
of moving parts. In all these respects, the liberal
arts have much to offer. Just in terms of career
preparation, therefore, a student is shortchanging
himself by shortcutting the humanities [1978, p.
15].

Thus voices in many quarters believe that general education can
play a role in enriching the quality of life and the checkbook,
too.

Recent Innovators

Champions of special programs for nontraditional students—women, minorities, and adults—view the developments in
general education with a mixture of anxiety and optimism.
Some are anxious because these special programs gained a foot-
hold in colleges and universities, at least in part, when many colleges dropped requirements during the 1960s and 1970s, thereby
making room in the curriculum for women's or ethnic studies,
for example. The current call to restructure general education
threatens to squeeze out these innovative programs by imposing
more requirements on students. Some are optimistic, however,
that their special programs may be incorporated into college requirements. Theirs, at best, is a fearful optimism.

A series of articles in the *Women's Studies Quarterly* provides a case in point. Carolyn Lougee, who chaired a Stanford
University committee on the undergraduate curriculum, dis-

cusses the issues confronting feminists in curricular reform. Stanford chose to design a new set of area requirements for all undergraduates. Many courses that meet the requirements study women and minorities, but no student is obliged to take a course with such a focus. The centerpiece of the program is the year-long course in Western culture. Lougee (1981) notes that women are neglected in this centerpiece course because it focuses on civic life during and following the Renaissance, the province of men; because the principle of selecting the readings stresses formal genres, such as drama or poetry, as expressed in the great works, most of which are written by men; and because the prevailing ideal is that of a cultivated, educated gentleman who transcends all cultures and eras. She confesses that she and many of her fellow humanists supported the proposed curriculum "because of our commitment to the importance of studying the humanities. We did so because we did not want our vision of the best to drive out our chance of grasping the good" (p. 7).

Feminists at Stanford submitted a number of proposals. First, they suggested a separate required course on women, which was rejected on the grounds that a special compensatory course for one group of students was inadvisable in the core curriculum for all. Second, some criticized the flawed understanding of women in Aristotle, Aquinas, and Freud, but Lougee counters, "I am less interested in three thousand years of misogyny than I am in *women,* and this strategy is not going to give us any *women* in our Western Civ courses" (p. 5). Third, they proposed that materials on women be integrated into existing courses. But Lougee retorts, "Because the pace, shape, and direction of change in the past have not been the same for women and men, integrating women into frameworks developed to explain men's past will not work" (p. 6). Thus, Stanford settled for the best option it found available, although a future rethinking of all subjects might yield a more gender-balanced curriculum.

Two reactions to Lougee's article reveal more of the controversy about the role of women's studies in the core curriculum. Froula and Munich (1981, p. 14) affirm "the importance of learning to read the literary classics of the Western tradition from a feminist perspective." Many classics, even those authored by men, profoundly illustrate women's oppression, and the task is to help students read these materials so as to understand the tensions between male and female. In a different vein, Wilson (1981) recalls: "We started out saying that women's studies was a practical *means* toward a transformation of liberal education into a nonsexist curriculum. Now I think we are tending to view women's studies as an end in itself because the battles fought, one class at a time, have been so enervating and time consuming. Because some of us have lost sight of our original humanistic goal, we cannot conceive of matching our effort of the last ten years in order to overhaul liberal education" (p. 5). Despite the difficulty, she calls for " 'mainstreaming' women's study, . . . a bold, sweeping redesign of departmental and college-wide programs (that) . . . would institutionalize for the first time a female Gestalt into the basic undergraduate liberal education; end the ghettoization of women's studies; and, if we are lucky, produce professional women who are more feminist than any previous generation—and more employable in non-stereotyped jobs" (p. 6).

The inclusion of special perspectives and ideas in the core curriculum also catches the imagination of proponents of minority students. Blake (1981) reminds us that since the purpose of liberal and general education is to make human beings whole, it must attend to the circumstances of minorities of all types: "Most approaches to the education of minorities start with a deficit model, therefore the discussion focuses on the problems the students present and how to meet their needs for remediation. This deficit model assumes that these students arrive at the institutional doors wholly bereft of any redeeming qualities, or lacking any positive contributions they might make—except on the sports field. However, both our research and our experience at Oakes College (University of California, Santa Cruz) shows us that these students bring with them a host of positive qualities and unique strengths." He argues that a program should build on strengths rather than try to attack deficits. Further, he reminds us that the experiences of minority groups cast fresh light on enduring national ideals such as social justice, equality of opportunity, and cultural pluralism. His is a persuasive argument for incorporating minority perspectives into the core of the curriculum.

Other innovators, such as those working with adults or using experiential learning, are even more skeptical of the emphasis on a common core. They note that adults have accumulated a fund of life experience and therefore their needs and goals differ from those of traditional students. General education in many adult education degree programs tends to employ more individualized curriculums or special delivery systems, such as the weekend college, to meet their students' needs. Advocates of experiential learning look askance at curricular reforms that stress common learning and similar, if not common, learning experiences, typically within the confines of the traditional classroom. While an occasional voice argues for intergenerational learning, it seems that the notion of mainstreaming, which captures the imagination of other innovators, does not intrigue practitioners of adult or experiential education.

These dynamics cast innovators of the recent past into the role of educational conservatives, defending their own precarious status quo. In protecting their own special creations, they resist change in the direction of common learning, just as their former antagonists resisted their individualized offerings. In some cases, those who resisted the earlier changes now find themselves in the forefront of the reform battle. Not only does the reform of general education produce curious bedfellows, but it sometimes even reverses their sides of the bed.

Students who are not well skilled in the basics represent yet another type of nontraditional student, and advocates of skills programs are also skeptical about proposals for general education that stress common learning and are less tolerant of diversity. These advocates feel that proposals requiring all students to meet the same minimal standards threaten to purge colleges of students who have potential but have not yet demonstrated an adequate level of achievement. The call for higher standards is regarded as a challenge to the principle of open access and to the common practice of helping individuals overcome entering deficiencies. However, Robert McCabe, president of Miami-Dade Community College, states that open access must continue, especially at community colleges, but, at the same time, higher standards must be met: "The college should assume responsibility to assist individuals to succeed, and an ordered curriculum should be instituted to deal with reading, writing, and computational deficiencies first, so that all benefit from attendance. However, the colleges must also be prepared to suspend students if there is no evidence of reasonable progress. At Miami-Dade, over 11,000 students have been suspended in the last three years" (1982, p. 5). Miami-Dade allows suspended students to reenroll after a semester, but they must take a special "intervention" course to aid performance and possibly take a reduced course load until their performance becomes satisfactory. McCabe claims that raising standards is the only way to ward off the mindless attempt to improve quality by imposing arbitrary admissions requirements, thereby denying many the benefit of a college education. Turning the argument around, he contends that the only way to guarantee that the open door remains open is to retain high academic standards.

The tensions between unity and diversity, conscription and freedom run throughout the debate on general education, but these issues weigh most heavily on those who defend the fragile innovations of the recent past. Precisely because they once attacked prevailing general education requirements, they find it difficult to support the effort to reconstruct the general curriculum today. But some see beyond defensive claims to the need to guarantee a quality program and, in many cases, to the opportunity to extend their offerings, in some fashion, to the whole of the student body. Both groups have much riding on the outcome of the general education debate.

Students

Students are conspicuous by their absence in the debate about general education. Unlike the curricular reforms during the late 1960s and early 1970s, which were stimulated by student demands for greater freedom, the campus debate today is carried on largely by faculty members and administrators. It appears that the faculty are determined to reestablish their authority over the curriculum; they seem to feel that reforms initiated by students have failed and that now the faculty must take charge. But to exclude students from the dialogue could prove catastrophic. A curriculum that is attractive to students could be an institution's first line of defense against the projected declines in enrollment. Requirements and courses that fail to attract and retain students could bankrupt institutions dependent on tuition income.

A survey of students was undertaken to discover their attitudes toward general education (Gaff and Davis, 1981). For the vast majority, over 90 percent, the goal of getting a broad general education is an important one. Other goals that enjoy wide support include "knowledge and skills directly related to a job or career," "self-knowledge and personal development," "understanding and mastery of some specialized body of knowledge," "ability to get along with people," and "intellectual tools to continue learning new areas by yourself." There is no evidence, by and large, that students are content to restrict their education to either narrow specialization or vocationalism.

Although students hold the ideal of becoming a generally educated person, they are very critical of the programs of study offered to this end. Asked to rate activities according to their contribution to overall intellectual and personal development in college, students gave coursework in disciplines outside their majors, both introductory and upper-level courses, the lowest ratings, lower than off-campus social, cultural, and work activities; talking or working informally with faculty; and campus activities, clubs, or social life. The highest ratings were given to coursework in their majors, followed by socializing with fellow students, and independent study and creative activities. Students were also asked to indicate the number of courses in which a set of learning outcomes was achieved. The alternatives were derived from rationales given for requiring breadth courses. Most of the students said that most of their courses failed to realize each of the following objectives: introduce them to significant ideas, concepts, or intellectual perspectives; contribute to a broad intellectual foundation for the study of their majors; engage and challenge their own ideas, assumptions, or attitudes; stimulate their curiosity and desire to learn more about those fields; and help master new methods of intellectual inquiry. Such results constitute strong evidence that general education courses are failing their students.

Students expressed specific ideas about the kinds of changes they prefer. When presented with a set of paired opposites, more than three of four preferred: choices among a set of alternative courses rather than a required core; active methods of learning rather than lectures; courses that are integrated rather than discrete; and practical or concrete topics rather than theoretical or abstract content. Smaller proportions, but still a strong majority, preferred courses in which value and social implications are explored rather than factual matters alone; courses tailored to different majors rather than uniform courses; programs of general education distributed throughout all four years rather than concentrated in the first two years; and courses stressing the personal needs of students rather than only intellectual issues.

These views are hardly radical; indeed, they resemble the ideas of many faculty members and administrators who want to strengthen general education. But students reject the commonly proposed solution of requiring more courses in conventional liberal arts disciplines. Rather, they hold that general education programs must be different—not just more of the same—if the ideal is to be realized. Students' views are important not only because their satisfaction affects enrollment, but also because they are concerned with the quality of their education, not with departmental politics or territorial infighting. This survey shows that students have important views about the purpose, form, substance, and methodology of general education, views which most institutions cannot afford to ignore.

The Harvard Plan and Its Critics

In the national debate about general education, Harvard University once again occupies center stage. But the Harvard Plan of 1978 differs from its predecessor of 1945 in two impor-

tant ways: it won the approval of its own faculty, and it is play-
ing to decidedly mixed reviews elsewhere. Indeed, the plan has
generated so much criticism that it has become a major topic in
the debate on general education. No one has criticized the ideal
of general education or Harvard's effort to strengthen this portion of its curriculum. But various educators have disapproved
of the plan's content, particularly its inadequacy as a model for
other institutions.

The general principles of the program are outlined in the
Harvard task force's report: "It is important to notice what is
not being proposed in the core curriculum as well as what *is*
being proposed. We are not proposing an identical set of courses
for all students, and we are not proposing an even-handed introduction to all fields of knowledge. The proliferation of knowledge makes both of these goals impractical, except at the cost
of severe simplification and the loss of either range or intellectual quality. We do not think there is a single set of great books
that every educated person must master, and we do not think an
inevitably thin survey of the conventional substantive areas—
humanities, social sciences, and natural sciences—is any longer
useful. Nor do we think a loose distribution requirement among
departmental courses can convey specifically enough what the
faculty believes to be the 'knowledge, skills, and habits of
thought' that are of general and lasting intellectual significance"
(Task Force on the Core Curriculum, 1978, p. 3).

The Harvard Plan requires a set of ten semester courses in
five substantive areas. In literature and the arts, three courses
are required: in literature, fine arts or music, and the contexts
of culture; in history, two courses: one on some aspect of the
modern world and another on the historical process and perspective; in social and philosophical analysis, one course on social analysis and another in moral and political philosophy; in
science and mathematics, one course in physical science and
mathematics and one in biological and behavioral science; and
in foreign languages and cultures, one course on Western Europe
or a major non-Western culture. In addition, proficiency is required in writing, mathematics through algebra, and foreign language at the level of minimal reading competence.

Among the other more prominent features of the program is the fact that the total number of courses acceptable to meet these requirements is only about 100, with students permitted to choose among several alternatives in each area. Guidelines for the content of each of these courses are detailed in the proposal. A standing committee oversees this segment of the curriculum, encouraging the development of appropriate courses and determining the suitability of courses that are proposed; subcommittees are responsible for each of the several areas of the overall program.

The response to the plan was immediate and clangorous. Dean Henry Rosovsky (1978, p. 41) recalls: "I was quite critical of the state of undergraduate education, and everybody seemed for the most part to agree with me. When you say things are bad, you don't get much disagreement, I learned. It's when you start offering solutions that things become more serious." He recalls some of the reactions, first from the campus and then from beyond. "We received hundreds of letters—all thoughtful letters —from the professors and from the students, and pretty soon all this was in the newspapers. There were some political reactions. Political reactions from the left. Political reactions from the right. . . . The student press opposed the new curriculum. They viewed it as recapturing authority. And some scientists were not sympathetic. They're not high on teaching science to nonscientists. . . . I've had some praise from quarters I don't particularly want it from—from people who oversimplify or from reactionaries who want to bring things back to what they call the good old days. The whole back-to-basics approach needs to be defined. I'm in danger of becoming a hero to some Neanderthals." Rosovsky's efforts stirred so much interest and controversy that he had to appoint a "minister of foreign affairs" to handle requests from interested outsiders for information, materials, and interviews.

The views of external critics are summarized by James Q. Wilson, the political scientist who chaired the task force on the core curriculum. Wilson points out that "We do not see Harvard as a model for what all colleges ought to be"; nonetheless:

> The emerging debate over curricular change
> has cast Harvard in the role of exemplar, assumed

that whatever it did ought to represent the ideal, and criticized it for falling short of that ideal. The nature of that ideal differs, of course, depending on the identity of the critic: Kenneth Lynn, writing in *Commentary,* wishes we had created a more coherent, humanistic curriculum based on the great books; Henry Fairlie, in a syndicated column, berates us for not becoming more like an idealized Oxford; Alston Chase, writing in the *Atlantic,* worries that the liberal arts have been so subverted by relativistic social scientists and pandering to student wants as to make any curricular change suspect; and Barry O'Connell, writing in *Change,* . . . protests that elite colleges perpetuate social inequality, a tendency likely to be made worse by a core curriculum. Each has his own explanation as to why Harvard should have failed to attain the critic's personal ideal: departmental provincialism, philistine professors, weak administrators, the temper of the times, the rottenness of society, or whatever [1978, p. 40].

The Harvard curriculum has become a lightning rod that attracts bolts of criticism from throughout the academic firmament. It illustrates the ways various voices come to bear on concrete proposals to change the general education program. Maher understands that, although Harvard did not set out to provide the definitive American curriculum, "the spotlight thrown upon its efforts by the popular press creates an inevitable 'fishbowl' effect. In effect, proposals generated at Harvard often become 'national' models" (1978, p. 3). His critique of the plan affirms that the quality of thought about general education is far richer than the Harvard program implies, that it neglects many contemporary ideas and innovative practices that hold promise for improving general education, and that its approaches should not be simply adopted by other, quite different colleges and universities.

Probably the most common reaction is that offered by Stephenson (1978, p. 4): "As Groucho Marx (who unfortunately, was never awarded a degree and therefore, one supposes, does not belong in the company of educated men and women) once said, 'There is less going on here than meets the eye.' " To many the program is but a warmed-over distribution scheme, a retreat to the past and to bankrupt forms, and too timid a response to the serious social and educational problems enumerated in Harvard's own report. Essentially a structural response, it offers little promise of either transforming the university's prevailing value system to emphasize the education of undergraduate students or commanding the loyalty of faculty to purposes larger than their departments.

Others criticize the requirements as overly constricted and arbitrary, compressing a vast intellectual and cultural richness into a few narrow categories and unnecessarily restricting students' freedom. The opposite danger is also cited, namely, that the plan does not provide the unity and integration that characterize general education at its best. These critics claim that the new scheme, although better than an indiscriminate, loose distribution system, does not restore a common curriculum that would capture the imagination and allegiance of students and faculty. Further, while the program does not require study in specific disciplines, these familiar categories lurk just below the surface. Although most disciplines are represented in the program, disciplinary separatism and fragmentation go unaddressed. Integration, synthesis, and interdisciplinary values remain shortchanged.

Still other critics point out that despite the guidelines for acceptable courses, there is no serious consideration of the conditions of learning. In the words of Katz (1978, p. 5), "No program for students these days is worth stating unless consideration is given to *how* the students are going to do the learning and what the chances are that the student will *retain* what is learned: such retention does not just mean memorized 'facts' but acquired skills, among them increased capacity for reasoning."

These criticisms notwithstanding, the program is proceeding apace (see Whitla, 1982). The science segment of the curriculum was offered for the first time in the fall of 1982, by a team of faculty members working together with three Nobel laureates. The faculty are more enthusiastic than some expected, developing new and stimulating courses, although it has been difficult to elicit courses in a few areas, such as moral reasoning. Students, too, are reacting positively; enrollments are higher than expected, as students are electing the courses even before requirements go into effect. And preliminary evidence indicates that the core courses, by and large, receive better than average evaluations.

As Dean Rosovsky concluded when the program was approved, "Look, this is not perfect, but it's a hell of a lot better than what we have now" (1979, p. A-23). Given the diversity of voices in the debate about general education, the miracle is not how well the plan is functioning but that a new program exists at all.

Chapter Three

Toward a New Philosophy

A curriculum is far more than a set of courses; most fundamentally it is a statement of an institution's philosophy of education. Kerr (1977, p. ix) puts it well: "In the final analysis, the curriculum is nothing less than the statement a college makes about what, out of the totality of man's constantly growing knowledge and experience, is considered useful, appropriate, or relevant to the lives of educated men and women at a certain point of time." Whether explicit or implicit, sophisticated or simplistic, an institution's assessment of intellectual and other values determines the curricular pattern it chooses. Thus although the focus of attention in the debate on general education tends to be the formal curriculum, far more important are the changes college faculties are making in their underlying educational philosophies.

Any curricular philosophy is a group product rather than the work of a single mind. It is, therefore, born of compromise and accommodation among several competing conceptions. And a curricular philosophy is expressed in action as well as in words; indeed, when they conflict, actual practices more truly represent the operative philosophy than do any verbal statements. Indeed, Cross (1975) identifies three curriculums that coexist at any school: the curriculum described in the catalogue, the curriculum the faculty teach, and the curriculum the students learn. If the discrepancies between an institution's stated philosophy and the faculty's practices or student's behavior are large, then the institution's educational philosophy is reduced to pious declarations and empty rhetoric. The resulting cynicism can destroy the very integrity of the institution.

One approach to devising a curricular philosophy is to consider the general aims of education. As we have seen, however, there is no consensus concerning the aims of general education. Riley (1980) enumerates six competing goals: developing critical intelligence, preparing students for jobs, transforming society and its institutions, transmitting a body of classical knowledge, providing students with skills, and developing the "whole person." While doubting the wisdom and feasibility of reaching any meaningful consensus on a national, regional, or state level, Riley argues that each institution can and must reach some consensus about goals, for "without a systematic review of the aims of education, colleges and universities will tend to reinstate mindlessly a 1950s model of general education" (p. 298).

A second approach is to define the qualities possessed by an educated person. Such an examination was conducted by the Tennessee Higher Education Commission (Branscomb and others, 1977). The authors conclude: "The general skills of writing, reading, speaking, and calculating are primarily the responsibility of elementary and secondary education. . . . Besides such specific skills, basic understandings are necessary for intelligent adult behavior, no matter what one's vocation. . . . We believe a general understanding of the concepts suggested under democracy and citizenship, history and geography, science, economics, literature, and self-directed learning is a must for all college graduates" (pp. 5, 10). In addition, they believe that college graduates should be able to reason and think critically, understand the major methods of intellectual inquiry, comprehend our form of government, exhibit a moral sensibility for both personal and institutional behavior, and manifest a heightened sense of personal awareness.

Such statements are not new, and most definitions of the educated person do not differ substantially from this one. It is significant, however, that many institutions are addressing this age-old question again and are reaffirming such traditional purposes. A second significant result of this exercise is that it focuses on the student. Unfortunately, curriculums have frequently been determined by the inertia of past practices, the interests of faculty, or other secondary issues. Further, the preparation of such a description affirms the importance of general education, since virtually all such goals fall under its province. A consideration of the qualities of an educated person provides curricular leaders with an opportunity to examine the purposes of education other than professionalism or specialization, and thus to prepare students for life outside the narrow confines of academia.

A third approach to reformulating or reevaluating an institution's curricular philosophy is to develop what Merton (1968) calls "theories of the middle range." Such theories are neither global philosophical statements nor specific, discrete prescriptions; the middle range seeks to avoid the amorphous quality of the former and the fragmentary character of the latter. Rather, middle-range theories are statements that relate ideas about general education to specific curricular practices. For example, some curricular review committees adopt the guideline that each curricular practice must have a stated rationale and that each general institutional goal must be realized in specific curricular practices. Such a guideline ensures that traditional educational practices, such as courses in Western civilization, are not reaffirmed simply because they are familiar, but because they express explicit convictions.

Many institutions have formed task forces to reevaluate their curricular philosophy and discuss germane topics. These task forces try to reach some agreement on basic principles, acceptable alternatives, and recommendations to their institutional community. They help their colleagues design courses and incorporate the institution's overall purposes into their individual course offerings. At its best, this process results in a coherent set of curricular principles that enjoys a working consensus and maintains institutional integrity, by ensuring that practices are consistent with stated philosophy.

Tenets of an Emergent Philosophy

Under the leadership of campus task forces and committees, new curricular philosophies are emerging. Fundamental differences exist among the philosophies of various institutions, and faculties sometimes reject propositions advanced by their task forces or unenthusiastically accept their recommendations. Nonetheless, a large set of tenets are shared by most institutions. Before enumerating these tenets, it is worthwhile to note that recent curricular philosophies for general education appear to be more eclectic than certain of those developed during earlier revivals; during such periods, whole institutions or programs were fashioned in accordance with the philosophies of Dewey's progressivism or Hutchins's essentialism.

Indeed, some critics charge that curricular philosophies are now not as strong or as pure as in earlier times, and that they are, therefore, suspect. In point of fact, during earlier revivals, very few colleges and universities embraced any particular school of philosophy. Furthermore, the national economy and demographic projections were then more favorable to the creation of new institutions devoted to new philosophies. Today the focus of attention is necessarily the improvement of existing institutions and the education of a variety of students, not the development of experimental colleges for special students attracted by a particular approach to education. This current trend might be called *practical idealism*. Thus while proponents of idealism, progressivism, essentialism, and pragmatism are found on every campus, most curricular task forces seek to reach broad areas of agreement rather than select one approach over another.

Among the most significant principles that characterize the current philosophy of general education are the following.

General education is compatible with specialization and is a necessary complement to it. Conventional wisdom regards general education as broadening and contrasts it with the depth afforded by specialization. Bell (1966) rightly recognizes this contrast as fallacious. The issue, he claims, is not "the specious one of 'breadth' versus 'depth,' which implies a nonsensical choice between superficiality and competence. The central problem is, rather, relevant breadth versus a limited and dangerously irresponsible competence." However cogent Bell's clarification, the distinction between breadth and depth arises repeatedly, and campus leaders concerned with general education frequently are confronted with various versions of this concern.

Mayhew (1980, p. 1) notes that "in discussing general education with members of our faculty, I often sense a measure of unease. Some appear to suspect that a strong emphasis on general education will hamper our students in the marketplace; others conjure images of the weakening of their departmental major programs. Suspicion that general education may be anti-science, or at least inadequately scientific, is also widespread." He tries to put some of these concerns at rest by explaining: "It is no doubt possible to take a radical stance on general education, arguing that the truly general and specific are incompatible and that all traces of specialization must be eliminated root and branch. Nevertheless, the aims of general education are not inconsistent with intensive major programs in science or in any other field; on the contrary, rigorous, in-depth study of a particular field is, I think, an essential component of good undergraduate education" (p. 1).

Other campus leaders take the position of Sir Richard Livingston, "A technician is a man who understands everything about his job except its place in the order of the universe" (cited by Bailey, 1977, p. 250). They do not reject specialization but see general education as a necessary complement to specialized studies, one which restores balance and allows specialization to occur within a larger context. Both breadth and depth are viewed as necessary to properly educate men and women: "In the polarity between diversity and unity, [we have] so attended to diversity and specialization that [we have] inclined toward the neglect of factors of connectedness and unity. This is why the question of general education has become critical in recent years" (Bucknell University, 1978, p. 2).

General education is a necessary part of professional education. Contrary to the views of Hutchins, who pitted general education against vocational education, many educators now assert their interdependence, claiming that a proper education in any professional area requires not only technical proficiency but also the ability to communicate with clients and colleagues, an awareness of larger social trends, a sensitivity to personal and social values, and the like. Ashby (1958, p. 84) describes this ideal as "technological humanism," which he defines as "the habit of apprehending technology in its completeness." He suggests that the student's specialty be the core around which a cluster of relevant courses is composed. Stating that "the path to culture should be through a man's specialism, not by bypassing it," he offers the example of a student who takes up the study of brewing:

> His way to acquire general culture is not by diluting his brewing courses with popular lectures on architecture, social history and ethics, but by making brewing the core of his studies. The sine qua non for a man who desires to be cultured is a deep and enduring enthusiasm to do one thing excellently. So there must first of all be an assurance that the student genuinely wants to make beer. From this is a natural step to the study of biology, microbiology, and chemistry: all subjects which can be studied not as techniques to be practised but as ideas to be understood. As his studies gain momentum the student could, by skillful teaching, be made interested in the economics of marketing beer, in public-houses, in their design, in architecture; or in the history of beer drinking from the time of the early Egyptian inscriptions, and so in social history; or, in the unhappy moral effects of drinking too much beer, and so in religion and ethics. A student who can weave his technology into the fabric of society can claim to have a liberal education; a student who cannot weave this tech-

nology into the fabric of society cannot claim even
to be a good technologist.

Several campus task forces have adopted the principle that general is not opposed to professional education but rather is a
necessary complement to it.

*Some knowledge is more important than other knowl-
edge.* The prevailing system of loose distribution requirements
typically permits a student to select from within broad categories, such as the humanities, social sciences, and natural sciences. Thus students can easily sidestep any particular field of
study, and graduate without having taken courses in specific
fields or having acquired particular skills. For example, students' inadequate writing skill is the subject of a report by the
University of California, Davis: "Roughly half of our entering
freshman fail the preliminary examination—a simple essay of
about four pages on a topic chosen from a list—that would
exempt them from English A. . . . Freshmen who fail the preliminary examination are required to pass one quarter of English
A with a grade of D-minus or better. Except for English A,
there is at present no campus-wide composition requirement.
. . . It is possible for a student . . . to go through college *without ever writing another essay,* or without the essays he writes
ever being corrected for grammar, spelling, organization, or
style" (Joint Steering Committee on General Education, 1980,
p. 7). The Committee recommended that the passing grade for
English A be raised to C-minus, that sections of the course be
limited to twenty students, and that there be a common final
exam graded by someone other than the section instructor. Further, it recommended that students be required to take two
additional courses that stress fundamentals such as coherent organization and concise expression. Writing, it declared, was
more important than many other topics.

The liberal arts and sciences are the major beneficiaries of
this reevaluation of priorities. Many institutions that had begun
to emphasize vocational and professional preparation are now
reaffirming the value of the liberal arts as the most generically
useful knowledge produced by the human mind.

Certain subjects should be required of every student. In the 1960s faculty and students rejected the notion of required courses in general education. Faculty disliked teaching courses to nonmajors, and students responded to their dislike by rebelling against the uninspired teaching and irrelevant instruction it produced. Today, having seen the consequences of the unstructured curriculum, many students and faculty alike are asserting that several key subjects should be required (Cahn, 1981-82). Harvard was one of the first universities during this revival to declare that some knowledge is sufficiently important as to be required of all students and to establish a set of requirements in the liberal arts.

Many small colleges now mandate a common core curriculum, a set of specific courses required of each student; such cores reflect their homogeneity of students, faculty, and institutional values. At larger and more diversified institutions, the tendency is to require certain subjects but to permit a degree of student choice among alternative courses. Although the specific requirements vary from school to school—both in terms of subject areas and levels of attainment—the trend is to require certain courses whose content is deemed essential.

Academic standards are too low and must be raised. Rightly or wrongly, many observers relate declining student achievement to the relaxation of standards and to the lack of structure in the curriculum. Many schools are raising their standards in a number of ways, including the imposition of more stringent curricular requirements. Allied changes concern limiting the use of credit/no credit grades; shortening the period during which courses may be added or dropped without penalty; raising the grade-point average required to remain in good standing or to avoid probation; and instituting college-wide competence testing in basic skills. Colleges are readdressing their responsibilities for defining and enforcing standards, thus attempting to ensure the value of the degrees they confer. Raising standards, indeed defining acceptable standards for a diverse student body, is a collective responsibility, because, in the words of one campus report, "Where credit-hour production is the name of the game, individual vigilantism in this matter can quickly lead to martyrdom" (University Educational Policy Committee/General Education Models Task Force, 1980, p. 7).

The course of study should possess a degree of coherence. The proliferation and specialization of courses results in a fragmented and less-meaningful program. Some colleges now limit the courses that are acceptable to meet their general education requirements. Such selectivity helps ensure that each acceptable course treats significant topics in ways specifically intended to contribute to coherence. Other colleges specify more precisely the nature of these courses and tailor them to achieve general education purposes. Some institutions require interdisciplinary, thematic, or problem-oriented courses; bolder efforts to achieve coherence include the creation of clusters of courses. SUNY, College at Old Westbury, requires students to take a cluster of integrated electives (Maguire, 1980). Faculty members in various departments jointly define the goals of their cluster's courses and are responsible for the cluster's coherence.

Colleges should place more emphasis on common learning. Many are affirming the value of having students take at least a portion of their studies in common, believing that common learning is an important part of collegiate experience. This emphasis on a community of learners is intended to correct the fragmentation that characterizes colleges and universities. Hill relates the eclipse of the academic community to "radically *unshared purposes* (or mismatched expectations) of faculty and students regarding the significance of undergraduate education; an astounding fragmentation and *atomization* of the undergraduate curriculum; and a resulting *privatization* of academic experience for both students and faculty who experience it in terms of isolation and nonengagement" (1979, p. 2).

To reassert its sense of community, SUNY Stony Brook created temporary learning communities, each of which federates existing courses around critical issues, such as world hunger or ethical issues in life sciences. This and several structural mechanisms allow students to experience, for a time, a genuine intellectual community that is qualitatively different from the rest of their college experience.

Other educators believe that a core curriculum can pro-

vide a center of gravity for students at institutions that enroll
many part-time, nonresidential, and diverse students, or those
that offer several special purpose, off-campus, and vocational
programs. Boyer and Kaplan (1977, p. 50) view the core curriculum as a means to counter the emphasis on individualism and
egotism in American culture: "In an era when the isolated self
dominates our moral thinking, our intellectual culture, our social relations, and our institutional designs, a strong case can be
made for a core curriculum based on commonality—commonality in time, on this globe, and together." Such emphasis on
commonality among all people illustrates our interdependence
and, they believe, prepares students to live more fulfilling and
productive lives.

  General education is everyone's business. General education was once parceled out to specific units, to the college of
basic studies, to the humanities departments, and to departments that provided introductory surveys of their academic
fields. Because responsibilities were delegated to various units
and individuals, many academics were able to wash their hands
of the matter. "General education," they reasoned "is taken
care of 'over there'." Colleges are now deeming this approach
unacceptable, as an interim report of the task force at Northeastern Illinois University shows: "Improving the general education of our students is too big and complex a task to delegate
to a few departments, special programs, or a congeries of otherwise unintegrated courses of wide individual choice" (University
Educational Policy Committee/General Education Models Task
Force, 1980, p. 7).

  Expression of this corporate responsibility for general
education takes various forms. Some institutions now appoint a
campus director of general education or a committee to super-
vise this portion of the curriculum. Others have new centralized
procedures for selecting and designating courses that serve general education purposes, no longer allowing departments or instructors to make such decisions. Some schools are revising their
faculty policies to explicitly state that all faculty are expected
to work in the program. Naturally, not all faculty must contribute in the same way; some may be more interested and effective

in teaching skills, others in conveying the essence of their disciplines, and still others in interdisciplinary studies.

Of course, some faculty and departments resist such responsibility, and the departmental structure encumbers coordinated planning. Yet many feel that general education is the *one* area in which everyone has a vested interest—it is the core of the curriculum that can either buttress or undermine every specialized course of study. If individual units see themselves as autonomous, or if faculty members feel more allegiance to their departments than to their institutions, then the campuses must reassert institutional authority and articulate common interests in such matters as general education. Many schools now stress the corporate responsibility and seek to elevate the views of faculty about their own interests and responsibilities in the general curriculum.

Strengthening undergraduate general education does not require abandoning research or graduate training. Colleges and universities serve a number of important purposes, only one of which is undergraduate general education. Some curricular committees, particularly at major research universities, work to reassure faculty members devoted to scholarship or graduate education that steps to strengthen undergraduate education are not an attack on other legitimate interests but are quite compatible with strong graduate programs and research capabilities. The goal is to achieve a balance rather than to stress any one purpose at the expense of the others.

The general education program should be distinctive, reflecting the character of the institution. During recent years general education courses throughout the nation became fairly similar; introductory surveys of academic disciplines and upper-level courses in subdivisions of traditional disciplines differed little among campuses. Such standardization provides some uniform measures of achievement and simplifies the transfer of credit. Perhaps to reassert their institutional identity or to better compete for enrollments, many schools are stressing the distinctive features of their general education programs. At St. Andrews Presbyterian College, for example, the design of a new curriculum included the following principles: "First, the design should be directly related to the college's identity and mission. Second, the curriculum should build on strengths of the college, its faculty, and resources. Third, the curriculum should be designed for the learning needs of the students who will be served —a balance between what needs the students and faculty perceive" (Crossley, 1979, p. 38). The college decided on a core curriculum called St. Andrews General Education (SAGE): "One distinctive value of a core curriculum is its visibility. That is, the program occupies a central place in our efforts and signals internally and externally that general education gets serious faculty effort and attention" (p. 54).

The search for curricular distinctiveness also can be seen at colleges with a religious affiliation, as in the Gardner-Webb plan, which not only requires course work in religion but is seeking to infuse religious principles (such as the notion of servant leader) throughout the curriculum.

A draft proposal circulated at American University stresses geographical opportunities for distinctiveness and explicitly mentions possible competitive advantages: "We believe that the proposed concept of 'America in an Interdependent World' will serve to maximize natural advantages offered by our Washington location, consolidate our many accomplishments of the past several years, and provide our university an exciting and promising future. We further believe that by giving our university a distinctive identity, we will enhance its overall visibility and power to attract superior students" (p. 1). The curriculum that was adopted relies on distributive studies but does require substantial work in the twin themes of the American experience and the global experience.

General education should incorporate recent advances in scholarship. Although the introduction of recent scholarship is fundamental to all higher education, general education courses have tended to rely on familiar content rather than to incorporate newer intellectual material. Many colleges are now asserting that such topics as international studies, the role of minorities and women, and recent advances in space exploration, the life sciences, and technology belong in the general education program. Some institutions, for example, now require courses in both Western and non-Western cultures. Similarly, schools that require physical education now include discussions of nutrition, drugs, and safety along with recreational sports, recognizing that recent research demonstrates that physical health is affected by factors in one's life-style other than exercise. Thus, even as some institutions are reemphasizing academic basics, they are also incorporating new advances in knowledge into their general education courses.

Faculty development is essential to general education. Although campus task force reports are worded diplomatically, many of them imply that the problem with general education lies primarily with the faculty. In a word, faculty are not broadly educated. Specialization fosters a narrowness of vision; academic disciplines work against serious intellectual discussion among experts in different fields; the emphasis on cognitive rationality all but purges values as a legitimate professional concern; notions of academic respectability prejudice faculty against working on fundamental, if messy, social and political problems; and the current retrenchment pits faculty members against one another and reduces debate about curriculum to self-serving statements and protective positions. These trends are now strongly being challenged, and many schools are encouraging faculty members to expand their vision and talents even as they are providing general education for their students. For instance, California Lutheran College provides faculty members with reading materials relevant to developing general education courses and offers opportunities for discussing the issues, both national and local, to increase their collective sophistication. A general education seminar at Columbia University provides a forum for the discussion of interdisciplinary value-laden issues that stimulate faculty and generate new general education courses. Other schools are encouraging faculty members to design new courses and teach in new ways. Interdisciplinary teaching in general education at the University of Wisconsin–Green Bay and at St. Joseph's College have spurred the faculty's professional development (Armstrong, 1979; Nichols, 1979).

General education reforms operate under a number of institutional constraints. As noted by a Northeastern Illinois University task force, public institutions face several constraints: "Idealism at a publicly funded and understaffed urban commuter institution . . . must be tempered by considerations of our students' needs, our faculty's availability and interest, our physical plant's limitation, . . . and the state's willingness to approve and support whatever it is we want to do" (University Educational Policy Committee/General Education Models Task Force, 1980, pp. 5-6). For example, a task force subcommittee suggested a required course on computer literacy: "If all UNI undergraduates, excluding Information Science majors, had to take this course, perhaps 100 sections a year need to be offered. However, Information Science already has one of the largest student-credit-hour loads per teacher of any department in the College of Arts and Sciences. Who then will teach these sections? New faculty? In a time when State officials are holding forth on the 'management of decline,' this option seems out of the question. And we have not even considered the availability of computer terminals or time" (p. 6). All institutions face various limits—faculty, budget, student interests, institutional mission—on the character of general education they can offer, and these limits must inform the school's operational philosophy.

Staffing of new programs must be reasonable and, in so far as possible, in accordance with past practices. As enrollments decline, faculty members are understandably concerned about the effects of curricular revisions on their futures. Many fear that curricular revision is a stalking horse for retrenchment. For that reason, proposals for curricular change sometimes mention staffing policies, including, for example, a statement indicating that all current faculty are expected to participate in the new program. Such universal involvement is common in small colleges as a means of stressing the responsibility of all faculty for general education and fairly dividing the obligation to staff the program.

Larger institutions sometimes take the opposite approach, reassuring faculty that no one will be required to teach courses that he or she is unwilling or unprepared to teach. Faculty are also reassured that work loads, summer teaching opportunities, and salaries will remain the same. Some schools also offer in-service training, primarily through summer workshops, and compensate faculty for time devoted to developing courses for a new curriculum. Despite these intentions and reassurances to support the faculty, Mary Sullivan, dean at the Rochester Institute of Technology, sounded a note of realism: "We are all in this curriculum endeavor together and unless there is a certain critical mass of enthusiasm and creativity in putting forth and volunteering for a set of courses that fulfill the purposes of a curriculum, there is no way that the curriculum can be adequately presented for students. There can be freedom and diversity in teaching so long as there are sufficient numbers of willing faculty to teach the diversity of courses that need to be taught" (1980, p. 3).

Case Example

The charge given to members of a general education committee at the University of the Pacific (1978) illustrates how these tenets can be unified into a coherent plan for reform. Committee members were told that their recommendation would be evaluated according to the following guidelines:

1. The proposed program of general education must be cost effective. The committee may recommend new programs, but the committee is responsible for making a revenue cost analysis of such programs.
2. The proposed program in general education should make effective use of existing university resources. Appropriate use of resources means full utilization of personnel and facilities.
3. The committee may ask programs and departments to engage in some redesigning of curriculum and methodology to meet the objectives of the proposed program in liberal learning.
4. The deliberations of this committee should generate discussion among members of the faculty of the university concerning liberal learning and establish a climate of opin-

ion which will support a university program of liberal
learning.

5. The general education program should allow and encourage experimentation by faculty and departments concerning the way in which they contribute to the goals and objectives of the program of liberal learning.

6. The goals of the program of liberal learning should be expressed in terms of outcomes. The application of this criterion means that instruction should be directed at producing discernible outcomes in students.

7. The proposed program of general education should include procedures for evaluation. The outcomes of courses
and instruction should be specifiable and a means of determining the success with which these outcomes are
achieved should be an integral part of the plan.

8. The proposed program in general education should include a monitoring process in which the system of accountability is university-wide.

9. The program must be designed so that it can be effectively
interpreted or presented as a coherent program to parents
and prospective students as well as to members of the university community.

10. The program in general education should be flexible and
adaptable to a variety of educational needs and goals of
students and to the programs of the schools and colleges
participating in this program. It must also be adaptable to
changing needs that emerge over time. The program should
contain orderly procedures for future modification and
adaptation.

11. The design of this program must be distinctive. It should
enhance the image of the university in comparison to
other institutions.

12. The implementation plan for this program should be one
which will allow the program of general education to be
adopted over a period of time in order to achieve an orderly transition from the several existing programs to a
single university program.

Thus the search for a new philosophy of general education is yielding a more robust agreement about the purposes and principles of general education today. The emerging conception of general education was expressed over a decade ago by Sanford (1967, p. 197): "Education aimed at developing the individual's potential as fully as possible is in the best sense *general education.* Introducing the students to a range of subjects and ideas, as in survey courses—sometimes called general education—is *not* the essential thing, though this may be a useful instrument of general education. Developing the generalist approach to inquiry, the synthetic function, is closer to the mark; and so is involvement in significant experiences with people and things. But this is by no means all. General education aims at development toward full humanity, and all the resources of a college should be organized to this end."

Chapter Four

Emerging
Curricular Patterns

The search for a philosophy of education is not an idle exercise, and the philosophical propositions discussed in Chapter Three are effecting changes in curricular patterns. Let us first consider changes in overall organization, such as the amount and structure of the curriculum, and then the content and various components of new programs.

Curricular Organization

The easiest way for a college to revise its curricular organization is to reimpose distribution requirements. This form of organization is so familiar that it need not be described here. Frequently, distribution requirements reflect campus politics rather than educational principles, but several other reasons motivate institutions to use this structure. First, the relaxation of graduation requirements in the 1960s led to a concern that many students fail to attain a broad and effective education, and the reinstatement of distribution requirements provides a corrective. Second, required study in the liberal arts reasserts the importance of these fields, which have been neglected of late in favor of more pragmatic vocational studies. Third, the return to a set of requirements distributed among traditional liberal arts disciplines is the form of general education that faculty members know best.

But history shows that general education tends to become ineffective when it degenerates into loose distribution schemes. Such schemes are marked by fragmentation, loss of educational purpose, and faculty and student disinterest—the very inadequacies that lead institutions to reconsider their general education programs. Distributed studies encourage rather than correct these problems, and the reinstatement of such a curriculum—in itself—is unlikely to be any more successful now than before.

Fortunately, many schools are more thoroughly examining the aims and structures of their curriculums, developing fresh approaches, and attempting to have their curriculums rise above campus politics. This chapter highlights the more thoughtful and creative curriculums that are resulting from extensive study and discussion. These innovative and promising ideas and programs are likely to set the trend for future curricular practice, and they may also serve to raise the sights and guide the actions of faculty members and administrators now in the formative stages of curricular review.

Some schools with distinctive general education curriculums have reviewed their programs only to reaffirm the value of their current offerings. A review at the University of Chicago, for example, concluded by describing and justifying current practices rather than recommending significant departures. Although a part of the current revival of general education, curricular reviews that reaffirm current practices are not as interesting as those yielding significant new conclusions and changes in existing programs; thus the latter are stressed here.

Amount. The number of general education courses required for a degree is, of course, a principal aspect of curricular organization. Among colleges that have recently reviewed their curriculums, the most common tendency is to increase the amount of general education. Of schools surveyed by the Association of American Colleges (AAC), 59 percent adopted revised curriculums that require more hours of general education, 36 percent did not change the number of hours, and 5 percent now require fewer hours (see Appendix A). Since these colleges made little or no change in the units required for the major, the increases in general education result in a decrease in free electives, the portion of the curriculum that had expanded at most schools. Thus the tendency is to redress the balance, not by eliminating student choice but by reducing it somewhat and by requiring essential areas of study to be included in each student's program.

A secondary trend is for schools to revise the content of the general education program without increasing the amount. Many colleges did not reduce the number of required hours at all during recent years, and others made only token reductions; rather than increasing the amount of time, they are seeking to revise the character of their programs without expanding their scope.

The actual amount of required general education varies greatly among schools. The mean amount of general education required in four-year institutions is 44 semester hours, which represents 35 percent of the total hours required for graduation, according to the AAC survey. Most schools require that between one-fourth and one-half of a student's four-year program be devoted to general education courses. For instance, Valparaiso University requires 62 semester credit hours of the 124 needed for the bachelor of arts degree; three hours less are required of students with proficiency in a foreign language and even less of students seeking the bachelor of science degree. The Rochester Institute of Technology requires approximately one-fourth of a student's program (54 quarter credit hours out of a total of 190) be in the college of general studies, consisting of humanities and social sciences; students in a few majors take less (Rochester Institute of Technology, 1980).

Community colleges offer two-year associate degree programs in academic and vocational areas, many of which are oriented toward general education. Recent curricular revisions have resulted in requirements that average 31 semester hours in general education (of the 60 required for associate degrees), according to the AAC survey. Among individual colleges, Miami-Dade Community College requires 36 semester hours; Community College of Denver, 30 hours; and Catonsville Community College, 27 hours. Even vocational programs, which once neglected the liberal arts, have recently made commitments to general education. The Denver district, for example, requires vocational programs to include four courses in a core curriculum. Of course, many community colleges offer courses for students not pursuing a degree, and these students may study any courses they wish.

Structure. The curricular structure is also being strengthened at most institutions (see Appendix A). Prescribing a limited range of courses that satisfy the requirements for study outside the major is practiced by 88 percent of the new programs. This approach takes several forms. Some schools simply limit the number of acceptable courses to a relatively small number. Harvard, for example, offers some 2,600 courses, but only about 100 are approved for general education purposes. Other schools devise a set of criteria, more or less explicit, that guides the development and certification of courses. The use of specific criteria allows more consistency in the certification of appropriate courses, helps ensure that courses serve accepted purposes, provides coherence, and makes for a clear rationale for the program. Many colleges with explicit criteria find it helpful to establish a committee to review and approve courses for this portion of the curriculum. For example, at the University of Southern California a faculty committee certifies a course for a maximum of three years, after which it is reviewed, with evaluative evidence about the course's effectiveness as a major determinant of recertification. These procedures provide for continual monitoring of the limited list of courses to assure that they are fresh and continue to meet the purposes of the program as a whole.

While some schools' requirements are pegged to conventional academic divisions, such as the humanities, sciences, and social sciences, many institutions use other categories. For example, the College of Liberal Arts at Northwestern University requires students to take two freshman seminars on topical issues and two quarter courses in each of six areas: natural sciences; formal languages, including mathematics, linguistics, philosophy, or computer studies; social and behavioral sciences; historical studies; values; and literature and fine arts. In addition, proficiencies in writing and a foreign language are required. The university provides an exceptionally clear and cogent rationale for the various requirements in its brochure for students (Northwestern University, 1980). Since these are intellectual rather than departmental areas, a department may offer courses in more than one area.

SUNY College at Brockport goes even further in breaking the monopoly some departments, such as English and history, traditionally have over particular requirements. Departments may offer courses in any distribution category, but each department is limited to four general education courses a term. For example, the philosophy department could propose as one of its four a course on the philosophy of science that would satisfy a science requirement. In the words of Robert Strayer, director of general education, "Faculty members have tenure—courses do not."

A second approach to curricular structure, used by 55 percent of the schools in the AAC survey, is an interdisciplinary core curriculum that provides a common learning experience for students. Typically, these courses are planned and sometimes taught by an interdisciplinary team. For example, Catonsville Community College is offering two new core courses: Explorations of Nature and Society, and Explorations of Ideas in Imagery. The former focuses on three topics: the dynamics and impact of change, as illustrated by the works of Darwin and Marx; the existence of an unseen reality, in the works of Curie and Freud; and the search for universal patterns, with the efforts of Einstein and Toynbee as examples. The second course examines these same three topics in the arts—in the works of Jan Van Eyck and Degas; Bach, Beethoven, and Webern; and in Goethe's *Faust* and Joyce's *Portrait of the Artist as a Young Man*. These two core courses, currently offered on an experimental basis, are supplemented by a limited distribution requirement to form a nine-course core.

A few schools, often small liberal arts colleges with a tradition of communal dialogue, have a more extensive core. St. Joseph's College, for example, replaced its lower-level distributive approach with a 45-credit, integrative and interdisciplinary set of semester courses spread over the four years. The course titles give a flavor of the character and rhythm of the core.

Freshman Year: The Contemporary Situation
                The Roots of Western Civilization
Sophomore: The Christian Impact on Western Civilization
                The Modern World
Junior: Man and the Universe
                Non-Western Studies
Senior: Toward a Christian Humanism
                Christianity and the Human Situation

Considerable debate continues about the relative advantages of a core curriculum and a distribution pattern (Boyer and Levine, 1981, pp. 23-34; Kramer, 1981). Indeed, a large number of schools making curricular revisions are opting for a combination of both. Most commonly a few core courses, whether disciplinary or interdisciplinary, and a limited distribution are required of all students. Although this pattern does not satisfy committed proponents of either form, it is a compromise that is appearing frequently.

A third common form of curricular structure requires specific disciplinary courses. Such requirements result from the conviction that certain subject matter is vital for all students; courses in history, English composition, or a laboratory science are commonly specified.

Perhaps most interesting is the AAC finding that loose distribution requirements are part of the revised program in only 15 percent of the schools surveyed. This reflects colleges' conscious application of criteria to provide courses specifically for the nonmajor and a commitment to assure that general education serves a broadening purpose.

Length. Many schools have recently extended their general education programs over their students' entire college career; 59 percent of the four-year schools responding to the AAC survey said their programs are not limited to the freshman and sophomore curriculum. This is further evidence that colleges are now rejecting an earlier concept of general education as simply breadth or a foundation for specialized study, carried out by means of a set of introductory surveys. Schools are affirming more sophisticated notions of integrating reasoning skills, values, and other elements of general education along with the study of a major and electives. Thus general education is integral to students' entire program of studies, rather than a hurdle that must be overcome before commencing serious work in the major.

Standards. Higher academic standards are now being established in all sectors of higher education, both within and without the general education curriculum. Among community colleges, where open access policies have most strained traditional standards, the new rules at Miami-Dade provide a useful example. President Robert McCabe, noting that taxpayers are becoming more dissatisfied that graduates of public colleges lack proficiency in basic skills, remarks: "the combination of lower entering skills and the need for strong academic standards has created a situation where community colleges, especially, are set up for failure. Unless we begin to adopt some reasonable policies, the open door is not going to remain open much longer. The alternative is going to be not letting in people who look like risks" (Middleton, 1981, p. 3).

All new students at Miami-Dade are now required to take placement tests in reading, writing, and computation. Those who fail—about 60 percent of the freshmen—must take non-credit courses in basic skills. Further, students who earn below a 1.5 grade-point average are either put on probation or suspended. Students on probation may take only a limited number of courses, and they must take at least one "intervention" course in remedial studies, study skills, or career counseling. Suspended students may return to college on probation after one term; if their grades still are not satisfactory, they are dismissed for at least a year. Further, the new curriculum requires all degree-seeking students to take five specially designed general education courses. These reforms are noteworthy in that students are expected to perform at a desired level, and the college is committing substantial resources to help students achieve that level.

Although Miami-Dade's particular effort is of interest, a great many schools are instituting higher standards. They are raising admissions standards, requiring more work and better grades of continuing students, and emphasizing that students are expected to work just as hard for a general education course as for one in their major. The University of Nebraska at Lincoln requires students to do a substantial amount of writing in general education courses, and faculty must respond in writing to student papers. This policy thus raises standards for faculty as well as students, because raising students' achievement levels imposes greater demands on teachers.

Academic Regulations. Similarly, colleges are reviewing their various academic policies and regulations; for example, some are tightening withdrawal and course repetition policies, and others are considering students' progress toward a degree as a criterion for financial aid. Illinois State University revised its withdrawal and course repetition policies, which once permitted students to withdraw from a course at any time prior to the fourteenth week of the semester. As Stanley Rives, former provost, explains: "Course withdrawal policies have been strengthened to encourage students to complete those classes in which they enroll. The time period in which a student may withdraw from a course without penalty has been shortened, with WF (Withdrawal Failing) grades now being computed in the student's grade-point average. This precludes a student from withdrawing late in the semester in order to avoid academic probation. Course repetition policies have also been strengthened so that a student, except in very unusual circumstances, may repeat a course only once in order to improve a grade for the purpose of meeting a grade-point average requirement for graduation or for avoiding academic probation. The net effect of these changes is to provide students a reasonable second chance to succeed without wasting state resources by allowing marginal students to repeatedly withdraw from and retake courses without making reasonable progress toward graduation" (1980, p. 2).

Other schools are limiting use of the credit/no credit grading option and increasing standards for probation, academic good standing, and dean's list. When several such policies are tightened, the net effect can be significant, even if the formal curriculum is unaltered. When these changes are made alongside a curriculum reform, the effect can be striking.

Curricular Content

In addition to organizational changes, many colleges are substantially revising the content of the course of study. Several of the more striking features of these efforts are highlighted below.

Liberal Arts. The liberal arts and sciences are being invigorated by a number of college-wide reforms. The trend is toward increased amounts of study in liberal arts fields—whether by means of a limited distribution scheme, interdisciplinary core courses, specific disciplinary requirements, or, most commonly, some combination of these. The humanities, the natural sciences, and the social sciences are all experiencing a revival, as most revised programs are designed to acquaint students with the range of human knowledge and the diverse methods of arriving at truth.

The disciplines benefiting the most from the current reforms are the humanities, the very fields that suffered most from the recent emphasis on more practical areas of study. Increasingly, curriculum planners are recognizing that an understanding of history, familiarity with some of the great works of literature, and acquaintance with basic philosophical principles are essential marks of an educated person. If courses on these topics are well designed and taught (a matter that is discussed in Chapter Five), they do possess practical value, according to current thinking. Such requirements give the liberal arts disciplines a chance to capture the interest and enthusiasm of a new generation of students, but their success will depend on their finding imaginative ways to compel the attention of today's students.

The Freshman Experience. The freshman experience is the subject of one group of curricular reforms. At issue is the proper introduction to college life and especially the role of general education in it. Oregon State University offers a freshman course, Connections, designed to overcome the separatism of disciplines, the lack of articulated rationale, and the often uninspired teaching that may accompany freshman courses. The syllabus describes the course as "an introduction to the realm of ideas through a critical assessment of the present moment of history," "an orientation to some of the modes of thought common to the liberal arts," and "an effort to call [students'] attention to various issues confronting today's world and to how these issues are connected to one another and to you as a thinking, valuing, feeling person" (Oregon State University, n.d., p. 1). Topics include mind manipulation, world hunger, and war and peace. The approach is interdisciplinary, and various activities—films, classroom exercises, lectures by outstanding teachers, student-led discussion sections, class logs, and attendance at cultural events—are designed to stimulate students' interest in intellectually rich issues and to foster their abilities to make significant connections among them.

A more complex assessment of what students need by way of an introduction to college life is provided by SUNY College at Brockport. Its introductory course, Dimensions of Liberal Education, seeks to accomplish four purposes: introduce students to the nature and purposes of a liberal education, orient them to the resources of the college, provide initial academic advising, and teach appropriate study skills. Sections are limited to twenty students, and about seventy instructors teach sections of the course. Faculty and staff prepare a special text of readings and an instructor's guide; teachers also participate in several training sessions regarding the conduct of a seminar on broad educational issues, while refining their advising skills.

Of course, different kinds of students need different kinds of introductions. More adults are now returning to college in midlife, and some schools have provided special assistance to them. Loretto Heights College, for example, launched Project Transition. At the heart of this program are four one-month seminars: Psychology of Adult Development, Values in Adult Experience, Perspectives on the Future, and Learning as Adults. Concurrent career development activities complement the seminars and help students clarify and focus their large number of life options. The activities are intended to expand personal and intellectual horizons within a supportive atmosphere, while at the same time sharpening vocational interests and career skills. This is but one of many efforts designed to assist the reentry of women into postsecondary education and eventually into employment.

A more radical critique has generated a different approach at Amherst College. The Select Committee on the Curriculum (1978) argued that two purposes are to be served by a curriculum for entering students, introductory and distributive. Currently the burden of introduction to liberal learning is largely carried by introductory courses in the various disciplines, an approach regarded by the committee as flawed because the very achievements of the disciplines "[lend] the impression that these distinctions represent natural fissures in what is known, or can be known, about the world"; disciplinary success "has become a sanction for the compartmentalization" of knowledge. The report concludes, "Given what we know about the insularity of the disciplines, it seems clear that an introduction to the intellectual life of the college must be established on some point of view exterior to the disciplines themselves" (p. 43).

The committee also rejected the notion of distribution requirements, viewing the traditional divisions as a bureaucratic convention having little internal coherence: by a divisional structure "the idea is insidiously created that the divisions actually divide knowledge in some rational or natural way, that in some fashion they represent fundamental compartments of knowledge" (pp. 44-45). The committee therefore recommended that divisional distribution requirements be dropped. Instead, the committee proposed and the faculty adopted a plan for freshmen to take three courses that would provide critical introductions to liberal studies. These courses are designed and taught by small groups of faculty in typically a small-group context. Each category is a broadly conceived area of intellectual

activity. Freshmen must take three courses from at least six offered, two in each of the three areas—Sign, Form, and Meaning;
Nature: Observation and Theory; and Social Life and Social
Change. Ironically, despite the disclaimers of the committee,
these categories serve as convenient intellectual foci for members of the traditional three divisions (humanities, natural sciences, and social sciences).

As these examples illustrate, several schools are concluding that a conscious introduction to college and to the life of
the mind is necessary for the general education of their students. The different mechanisms represent efforts to make the
transition into college more effective than usual compartmental
disciplinary introductions. Further, each seeks to set the tone
and provide a rationale for the students' overall course of study,
especially that portion lying outside the major. Colleges also
hope that such special procedures will help attract and retain
students.

Skills. The role of skills in general education has always
been a subject of controversy. On the one hand, skills such as
critical thinking, analysis, and synthesis have always been considered central. Hutchins, for example, maintained that the major purpose of general education is to train the mind rather than
to fill it with any particular body of knowledge, because existing knowledge is always being eclipsed. On the other hand,
some regard skills as unworthy of special attention, intellectual
substance being the stuff from which solid programs are made.
Open admissions and increased access policies have refired the
controversy as more students who lack basic skills enter college. One state university reports that one-fifth of its freshman
class is unable to read at the tenth-grade level. Even worse,
many students graduate still unable to read, write, or think
effectively.

Thus the enhancement of learning and thinking skills, at
both basic and advanced levels, occupies a dominant place in
the current reform of general education. The AAC survey (see
Appendix A) reveals that among the basic skills writing is a part
of virtually every new curriculum; mathematics is included in
four of five; and speaking is stressed in three of five. The revised

curriculums show a strong tendency to increase attention to basic skills, but higher-level skills also are receiving renewed attention. Critical thinking, problem solving, and research or library skills are stressed in most new programs. Foreign-language training, one of the traditional skills associated with general education, and computer literacy, perhaps the newest, are also common.

Basic skills, in particular, are of greater import now than in earlier revivals of general education. Colleges are discovering that it is fruitless to blame the students or their high schools; simply put, the students are in college, they lack basic skills, and they must be taught them. Many institutions have established remedial courses, typically noncredit, for those students who need special attention. Others have set up learning assistance centers that provide special support services such as diagnostic testing, tutoring, a writing laboratory, study skills courses, and personal counseling for students having special problems (Maxwell, 1979). This movement regarding the improvement of basic skills is so extensive that the Council of Writing Program Administrators, founded in 1976, has members from more than 400 institutions (Wiener, 1981).

Clifford Hand, academic vice-president of the University of the Pacific, attacks the simplistic dichotomy between skills and content and provides a rationale for the importance of including skills in the curriculum for all students, whatever their level of ability: "We proceed on the assumption that writing is not a marginal 'skill.' . . . A student's powers of perception are closely related to his powers of expression; one becomes aware of what he knows and of what is known in proportion to his ability to express it. As a person realizes his ideas and feelings in a written form, he becomes more aware of them and improves his facility with language and abstract expression" (1979, pp. 1-2). Similar justifications can be adduced for the other basic skills such as speaking and computation.

The simplest curricular response to the need for greater attention to basic skills takes the form of requiring a course or two in English and mathematics. These requirements may be an improvement over previous inattention that allowed students with deficiencies to escape detection, much less take steps to correct them. But many schools have learned that the English department by itself cannot overcome the enduring effects of all prior schooling, of countless hours of television, and of cultural expectations that tolerate poor expression. Therefore several schools are devising new remedies.

"Writing across the curriculum," in which faculty members incorporate writing into courses ranging from physics to history, is one such effort. Pioneered by the Bay Area Writing Program at the University of California, Berkeley, which teaches faculty members from various disciplines how to incorporate writing in their courses, and at Beaver College, first to adopt writing across the entire curriculum, this approach has been eagerly adopted by many other institutions. Central College, for instance, has a policy of "departmental endorsement" concerning communications skills: "Rather than imposing an institution-wide standard, which would have the effect of taking away the responsibility that every department was committed to sharing, each department determines the communication demands that its graduates face, describes the kind of linguistic maturity that its graduates must have, and then designs a program to ensure students' development. All students, then, must demonstrate to their major department, that they are competent in reading, writing, and speaking (and in some departments, mathematical manipulation) in order to be certified for graduation" (Cannon and Roberts, 1981, p. 5). Other features of the program include testing of incoming students for reading, writing, speaking, listening, and study skills; use of the results to counsel students; designation of about a quarter of all courses as skills courses that provide instruction in both subject matter and skills; month-long summer workshops in which faculty learn to create and evaluate assignments that incorporate basic skills; and a skills center that is used by about 65 percent of the freshmen and over 40 percent of the entire student body.

Variations on this approach are many. At DePauw University, students must pass specially designated skill-intensive courses in writing, speaking, and quantification. Students receive two grades for these courses, one for the regular coursework and the other for the skills certification, and several courses in each skill area must be passed before graduation. Gonzaga University offers special one-hour adjunct writing courses along with regular upper-division courses as a supplement to freshman English courses. In these adjuncts students work with English instructors to review drafts of papers for organization, style, grammar, and format. The university's pilot test showed that about a third of the students in each participatory course elect to take the adjunct. Of course, faculty workshops and seminars are essential to such wide-ranging programs.

A competency-based approach is being used elsewhere. Florida A & M University, for instance, requires an interdisciplinary series of three five-hour courses in listening, speaking, reading, and writing skills. Preentry assessment and placement determine the appropriate course section for each student. Based on the concept of mastery learning (Bloom, 1971), the courses are divided into modules through which students progress at their own pace; they must pass an examination for each module before attempting the next one. The university also requires competency in mathematics, and those courses are also modular and self-paced. This arrangement allows individualized instruction to accommodate the diverse backgrounds of students, while assuring that they reach an acceptable level of achievement.

Instruction in higher-level thinking skills frequently builds on the contributions of psychologists who have studied cognitive developmental patterns. Both general theorists, such as Jean Piaget and Erik Erikson, and those who have developed theories regarding college students, such as William Perry and Arthur Chickering, posit stages of intellectual development. Most cite a progression from concrete to abstract thinking, from simple to complex mental operations (see Piaget [1932], 1965; Erikson, 1963, 1968; Perry, 1970; and Chickering, 1969, 1981). Active learning methods, conscious attention to thought processes, and frequent feedback from others are thought to facilitate more advanced reasoning ability. Sadler and Whimbey (1980) present evidence that students at all levels of thinking are initially able to increase their sophistication through instruction oriented specifically to the cultivation of skills.

Through the Development of Operational Reasoning Skills (DOORS) project at Illinois Central College, course material was developed for six courses—mathematics, English, economics, history, physics, and sociology. Each course introduces students to exploratory learning activities and progressively moves toward abstract generalizations, and a great deal of student participation in learning is demanded. After finding that the courses not only promote students' thinking processes but also enhance the likelihood of their graduating, campus leaders created a consortium of nearby community colleges to adapt basic features of the program to other settings.

A series of skills courses offered by the University of Rhode Island includes critical thinking in the humanities and social sciences, experiencing the arts, quantitative thinking, and communication courses. The critical-thinking courses stress methods and techniques used to solve problems in various disciplines as well as standards for evaluating the solutions. The quantitative skills course teaches students to abstract information from tables, graphs, or equations, thereby translating ideas and observations from one medium to another. By using examples and problems from many disciplines, the instructors seek to demonstrate the flexibility and wide applicability of quantitative methods. Courses in the arts provide interrelated introductions to dance, visual art, music, theater, and esthetics, with an emphasis on the development of creative self-awareness by means of active participation in studio projects. Evaluations of these courses during the experimental phases have been generally positive.

To summarize, most new general education programs include skill components, although schools differ in the skills that are included, the level of achievement expected of students, and the degree of sophistication of their programs. But virtually all institutions making reforms in one way or another attempt to ensure that today's students are better able than their predecessors to think and learn independently. They are intent on giving students the tools for lifelong learning, not merely the content that soon becomes outdated.

Global Perspectives. Statesmen claim that Americans must think in global terms and become more knowledgeable about peoples beyond our shores. We live in a world ever more interdependent, drawn together by rapid transportation and communication and by trade and security pacts, a world ever more threatened by acts of international terrorism and environmental degradation. Thus contemporary education can no longer be confined to this continent, or even to the Western tradition, and most colleges and universities are incorporating global perspectives into their revised curriculums. They are working toward the agenda proposed by Robert Leestma, a former U.S. government official: "Educators are the single most important group in helping generate a critical mass of citizens capable of recognizing the global age, its impact on their future life, and their responsibilities as American citizens in an interdependent world. Every educator—and every student—is a prospective founding father for the future. Among other competencies and sensitivities, each needs to develop: (1) some basic cross-cultural understanding, empathy, and ability to communicate with people from different cultures; (2) a sense of why and how mankind shares a common future—global issues and dynamics and the calculus of interdependence; (3) a sense of stewardship in use of the earth and acceptance of the ethic of intergenerational responsibility for the well-being or fair chance of those who come after us" (1979, p. 3).

"Global perspectives," despite its currency, is not a unitary concept; rather it comprises three quite distinct parts: knowledge, affect, and language (Barrows, Clark, and Klein, 1980). *Knowledge* concerns a student's grasp of facts about international events; *affect* is defined by attitudinal measures that are predominantly, but not exclusively, political in nature; and the *language* component is defined by foreign-language abilities, learning experiences, and attitudes toward foreign-language study. Let us briefly examine how some schools are meeting each of these needs.

Knowledge is provided largely by courses and academic programs, and virtually all colleges and universities offer some courses that include international dimensions. Indeed, a good number have major programs in international studies, concentrations in area studies, and specialized research centers focusing on various parts of the world. Ramapo College recently inaugurated an interdisciplinary major in its School of American and International Studies. Majors are required to take a four-course core that includes both domestic and comparative studies and then select either one of the traditional disciplines, or international studies, American studies, or the business comajor.

In addition to providing new specialized courses and programs for students majoring in international studies, schools are following the recommendation of the National Assembly on Foreign Languages and International Studies (1980, p. 4): "The first priority is to implant a strong international dimension into the core of general education requirements." The assembly further recommends that "The curriculum should be expanded to introduce students particularly to non-Western cultures" (p. 4). Several schools have met this challenge by requiring a course in a non-Western culture; Antioch and St. Olaf both have this requirement.

Brooklyn College (1981) requires a course specially designed to bring students into contact with less familiar cultures: "One goal of the curriculum is to develop an appreciation of cultures other than one's own. . . . This course will not introduce all the world's cultures, or even civilizations, but it has a twofold objective: (a) a kind of cultural empathy—the ability to project imaginatively into different cultural worlds and to appreciate that people live, or have lived, rich, complex, important lives there; and (b) a sense of cultural relativity—that other ways of life are just as valid as one's own and that understanding them can bring new perspectives on one's own familiar world" (p. 16). The course has three units, (on African, Asian, and Latin American cultures), and each is an intensive exploration of one particular theme rather than a survey of the area.

The predominant way to deal with the affective dimension is by direct individual experience, preferably over a sustained period of time. For example, an exemplary exchange program is operated by Goshen College, a small Mennonite college in Indiana. The heart of its study-service trimester is required interdisciplinary study and service in a foreign culture, most commonly in a non-Western country. Usually led by a faculty couple, groups of students begin by studying the language and culture and then disperse to work in service projects, often related to their major interests. They usually work under the supervision of a local person and live with a native family. Students abroad pay the usual fees, as the cost is about the same as campus instruction. Since its inception in the 1960s, only about 20 percent of the students have opted for the alternative, an equivalent set of on-campus courses. Kalamazoo College has a similar program.

Study abroad courses are not a luxury confined to small private schools. Among public institutions, Rockland Community College, under the leadership of President Seymour Eskow, has recently created three units to foster international understanding. The Center for International Studies encourages foreign study through structured service-learning, independent study, and enrollment in courses in overseas universities. In the largest of its programs, 200 students travel to Israel each semester. The International College offers interdisciplinary studies in ethnic, religious, and geographical issues. It also offers language instruction and creates public policy forums on a variety of topical issues. And the Center for International Students serves 200 international students as well as additional hundreds of immigrants with English instruction.

Language instruction, the third part of the global agenda, has always been a struggle for Americans. Many do not recognize the value of learning a foreign language because—unlike many other countries—foreign tongues are not a part of our daily routine. During recent decades, some Americans have even come to believe that all the world should speak English. Only the recent economic inroads made first by Germans, then by Japanese, and more recently by the Middle Eastern oil-producing countries and others with special leverage have shaken this smugness. It is obvious that Americans need to speak foreign languages in order to serve the nation's interests, including peace, diplomacy, trade, environmental quality, and others. And larger numbers of foreign travelers and foreign products provide reminders of our linguistic limitations.

Talk is heard on many campuses today about reimposing a foreign-language requirement. Stanford, for example, after having dropped it in 1969, reinstated a language requirement for freshmen in 1982 ("Foreign Language Requirement . . . ," 1981). With this action, it joined Chicago, Columbia, Cornell, Harvard, Radcliffe, Pennsylvania, Princeton, and Yale, each of which has some kind of requirement. At Stanford the requirement can be met by completing three years of a language in high school (which about a third of new students do), by passing a competency test, or by taking courses through the first-year level. Other leading universities, including Brown and the Massachusetts Institute of Technology, do not require linguistic proficiency.

Less-prestigious institutions less frequently require a foreign language, partly out of fear that such a policy would make the college less competitive in recruiting students. Furthermore, the common curricular step is to require competency in a familiar Western language—French, German, or Spanish. Although useful, less-familiar languages are becoming increasingly important in our world—Arabic, Chinese, Japanese, Russian, Swahili—but colleges are ill equipped to offer instruction in them. Few language faculty are qualified in these languages, and poor enrollments in language departments do not justify hiring new faculty.

For these reasons some schools are undertaking creative experiments. Ohio State University tested instruction in Arabic, French, German, Latin, Russian, and Spanish by means of individualized self-paced modules ("Taking Foreign Languages Out of the Classroom," 1980, p. 9). When given a choice between the regular and new approaches, about 25 percent of the students studying the six subjects chose the individualized approach. The individualized courses tended to attract a larger proportion of older students, part-time students, and students from nearby colleges that did not offer language instruction.

The new approach was no more expensive, and in many cases less so, than regular classroom instruction. Schools that feature foreign study have long relied on self-instructional methods, particularly for teaching less-popular languages. For instance, Rockland's self-study language center provides training in some thirty languages through tapes, readings, and native-speaking tutors.

Although schools may strengthen their program in global studies by stressing knowledge, affect, or language, there is an obvious interaction among these three components: "The widest and most neglected frontier of U.S. educational reform is no longer international studies. It is a global perspective on *all* studies" (Cleveland, 1980, p. 19). Nothing less than comprehensive programs that involve the examination of the content and structure of the entire curriculum can satisfy this call.

Johnson County Community College, near Kansas City, has begun such an examination. An international studies task force of administrators, faculty members, and students was appointed in 1979 and developed a three-year plan. The plan mandates the preparation of instructional modules on East Asia, Latin America, the Soviet Union, the Middle East, and Africa. Each module is to include a set of readings, study guide, bibliography, audiovisual material, and suggestions for incorporation into existing courses, for they are to be phased into existing courses over time. Second, new courses are to be developed to study the language, ideas, philosophies, and politics of other civilizations, particularly non-Western. Third, an ongoing faculty development program will include a colloquium on integrating international perspectives into existing courses. Other proposals include: offering short courses in international affairs for the business community, expanding the foreign-exchange program, strengthening instruction in English as a second language, and encouraging foreign students in the area to serve as resource persons. Although it is unlikely that all these initiatives will be fully realized, this example illustrates how an institution can promote the introduction of global perspectives into all segments of the curriculum.

Thus some institutions are responding to the global challenge with their curricular revisions, and in very creative ways. But, as Bonham reminds us, "when seen across the academic landscape as a whole, such integrative teaching efforts are still vastly insufficient to inspire hope for a globally aware national studentry" (1981, p. 2). Clearly, much is being accomplished, but much more remains to be done.

Women's and Minorities' Perspectives. General education has traditionally placed strong emphasis on understanding one's heritage and culture. During the current revival, historical and cultural knowledge are again being affirmed as important to an educated person. Schools often require courses in history, the most common form of which is some variation of the familiar Western Civilization course, in which several highlights of the Western tradition—ideas, events, creations, or people—are singled out for attention. World history courses that introduce students to both Western and other civilizations and proceed to comparative analyses are a contemporary variation that is being tried at the University of California at Riverside and Dennison University, among others. American history courses, too, are part of the changing undergraduate curriculum.

But the matter is far more complicated than it used to be. As we noted in Chapter Three, schools are asking which, or more pointedly, *whose,* heritage and culture is to be taught. A good deal of recent scholarship has revealed that sexist and racist biases still permeate some curriculums. Some schools have established requirements in history and other areas without any special regard for the perspectives of women and ethnic minorities.

Other schools are attempting to create a more balanced curriculum by incorporating new perspectives and scholarship. The University of Tennessee, Knoxville, requires a course in ethnic studies or women's studies from an approved list. The practical advantages to this approach include its conceptual simplicity and its ease of administration. Yet other colleges are expanding their offerings in world history courses. As Donald Schilling, who teaches a two-course sequence at Dennison, explains: " 'World history is a compromise between those who want to study Western civilization and those interested in the Third

World' " (Winkler, 1982, p. 7). World history is more intellectually defensible if it introduces a comparative perspective on
the values of modernization and incorporates traditions that lie
outside the Western world.

While Antioch College does not require a specific course,
it has reaffirmed its commitment to include women and minorities in the distribution courses. The college's curriculum committee reviews departmental offerings "to assure that Antioch's
commitment to cross-cultural education and to presentation of
the contributions and concerns of women and minorities is met
by an appropriate and sufficient number of courses" (Antioch
College, n.d., p. 2). And Arizona State University is incorporating material on women and on the topic of gender into basic
humanities courses through faculty development seminars.

A group working with the Organization of American Historians is preparing curricular materials to help professors integrate the history of women into basic European and American
survey courses. Teams of historians are developing proposed
syllabi, suggested readings, sample examination questions, and
possible lecture topics that can be used to enrich current courses.
Much of the material comes from research in the newer approaches of social history, especially regarding everyday life,
community structure, and family life. Users of the materials are
urged to freely adapt any ideas or suggestions for their own
courses.

The approach with greatest potential for revising traditional curriculums is a form of mainstreaming. Proponents explain that although there are hundreds of women's and ethnic
studies courses, these tend to be concentrated in peripheral
units or special departments. Radzialowski urges colleges to
move ethnic studies courses to the center of the liberal arts curriculum because they can make two distinct contributions to
liberal education: "First, they can serve as an introduction to
the many areas of the world to which American ethnic groups
trace their origins. . . . Secondly, the new insights which recent
research in ethnic studies has given us provide an ideal locus for
a discussion of the nature of American identity and the meaning
of pluralism" (1981, p. 2). Similar arguments are made by pro-

ponents of feminist perspectives. For example, Sandler (1981, p. 1) writes: "A central, unachieved goal . . . is the mainstreaming of women's studies—the implementing of change in the traditional curriculum (especially in required introductory courses) so as to incorporate into them the materials and perspectives of women's studies. Such mainstreaming would broaden the educational experience of *all* students—both men and women—by recognizing women's contributions and experiences as they related to the established academic disciplines, and would enhance the general educational climate for women students and faculty by integrating the achievements, roles and concerns of women into primary course content and overall institutional context." A few schools are starting to work on this ambitious task.

A particularly promising effort is underway at Wheaton College: "Wheaton is engaged in integrating the study of women into the core of the curriculum through a systematic examination and revision of introductory courses in all disciplines where faculty express a conviction that research on women is relevant" (Schmidt and Spanier, n.d., p. 1). After an initial faculty conference to raise key issues, several departments started to review the scholarship on women in their domains, collect and evaluate relevant materials, and develop a plan for incorporating new material into introductory courses. An intensive workshop on this new scholarship, held during the midyear intersession, featured outside scholars, and participants received a stipend to purchase books on feminist scholarship related to their interests. Several faculty visited other schools and attended conferences; consultants were invited to the campus; and a student essay contest was held to solicit perspectives on women in the liberal arts. With the assistance of a faculty advisory committee, faculty members are developing, testing, and assessing new curricular materials. Bonnie Spanier, a biologist and coordinator of the project, mused, "It may seem strange that a college committed to quality education for women should admit to having left women out of the content of its courses. But Wheaton (was) no different from other colleges and universities in this respect" (cited by Leitert, 1981, p. 3).

Values. Courses in values are becoming part of some revised general education programs, which reveals that "institutions are now willing to accept responsibility, in the curriculum, for helping students make discriminating moral judgments" (Wee, 1981, pp. 41–42). Treatments of values have always been problematic in colleges and universities, because there are no moral experts and no universal standards of judgment. Particularly during the twentieth century, the role of values has been questioned, and periodically various accepted "objective" methodologies have eclipsed the value dimension of the search for truth. Yet most educators agree that just as there are no objective standards of value that would justify the inclusion of values in the curriculum, so too is there no such thing as completely objective knowledge. General education traditionally has addressed values, as, for instance, when Columbia developed its influential Contemporary Civilization core course to study war and peace issues following World War I. Today's revival of general education is once again fostering the inclusion of values in the curriculum.

Which values are to be stressed and how can they be taught? A wide range of value-related topics are included in new curriculums. For instance, in the Federated Learning Communities at SUNY Stony Brook (which is discussed more extensively in the next section) interdisciplinary learning communities have been organized around six topics: World Hunger; Cities, Utopias, and Environments: Designs for Living; Technology, Values, and Society; Human Nature; Science for Public Understanding; and Social and Ethical Issues in the Life Sciences. For example, a brochure describing the last-mentioned community explains: "Headlines scream of test-tube babies, cloning, organ transplants, the Karen Quinlan case, lawsuits about 'deprogramming,' involuntary drug research, and hitherto unimaginable surveillance techniques. The average person even when well educated, does not know enough about the scientific findings, about how they are likely to affect us as individuals and as a society, or about the ethical issues forced upon us by these events. . . . Our main objective will be to provide as many perspectives as possible upon the human condition, upon the technological instruments we use to explore or to control that condition, and upon how we can assess the social and ethical implications of using (or refusing to use) those instruments" (State University of New York at Stony Brook, n.d., p. 1). As this passage implies, values education does not seek to indoctrinate students with a particular dogma or stance; rather, it seeks to provide students with an antidote to indoctrination. The task is to identify a cluster of related values, explore the issues involved, analyze the facts and themes related to the issues, examine the implications of factual matters, and discuss the action or policy alternatives. Thus the inclusion of values also contributes to the recovery of wholeness in undergraduate education.

One of the simplest ways to integrate values in the curriculum is to offer elective courses. The University of California at Los Angeles has created a Freshman-Sophomore Professional School Seminar Program. Although some of this university's professional schools do not regularly offer undergraduate instruction, through this program faculty members in medicine, psychiatry, public health, dentistry, nursing, engineering, education, architecture, urban planning, social welfare, librarianship, and management offer seminars on topics that meet the general education needs of lower-division students. Sample courses include Planning and Design for Diverse Life Styles, Education as a Profession, Engineering: Its Role and Function in Society, Personal Freedom at Work, and Drug Abuse and Drug Research. Similarly, the University of Florida offers a program, Humanities Perspectives on the Professions, that relates the perspectives of the humanities to the events and issues that preprofessional students will confront in their vocations. Courses are designed, and often taught, collaboratively by preprofessional and humanities faculty. Core courses acquaint students with a range of views on their specialization, special topics courses focus on specific issues (for example, Philosophy and Mental Health), and basic interdisciplinary courses combine materials from several fields (for example, Critical Thought and the Scientific Mind).

Another approach is to require students to complete a course on contemporary issues. SUNY College at Brockport requires an upper-level course in which students examine the ethical, moral, and value dimensions of compelling current issues.

Sections of these courses are limited to twenty-five students to encourage the give-and-take discussions that complex issues demand. Unlike courses designed to enlighten students about value issues related to their specialization, these have a scope broader than the major or cognate fields.

Schools with close ties to the church and fundamental religious beliefs find general education reforms an occasion to strengthen or reaffirm religious values. One hour of daily Bible study is an inviolate practice at the strongly religious David Lipscomb College, a practice the school's general education review committee assumed as a given. Schools with weaker church ties or less-doctrinaire practices seek only to bring students into contact with their religious tradition. Eckerd College, for example, requires a course that focuses on contemporary issues—social, political, philosophical, ethical, esthetic, or scientific—from a Judaeo-Christian perspective. The course uses the Judaeo-Christian tradition to illuminate perplexing contemporary issues; and attention to non-Christian perspectives provides contrast and clarity (Eckerd College, 1980). Eckerd also explicitly treats values in its Western Heritage sequence, in a senior seminar, and in distribution courses. Thus, the concern for values pervades the entire general education program. St. Joseph's College, a Catholic school in Indiana, has adopted a similar approach.

Although several schools are giving renewed attention to values and to the greater sense of wholeness that connotes, there remains some concern about how thorough these reforms are likely to be. As Susan Wittig, former Dean of Newcomb College, comments on her college's revised curriculum: "I am very pleased about the category called 'Reflection on Values,' which requires students to take one course specifically related to values thinking. However, here's the catch: the courses that have been placed into the categories are simply our old courses (some retitled)—there isn't much thinking going on about the *basic* meaning of liberal learning, I'm afraid" (1981).

If value requirements are taken seriously, if the courses are carefully designed and carried out, they can potentially shift the balance of facts and values in undergraduate education and restore a more holistic approach.

Integration. Most curricular review committees are disturbed by the fragmentation of their school's baccalaureate programs. Among the methods being used to provide greater coherence for students are several approaches discussed earlier: courses in the freshman experience, global perspectives, and values. Other means specifically designed to integrate knowledge are also being introduced in general education programs. According to the AAC survey, 69 percent of the revised programs require interdisciplinary or other integrative study (see Appendix A).

An approach particularly popular during the 1960s and early 1970s is the creation of alternative interdisciplinary programs that offer new opportunities to integrate the curriculum and life outside the classroom. Several cluster and residential colleges were created by schools as separate units devoted to interdisciplinary education and other innovations. The Residential College at the University of Michigan, the Hutchins School of Liberal Studies at Sonoma State University, and the Paracollege at St. Olaf College are examples of cluster colleges that enhance the integration of learning.

More recently other integrative curriculums have been instituted, often holistic programs that serve as an alternative to the usual distribution requirements. Pacific Lutheran University, for instance, created a two-year integrated studies program whose four sequences consist of nine interdisciplinary, team-planned, and originally team-taught, courses. This program was initiated by a small group of faculty who were interested in integrative learning and disillusioned with a curriculum reform that resulted in only a minor shuffling of the standard distribution requirements. Similarly, Valencia Community College in Florida operates a two-year interdisciplinary studies program in general education. Students take eight courses, two a semester for four semesters, in which English, mathematics, social sciences, natural sciences, and the humanities are integrated in a historical framework.

Other schools provide integrative opportunities for a portion of the students' general education. One of the most imaginative efforts was devised by Patrick Hill at SUNY Stony Brook.

Six existing courses are "federated" around a theme, such as world hunger. But, as Hill (1981) argues, having students take three courses in common in each of two semesters cannot overcome the fragmentation of the academic community that results from the atomization of learning in discrete courses, the mismatched expectations of students and faculty, and the privatization of the academic experience; thus, additional structural features are included. A core course brings together the three instructors each semester to discuss the relationship between their disciplines and the central theme. And since the students—not the faculty—experience all three courses, they meet in a program seminar to relate and synthesize all the material. A new kind of professional, a master learner, is pivotal in the program. This is a faculty member who attends all three courses and thereby spans the instructors' specialized knowledge to meet the students' integrative needs. The master learner provides useful evaluative comments to the instructors about their teaching, assignments, and other pedagogical matters.

Although all these approaches have received laudatory evaluations, each reaches only a portion of a school's student body. Many educators are now concerned about the great number of students who graduate without participating in a learning community or examining interdisciplinary or even intradepartmental relationships among discrete courses. Accordingly, schools are attempting to incorporate such perspectives into their general requirements.

One of the simplest methods is to require one or more integrative courses as a part of the general curriculum. Some schools require a cluster of related courses. At SUNY, College of Old Westbury and at the Rochester Institute of Technology, for example, faculty members discuss their interests and plan a series of thematically related courses. Students then complete the cluster in which courses are intentionally and continuously integrated. Reports from Old Westbury are that this technique, like many of the others, not only works for students but also has enormous benefits for the faculty; it expands their horizons and enriches their understanding of areas close to their specialties.

Another approach is used by California Lutheran College,

which is experimenting with a loop sequence. Each loop consists of two regular courses and a third that bridges them. The regular courses meet for two weeks, then the course that completes the loop meets for one week; this pattern continues throughout the term. All the instructors and all the students enrolled in the two regular courses are involved in the bridge course, which is led by a designated instructor. The three loops thus far developed are: a core curriculum loop with history, religion, and English; a thematic sequence on peace and justice including English, religion, and sociology; and a major sequence of macroeconomics, international business, and English. All seek to foster greater integration while relying heavily on traditional academic disciplines.

Another approach stresses ways of knowing. The University of Maryland prescribes two upper-level integrative courses, one focusing on human problems and the other on the epistemology of knowledge: "It is intended that these be broad, synoptic courses that, through any appropriate subject matter, introduce the student to the epistemological bases, the modes of discourse, the standards of 'truth' and the value assumptions" of the academic disciplines (University of Maryland, 1979, p. 2). Such an approach involves a major commitment by such a large university to a level of integration above that provided by individual disciplines. Robert Shoenberg, dean of undergraduate studies notes that implementation will "require a considerable reorientation in faculty teaching patterns to offer two such courses for each of some 4,500 seniors every year. The prospect, frankly, scares me to death, though it is, at the same time, exhilarating, and offers some incredible opportunities" (1980). This is one way even a large university committed to specialized scholarship can contribute to the integration of undergraduate education.

Finally, the familiar idea of senior seminars and projects is being revived. Several institutions have determined that it is valuable for students to integrate various portions of their undergraduate education in an academic product that demonstrates the abilities to define issues, do research, communicate results, and draw valid conclusions about topics of importance.

A variation on this approach is the interdisciplinary baccalaureate essay required of juniors at Hobart and William Smith Colleges. The advantages of a junior-year requirement are that students are not distracted by decisions about careers and graduate
schools, and that high standards can be maintained when failure
does not pose an immediate threat to graduation.

Conclusion

Although this discussion of changes in overall curricular
organization and content is necessarily selective, we have examined the dominant tendencies. Obviously, no one school offers a
curriculum that incorporates all the features discussed here, but
several institutions are making artful combinations. One may
wonder which of these structures and components of the curriculum work best. Apparently, each of these practices works well
in its own context; and each may be of value to other colleges
or universities, but none may be assumed to be automatically
effective elsewhere. Although one can learn from other institutions and programs, each college or university must develop the
curriculum best suited to its circumstances. (For a discussion of
the procedures by which schools can best construct an appropriate curriculum, see Chapter Seven.)

Collectively, the reforms redress imbalances that have
arisen in the undergraduate course of study. They reemphasize
the broad aims of education, rather than narrow specialization
and career preparation. They provide structures designed to
achieve desired educational purposes, rather than a laissez-
faire curriculum. And they give a rightful place to general education, rather than to programs dominated by the major and
free electives. Once again colleges and universities are moving
toward a curriculum that includes attention to the liberal arts;
introduces the life of the mind; promotes thinking skills; provides special perspectives on international, women's, and minority issues; and emphasizes values and the integration of knowledge—all central features of a sound general education. In each
of these ways, colleges and universities are improving the quality of their undergraduate curriculums.

Chapter Five

Rethinking Courses, Teaching, and Faculty Development

Despite the attention focused on the curriculum as a whole—its philosophy, organization, and components—individual courses are the building blocks of any curriculum. A general education curriculum, however creative or distinctive, is only as strong as the courses that compose it and the quality of instruction they provide. Indeed, if a school has no overarching curricular philosophy, individual faculty members must rely on their own best judgments about the appropriate content, goals, and methods of general education courses in their field. In such cases, for a school to improve its general education means essentially that it enhances the quality of instruction in those courses.

When general education has been neglected for too long, the ills become so severe that they cannot be remedied by separate actions on the part of individual faculty members, however well meaning. The program as a whole must be reviewed; the college must redefine its vision of the generally educated person and decide how the instructional program as a whole can foster the development of such a person. A new curriculum thus represents an institution-wide agreement about the general character of individual courses and their roles in educating students. Once this new understanding of the nature of the curriculum is reached, individual courses again come to the fore as a focus of concern for enhancing general education. For courses both convey to students the purposes of the curriculum as a whole and also reflect the expertise and judgments of many individual teachers.

Thus to discuss general education courses is also to discuss the teaching of those courses. The pronounced interest in faculty development among higher education professionals during the 1970s yielded important insights regarding the improvement of teaching. Every effort should now be made to draw on those lessons, to use the techniques and procedures developed during the last decade to design courses and a pedagogy that will once again make the core of the undergraduate curriculum a vital and exciting center of learning.

Courses

General education courses differ in important ways from other kinds of courses. But the lack of unanimity about the purposes of general education is, of course, reflected in disagreements over appropriate coursework. At a broad level of analysis, Berry (1977) argues that liberal (or in this context, general) education is an attitude and an approach to a course; it is not simply a matter of content. According to this formulation, virtually any body of knowledge can be taught in a general or in a specialized manner. Mayhew (1980) proceeds to clarify the attitudes embodied by general education courses, noting that faculty often "pay inadequate attention to the general education ends of our major programs and our individual courses, letting the subject matter speak for itself, rather than seeking to clarify (to both our students and ourselves) the higher educational ends of our teaching" (pp. 2-3). But this approach is inadequate: "Each course is founded on a conception of what the course is 'about' in the sense of its educational aim. Courses can no more 'speak for themselves' than facts. To assert that facts speak for themselves is to ignore the selection by an observer of particular facts to do the speaking and the choice of which aspects of the facts that the observer describes; factual statements are embedded in concepts, approaches, strategic choices—in a word, theories. Similarly, our courses are organized selections of materials, implying a theory of what the whole concoction is about" (p. 3).

Calling theories about courses "metatheories," Mayhew finds the most common metatheory held by faculty members to be that of covering the material. But this theory is inadequate:

> There are two basic theories of coverage: we say, in effect, "I try to cover the material implied by the course title," or we say "I try to prepare students for future courses in this field." I call these the *name* and the *sequence* theory respectively. Both these theories have a certain pedagogical logic. After all, they may be said to reflect our responsibilities. The name theory corresponds to the requirement of truth in advertising and the sequence theory to our obligation to colleagues who will teach all those future courses. And, of course, the theories are very convenient; they help us to avoid the greatest difficulties attendant to defining our more long-run aims. On the other hand, if we want to establish or clarify the ends of our teaching, then neither of the two theories of coverage seems a particularly ambitious pedagogical approach. Seeking to cover material is a narrow, static, time-bound approach to teaching. . . . even under optimal conditions, the metatheories of name and sequence remain worse than narrow: they are intellectually shallow. The best postsecondary education provides instruction not in content but in method. It teaches not conclusions per se but how conclusions are reached, and once reached, how

they are used to build new conclusions and novel applications. Higher education should help students to become active participants in the process of inquiry, not passive receptacles for received thought [pp. 3-4].

Having rejected the coverage metatheories, Mayhew suggests a way to arrive at a more satisfactory conception of pedagogy: *"What and how would you teach if you knew that no student in your class would ever take another course in that discipline again?* ... the question should be asked of every course, not necessarily with the idea of radically altering every existing offering, but as a heuristic device for establishing a layer of general educational goals as a foundation for effective teaching" (p. 6).

Criteria. Mayhew's analysis of metatheories leads us to a consideration of the distinguishing marks of a general education course. Four primary issues are of concern. First, should the institution explicitly specify criteria for general education courses or should individual instructors be guided by the rationale contained in their program's description and departmental debates that preceded their adoption? Individual faculty members have typically been left more or less to their own devices in designing and teaching such courses, and this approach is being taken by many schools now revising their curriculums. But more institutions are stating key criteria for various types of courses, thus guiding faculty in their instruction. Increasingly, faculty committees certify courses as meeting general education purposes.

A second issue confronting those schools that decide to establish criteria for different courses is how specific they should be. Most institutions recognize the need to balance the overarching institutional purposes with the individual purposes, expertise, and styles of faculty members. At Los Medanos College, California, the following principle is used: "Each criterion is necessarily broad and encompassing. It will not spell out exact, specific ways in which a course outline should satisfy the criterion. That specificity is best supplied by those best suited to be specific, that is, instructors in the disciplines" (1981, p. 8). Ideally, a school's criteria are specific enough to guide instruction but flexible enough to permit faculty to take advantage of their interests and expertise.

A third issue is whether to establish broad criteria that apply to every course or to devise area-specific criteria that pertain to certain subject areas, such as the natural sciences or humanities. Los Medanos, for instance, decided to adopt generalized criteria that pertain to all courses in the distribution portion of the program. A draft proposal lists eight questions that are to be asked of every general education course:

1. Is the course interdisciplinary?
2. Does the course teach the modes of inquiry indigenous to the discipline?
3. Does the course teach about the esthetic qualities of the knowledge of the discipline?
4. Does the course explore these implications of the knowledge of the discipline: values, ethics, and future?
5. Does the course provide opportunities for learners to develop higher cognitive skills through reading and writing?
6. Does the course provide opportunities for learners to enhance their effectiveness in thinking?
7. Does the course introduce creative processes and examples of human creativity?
8. Does the course encourage learners to consider the variety of perspectives, experiences, and persuasions that impact on the society?

Finally, at some schools criteria are established by the entire faculty, while others establish subgroups to develop criteria for particular areas. Relatively small, homogeneous colleges with a tradition of interdepartmental cooperation may be able to arrive at a working consensus by means of a committee of the whole. Many larger institutions, however, work through decentralized groups, such as committees representing clusters of related departments. Occasionally, as at Valparaiso University, courses are developed by departmental teams aided by faculty members from outside the area of specialization who function as a kind of "consumer advocate" of the general perspective.

However they are fashioned, criteria serve two important functions. They direct course design and instruction to desired ends, and they provide the campus' general education committee with a basis for approving courses for the program and for monitoring their effectiveness. The test of any set of criteria, of course, is how well they work. Usually an initial set of criteria will be revised in light of their effectiveness; they are regarded as first approximations to be revised through experience rather than perfect formulations that are set in concrete.

Several features are frequently used as guidelines for designing courses or as criteria for selecting from among several that best serve general education purposes. Perhaps the most common is a focus on the special needs of nonmajor students. Nonmajors, who may never take another course in the discipline, need to grasp a few basic concepts or ideas; learn how the perspectives, ideas, and language of the discipline relate to those of other fields; and develop the interest and motivation to continue informal learning and reading about developments in that area. Prospective majors, in contrast, require an introduction to the discipline's range of subspecialties and a firm foundation for advanced courses in the field. Although a single course may serve both introductory and general purposes, some schools do not allow courses that count toward the major to be used to satisfy general education requirements. At the University of Southern California, for instance, no more than two courses counting toward a major may also fulfill general education requirements. Even when such a principle is not officially adopted, often the specialists must demonstrate that their courses address the particular needs of nonmajors.

A second common criterion for a general education course is that it include a substantial amount of writing. The University of Nebraska, for instance, specifies that courses taken for general education credit must require some writing to which the instructor responds in writing. The latter expectation involves a pedagogical assumption about the value of written criticism and also seeks to redress the ills of the large survey course as well as some of the newer instructional techniques, which tend to utilize simple check marks to assess learning, require little personal investment in expression by either students or teachers, and give students little or no practice in forming or expressing their ideas.

Other criteria of interest are specific to various institutions; various schools expect their general education courses to:

- reflect a departmental perspective or the specialized skills of faculty members involved
- address the fundamental issues in the area of study
- make use of primary sources wherever possible
- be comparative in character and introduce students to relativity of perspective, limitation of method, and distinctiveness of approach
- provide opportunities for active modes of learning
- allow students to reflect about knowledge as well as present the knowledge itself
- be concerned with the relation of the students as individuals to the discipline, especially in terms of the discipline's contribution to the students' personal growth

Of course, when a new curriculum is approved, the roles of existing courses and newly developed ones must be considered. Some schools attempt to merely fit existing courses into new categories, to simply rename the old wares. But unless new courses are developed, curriculum reform amounts to little more than a rearrangement of existing courses. However, a school should not devise all new courses before carefully reviewing current offerings to determine which may serve the new purposes, for it is foolish to substitute the untried for courses with proven effectiveness. Most new programs use some combination of new courses and existing ones, perhaps with some modification. Of Harvard's new core, for instance, about 60 percent of the courses are new and about 40 percent are old, often with some revision. St. Andrews Presbyterian features two tiers; the first consists mostly of existing courses in the disciplines, the second mostly of new interdisciplinary core courses.

To illustrate some specific criteria that pertain to various area courses, Document 1 at the end of this chapter discusses the requirements in force at Franklin and Marshall College.

Related Practices. In addition to framing the character of courses, some institutions provide classroom supports intended to better allow general education courses to achieve their intended purposes. For example, the University of Southern California, among other schools, requires that general education courses be taught by full-time faculty. The rare exceptions to this rule must be approved in advance by the general education committee, and the rule applies to all sessions of the university, including the College of Continuing Education evening classes, summer session, and courses taught off-campus and in foreign countries.

Other schools limit the enrollment in general education classes. For example, the freshman courses at SUNY College at Brockport are restricted to twenty students, thus facilitating the courses' orientation, advising, and seminar functions. A course on contemporary issues, which stresses a cross-cultural perspective, is limited to twenty-five students, allowing discussion and class participation. Other schools, such as Harvard, do not limit class size but do offer many small discussion sections, typically led by teaching assistants.

Schools also provide faculty with retraining and assistance in course development. For it takes a good deal of time and creativity to design a new course, especially one that is to realize the ambitious aims of general education or that is to use certain pedagogical techniques unfamiliar to the faculty. Florida A & M University adopted a competency-based approach to communications and mathematics skills, and offered faculty members support during the summer to design self-paced modules and tests. Similarly, a statewide program in Florida for faculty retraining helped some faculty members to acquire expertise in new areas that could be used in the program. Several other institutions have faculty or instructional development centers or programs in which in-house consultants assist in the design of courses and in the development of new pedagogical strategies. The Center for Instructional Development at Syracuse University, for instance, played a major role in the design of interdisciplinary core clusters. Such special support programs complement a school's other efforts to develop courses that carry out the purposes of their new curriculums.

Teaching

"Requiring courses does not guarantee learning in courses," reminds Irving Spitzberg, general secretary of the American Association of University Professors (1980, p. 426). It is an unfortunate truth that no educational practice can guarantee that all students will learn the information or skills intended. Clearly, courses, even well-designed ones, are insufficient without effective teachers who can stimulate students and assist them in learning.

The quality of teaching in general education has been very uneven. On the one hand, too often general education courses have been cursed with less than inspired teaching, having been left to those at the bottom of the academic pecking order. On the other hand, general education teaching sometimes has represented the best of undergraduate education. The late Lionel Trilling, reflecting on his distinguished career as a college teacher, thus described his experience: "I inhabited an academic community which was informed by a sense not merely of scholarly, but of educational purpose, and which was devoted to making ever more cogent its conception of what a liberal and humane education consists in. . . . it is indeed a striking and impressive circumstance that in our country in our time it has been possible for there to be so pertinacious a concern with questions of what is best for young minds to be engaged by, with how they may best be shaped through what they read—or look at or listen to—and think about" (1980, pp. 45-46). This sense of educational purpose animates the best of the professoriate and generates excitement in the classroom that carries over into conversations in faculty offices, lounges, student dormitories, indeed throughout the college community. The regeneration of this spirit is necessary if the reforms of general education are to fully realize their goals.

The poor quality of teaching in general education is a

part of the neglect of teaching in general: "General education falls prey to a whole set of abuses and impediments that are common across undergraduate teaching. These include: faculty who lack preparation for teaching; preoccupation of the best-qualified teachers with research and publication instead of teaching; an advancement system which rewards research and publication more than teaching; assignment of great portions of undergraduate instruction to the least-experienced instructors and to graduate assistants; strong traditional acceptance of amateurism in college teaching; academic myths (for example, good teachers are born not made, knowledge of a subject matter is synonymous with the ability to teach that subject); failure to obtain and use feedback; conservatism regarding change in teaching methods and styles; misuse of the concept of academic freedom resulting in a shield for incompetent teachers and administrators; and preoccupation with what is immediate and obvious rather than with what is important" (Redwine, 1980, p. 85).

In addition to these difficulties, several others are endemic to general education; for instance: teaching in this portion of the curriculum lacks standing in the academic status system; faculty and students do not have a clear conception of general education and how particular courses contribute to a holistic education; and many see general education as bread-and-butter courses that support more specialized and advanced courses. All these factors contribute to perhaps the most pervasive image of general education pedagogy: a large class in some required subject taught by a junior faculty member, possibly with teaching assistants, lecturing to passive students. Although this is a caricature—not all classes are large, not all instructors are junior faculty, and not all lectures are dull—it captures the pervasive spirit of passivity of learning that characterizes this portion of the curriculum.

To change this image, to stimulate faculty and students alike, some schools are using active teaching and learning methods in their general education courses. The AAC survey of institutions involved in reforming their general education programs found that 86 percent of the respondents were developing teaching methods to supplement the lecture (see Appendix A). Let us consider some examples of approaches to engage students, to make learning more active, to stimulate and motivate them.

Oregon State University requires a freshman course, Connections, that serves to introduce general education by raising several critical issues and various perspectives for understanding them. Because the course enrolls several hundred students and takes place in an auditorium, the teachers have brought a great deal of creativity into the cultivation of active modes of learning. These include having students write a paragraph in response to the main points or central message of each class; preparing handouts that free students from taking notes and thus allow them to listen and participate; showing films that heighten students' awareness of abstract ideas and having students write short responses to them; requiring students to participate in discussion groups led by specially trained students; and requiring short essays on assigned books. Further, some classroom sessions involve active participation. For instance, a session on world population and world hunger involves a simulation. Students are divided into countries according to their population and given candies in proportion to their wealth, very few to India despite its large population and large quantities to the United States, despite its relatively small population. When the "countries" engage in trade and aid to feed their people, the effects of the unequal distribution of food and the factors that impede more equitable distribution strike students with considerable force.

The case-study method is being developed at St. Andrews Presbyterian College as the major approach of its two-course sequence on human choices and global values. The focus of the first section of the course is on personal, family, and community issues, while the second deals with national policy, international, and global issues. Since the subject matter is such that there are no right answers, and the situations studied are in constant flux, the case-study method seems to convey an appreciation for the open-ended quality of knowledge. It also draws out the best thinking of faculty members and of students as they focus on various issues and offer different perspectives on complex realistic situations. Further, the three-course sequence on Christianity and world cultures is taught by interdisciplinary teams. These history courses employ a "block-and-gap" approach, highlighting certain ideas, people, and periods. Their content varies from year to year, depending on the faculty members involved and the issues that call for attention, but the course employs a common syllabus and involves library research and writing. Every faculty member at the college contributes to the general education program by teaching one core course and one breadth course each year.

Experiential learning is featured in several new programs. As the University of Maryland prepared to implement its new breadth requirements, it became apparent that standard classroom teaching methods would not address the stated goals for student development. The goals were concrete experience, reflective observation, abstract conceptualization, and active experimentation, which relate to different stages of individual development as well as to different aspects of the experiential learning process. Two groups of seven faculty members each are working with the university's office of experiential learning programs, which coordinates service learning, internships, and cooperative education, to design experiential features for general education courses. Each faculty member works in a team with a learning theorist and an experiential educator to design, test, and evaluate a general education course. Although the courses of the group are large, averaging over forty students, the instructional strategies involve active learning. In a similar vein, American University encourages some off-campus internship experience as a part of its new general education program. This allows students to take advantage of the unique learning opportunities provided by the college's location in the nation's capital (University Undergraduate Studies Committee, 1980). Antioch College, which pioneered the cooperative learning approach, has often grappled with relating its formal curriculum and classroom content to students' out-of-class experiences. The faculty recently approved a curriculum that stresses both knowledge and skills; while knowledge requirements must be met by coursework, two of the nine skills requirements *must* be met through co-op jobs that are approved for that use, and two more requirements *may* be satisfied by participation in activities of the college community, such as community governance, publications, perceptorial groups, or special task forces. Further, preplanned independent studies related to the co-op or community experience may be used to satisfy a portion of the seven knowledge requirements.

Yet other institutions stress a competency approach, particularly in regard to the development of skills. Brigham Young University employs a competence-based general education program that is carried out by means of individualized, self-paced modules. Students are expected to complete the materials that have been prepared by faculty members and pass a test at the end of each module, before proceeding to the next one. Although few colleges and universities are embracing the competency approach to this extent, several do employ it for limited purposes. Communication, foreign languages, and mathematics, for instance, are often handled in much the same way, with diagnostic testing for initial placement and proficiency testing to certify mastery. Some institutions have established a computer-literacy requirement in which students must learn a certain amount of programming. This requirement sometimes can be met by a course but sometimes by means of a special module developed and administered by staff members at the computer center.

As Maher (1980, pp. 8-9) cautions, new pedagogical methods must be complemented by new evaluative methods; traditional tests are often insufficient: "If we simply look at the kinds of tests which are given in most introductory courses, we realize that, in most cases, we are essentially encouraging and testing the development of memory—an essential component, but not the totality of an educated person. In introductory level courses, we, generally, do little with true analysis, synthesis, and especially, development of judgment. Too often, the sheer weight of numbers in these courses precludes a variety of teaching styles which would move the class beyond a memory exercise." Although a variety of evaluative techniques allow even large courses to be more than memory exercises, such techniques are used all too seldom. Instructors must design examinations that require more active thinking, higher-level thought processes, and more creative expression.

An extensive description of well-designed courses that contain a variety of useful pedagogical techniques is presented by Guroff (1981). A report of the Quality in Liberal Learning Project, the volume is an account of sixty-two course development projects funded by small grants from the Association of American Colleges. Three areas of improvement of liberal learning are stressed: interdisciplinary studies, liberal learning in career education, and liberal learning in continuing education.

In summary, well-designed courses that employ engaging and stimulating pedagogy are necessary if the core of the undergraduate curriculum is to be rescued. Although many institutions are moving beyond the lecture and developing new pedagogy, these steps may not be sufficient. More extensive and long-term efforts directed at the comprehensive development of faculty will be required in most cases.

Faculty Development

"Faculty development" is a phrase heard on most college campuses during the 1970s. Facing the prospect of retrenching, witnessing reduced faculty mobility, and becoming "tenured in," colleges and universities turned to faculty development. Schools enrolling larger numbers of nontraditional students—adults, women, and minorities—saw in faculty development a means to help faculty adjust their instruction to the changing clientele. Others, looking ahead to smaller numbers of traditional college-age youth, determined they must deliver more effective instruction and retain the students they recruited. All these factors pointed to the professional development of faculty members as essential to the renewal of institutions.

Professional development for faculty is not a new idea. The tradition of encouraging faculty to keep current in their fields of specialization and to conduct research is an old one. But approaches that transcended the acquisition of knowledge were needed to achieve the new purposes: approaches that focused on faculty instructional roles, career progression, and contributions to the effective functioning of the institution. At the start of the 1970s the broadened meaning of faculty development was a shiny new concept, and by the end it was another human technology. It had been put to the test and was shown to work (Gaff, 1978; Nelsen and Siegel, 1980). Fortunately, all that has been learned can be brought to bear on today's agenda to strengthen the core of the undergraduate curriculum.

Consider a few of the accomplishments that can assist in the implementation of a revised general education program.

- Many materials for use with college faculty are now available, often at modest cost. The three volumes of the *Handbook for Faculty Development* (Bergquist, Phillips, and Quehl, 1975-1981) contain the best collections, but the variety of other materials includes questionnaires, interview forms, summaries of research on teaching and learning, guidelines for designing workshops and other campus events, and video- and audiocassettes on aspects of instruction, simulations, and games.

- The professional literature has expanded. Several books and many journal articles provide descriptive, analytic, critical, and evaluative treatments; the booklet *Professional Development: A Guide to Resources* (Gaff, Festa, and Gaff, 1978) is a useful guide to this scholarship.

- A cadre of new leaders has emerged to provide development services for faculty members. As they have gained experience in their campus work, many practitioners have added to their expertise by attending conferences and special training workshops. Predictably, they have formed professional organizations, including the Professional and Organizational Development (POD) Network in Higher Education and a counterpart group for staff development specialists in community colleges.

- Evaluations of campus programs and activities are encouraging. Although the results are far from conclusive, benefits for both faculty members and institutions have been documented. Indeed, the demonstrated benefits extend to faculty members at all levels and from all areas of the academy—senior as well as junior faculty, those in the liberal arts as well as professional fields, and those with different teaching aims, styles, and abilities.

Faculty development programs can be initiated and sustained using the staff and resources already available on most campuses. Many schools have vested leadership in a small group of teaching faculty, often aided by administrators and students. Assistance is sometimes needed from experts, external consultants, and campus specialists, but the primary leadership can be taken by teaching faculty on virtually any campus.

Of course, faculty development, like any other venture, has its failures; its techniques can be subverted or misused. Further, it is a set of perspectives and skills that require study and experience to master. But substantial progress has been made by schools working directly with faculty members in the design of their courses, the enhancement of their teaching styles, the improvement of their relationship with students, and the renewal of instructional programs. All these lessons can now be applied to assist those who are designing new courses, developing an engaging pedagogy, and generally strengthening the quality of general education.

Despite the success of faculty development activities, most leaders in general education have not fully utilized this approach to improve their programs. Perhaps those institutions actively involved in reviewing their curriculums are not yet ready to address course design and pedagogy, central issues to faculty development; many are still debating the limitations of the current program, considering educational philosophies, or deciding on curricular structures. Since the greatest advances in faculty development have been made with course design and teaching, perhaps the widespread application of such techniques to general education lies ahead.

But there is another, deeper, reason that they have not drawn much from each other even though both aim at improving academic quality: they represent quite different conceptions of educational improvement, different ideas about major problems, proper solutions, and effective strategies. In broad terms, the basic purpose of general education reform is to improve the quality of student education. But the primary goal of faculty development is to provide for the continual professional growth of faculty members, thereby renewing instructional programs, even whole colleges and universities. The focus of concern in general education reform is the curriculum, particularly the general education portion. Curricular reform involves defining minimal standards for the student body as a whole. In contrast, individual faculty members and their courses are the focal points of faculty development, as efforts are made to assist instructors in better realizing their own purposes. Thus curricular reforms are usually large in scope; they are revisions of the institution's central activity. But faculty development programs operate on the periphery of the institution; they tend to be small in scope and budget, and they serve as additions to the current program. Although virtually every department, division, college, committee, and faculty member is affected by curricular reform, few individuals or groups are so affected by faculty development, and thus few have vested interests to protect.

Whereas students must comply with their institution's curricular changes, faculty participation in development programs typically is voluntary. Indeed this is necessary to build a constituency for the activities of the program. As a result, faculty development relies on conservative inducement strategies to entice faculty to attend seminars or workshops, discuss their ideas, and try out new skills—without rocking the boat and challenging existing academic structures. This contrasts directly with the need to alter existing general education requirements using the kinds of consensual holistic strategies that will be discussed in Chapter Seven.

Campus leaders of curricular reform include administrators and faculty members with expertise in the subject matter treated in general education, faculty members respected for effective teaching in general courses, and those who embody the ideal of a generally educated person. While administrators and outstanding teachers play key roles in establishing faculty development programs, such efforts are staffed by persons who have either process skills with which to draw out their colleagues and get them working together or technical skills with which to assist in designing courses, developing instructional materials, or conducting evaluations.

Concern for general education has emerged as a part of a national trend toward conservatism and fiscal stringency. Faculty development, however, emerged during the 1970s, which began with a spirit of radicalism and individualism and ended with a growing awareness of the need for academic retrenchment. Each movement reflects the spirit of its times.

These different aims, programs, and strategies are appropriate to each set of concerns. But their many differences go a long way to explain why activists in the two movements, both devoted to educational improvement, have failed to cooperate more fully. Now these complementary endeavors must begin to work together. Curriculum, courses, teaching, and learning in general education can best be enhanced by developing the full talents of faculty members and by ensuring that their interests and growth are furthered through general education. Indeed, unless general education curricular reforms are carried through in the courses and the quality of teaching, and unless faculty members find that they derive intellectual and personal stimulation from working in that context, the new programs are not likely to have a very long or satisfactory life.

Various institutions have begun to use the techniques of faculty and instructional development to complement their curricular revisions. Let us briefly survey some recent examples:

- Faculty development specialists can gather background material and help an institution launch a full-scale curricular review. Their expertise in research, analysis, and reporting should not be overlooked, and their knowledge of educational improvement and institutional strategies for introducing changes are valuable contributions to institutional planning groups.
- Instructional development experts can use their expertise in the design of courses and learning materials to help faculty

members design specific courses to achieve goals of general education. Campus specialists can help faculty members specify objectives, adapt new instructional methods, and evaluate students' achievement.

- Faculty development staff members can use their skill in designing professional development activities to plan and organize workshops or seminars to provide training for faculty. For example, when DePauw University adopted a plan that required courses throughout the general curriculum to address writing skills, speaking, and mathematics, faculty had to learn how to incorporate instruction in these skills into their courses. Workshops on student learning styles and development, intensive work among a small group of faculty members, use of expert consultants, and follow-up assistance helped faculty acquire the competencies requisite to the general education program.

- Faculty development relies heavily on inducement strategies, and thus directors of those programs are able to assist with the recruitment of faculty to teach general education courses. Interdisciplinary core courses, global studies, or values-oriented courses often do not have a natural faculty constituency, and faculty members must be recruited and often given some training for the unfamiliar task. Developers can help faculty understand the potential professional and personal benefits of the new assignment.

- Faculty development specialists also possess group-process skills, which they can use to help groups of faculty members work together to fashion a consensus about the shape of a new course or component of a program. The instructional development staff at Syracuse University, for instance, worked with interdisciplinary groups of faculty to design thematic clusters of courses in related liberal arts disciplines, a central feature of its new general curriculum.

- Development specialists can use their knowledge of evaluation methodologies to help prepare and conduct the evaluation of the new curriculum. They can assist in the development of tests to measure students' accomplishment of general education purposes, in the assessment of teaching in certain courses, or in the evaluation of the program as a whole.

Obviously, not every faculty or instructional development specialist has each of these abilities, nor are these skills
found on every campus. But these competencies are possessed
by many practitioners, and many institutions have such talents
available on campus. Consider the following example of how
the principles of faculty development aided curriculum reform
at Pacific Lutheran University.

Curtis Huber, a professor of philosophy at Pacific Lutheran, was dissatisfied with the distribution scheme. He gathered a
small group of like-minded colleagues to explore the possibility
of creating a more integrated core curriculum. First, they enticed thirty-two faculty members to participate in week-long
summer workshops: "Through this exercise in creative humilia-
tion, we learned to understand each other's jargon, share concerns about our teaching more openly and learn from carefully
chosen consultants some of the existing options for interdisciplinary curricular structure and teaching methods. Trust levels
and cooperative behavior were heightened. Participation in
these workshops was linked to the creation of team-taught mini-
courses immediately following the workshops, using the information and skills in the week-long experience. The reinforce-
ments thus provided gave faculty some confidence in attempting new instructional techniques and evaluative reaction from
hundreds of students. The experience was thoroughly successful
largely because faculty development was tied to specific tasks of
curricular change" (1977, pp. 160-161). A series of follow-up
activities were inaugurated: "Accompanying these efforts was a
continuous process of positive reinforcement provided largely
by the participation and consent of the administration. Perqui-
sites, luncheons and dinners, some in the hallowed presidential
dining room, were provided for the periodic day-long meetings
at which forty or more faculty subsequently developed course
proposals and examined, criticized, and sorted curricular designs. Our efforts and their results were widely publicized
among the entire faculty" (p. 161).

Eventually, a series of four sequences, each consisting of
two related interdisciplinary courses, was devised; the sequences
composed an integrated approach to the overarching theme, the

dynamics of change. A culminating seminar provided additional integration to the program, called the Integrated Studies Program but known among students as the "hard core." Over fifty faculty members have participated in the program; a careful evaluation of the effort and of its effects on students and faculty has been conducted; revisions have been made in light of the early experience; and a strong sense of intellectual community has evolved. New integrated course sequences are now being introduced, and new faculty members are teaching in the program.

Because faculty development activities were so successful in preparing faculty to plan cooperatively and to teach as members of an integrated program, all new faculty participate in an interdisciplinary workshop and work with their colleagues to design their courses to fit the program. Huber (p. 169) concludes: "Far from being a 'frill' or 'fad,' we have found this kind of in-service learning and sharing among peers to be one of the most potent methods of dissolving the national and institutional barriers to educational integrity and coherence. The crucial factor has been that faculty development has been directly related to specific curriculum development instead of being pursued as an end in itself or to serve the occasional need or interest of the individual." This lesson is one that leaders of general education reforms cannot afford to ignore: curricular change requires attention to faculty development if it is to achieve its purposes.

Conclusion

The conditions of learning are essential concerns in an effective general education program. General education courses are different from others, primarily in that they are meant for students who may never take another course in the subject. The most promising reforms identify the special qualities of general education and use them as criteria for selecting courses and for guiding instruction. Exemplary programs also incorporate specific steps—including efforts to make learning active, individualized, and communal—to prevent a succumbing to the routine pedagogy that doomed their predecessors.

Faculty development, especially activities that emphasize teaching roles, is necessary to accomplish some of these ends. Faculty development programs not only give faculty members a detailed understanding of how their instruction relates to the entire general education program but also assist them in acquiring the sensitivities and techniques to teach skills, explore values, foster the integration of knowledge, or achieve any of the other purposes of general education. The opportunity to work in a vital program organized on such principles is itself a powerful force for the renewal of faculty. Indeed, faculty who work in distinctive programs of general education report that such teaching is among the most valuable experiences in their careers. Such renewal results from working in a challenging program with colleagues and students engaged in a common enterprise and devoted to the general education of all. This is the spirit that animates general education at its finest.

Document 1. Criteria for General Education Courses at Franklin and Marshall College.

Scientific Inquiry

This requirement involves the student in a systematic study of the physical and/or biological world and consists of two courses each of which must involve laboratory work. These courses must focus primarily on the study of the general subject matter of the discipline. Through that study, a course fulfilling the scientific inquiry requirement must:

1. introduce major concepts of a field of science, providing insight into the breadth of the discipline and its relationship to other disciplines;
2. illustrate the relationships which exist among experiments, models, theories, and laws;
3. involve systematic data collection using experimentation and/or observations, with one or more of these sets of data being treated in a quantitative manner;
4. discuss the limitations of data and the possibility of alternative interpretations;
5. address relationships between exemplary scientific principles and (a) the historical and cultural context in which they arose, (b) public policy issues.

At least one course of the scientific inquiry requirement must have been completed by the end of the fourth semester.

Social Analysis

This requirement consists of two courses, each of which provides the opportunity to study institutionalized human social behavior in a systematic way. A course fulfilling the social analysis requirement must:

Source: Franklin and Marshall College (1980, pp. 4–10).

1. focus one or more of the following units of analysis: families, organizations, communities, economies, or governments;
2. illustrate particular areas in which the discipline merges with other disciplines;
3. explore several of the alternative theoretical frameworks which have been used to offer meaningful explanations of social phenomena in that discipline;
4. illustrate and evaluate methods of data collection and analysis, including quantitative methods used in that discipline;
5. consider a significant social issue from the point of view of alternative analytic models used in that discipline and evaluate their relevance for deciding social policy questions;
6. introduce the origins and breadth of the discipline with which the unit of analysis is being studied.

At least one course in the social analysis requirement must have been completed by the end of the fourth semester. The social analysis requirement must be satisfied by one course in each of two different disciplines.

Historical Studies

This requirement is intended to introduce students to a substantial and coherent body of historical knowledge within Western culture and to the nature of historical inquiry.

A course satisfying the historical studies requirement must:

1. survey a major culture over a significant period. This may be done thematically, if the theme is itself substantial (for example, the scientific, political, or religious history of ———);
2. provide experience in the critical use of sources and evaluation of evidence;
3. encourage knowledge and understanding of a variety of historical interpretations;
4. include discussion of the nature of scholarly inquiry and the limitations of scholarly authority;

5. employ associations (for example, analogical) with contemporary thought and institutions;
6. increase in student's knowledge and understanding of the complexities and varieties of human events.

Courses satisfying this college studies requirement must attempt to familiarize students with important developments in the history of Western culture as one of the mainstreams of world history.

Literature

This requirement is intended to encourage, enhance, and extend the student's response to literary art, by introducing the processes of thoughtful literary analysis. It will also further the student's understanding of the Western literary tradition as a major body of knowledge about the human condition, by focusing on classic texts from that tradition.

A course satisfying the literature requirement must:

1. teach the student to read independently and with careful attention to the text;
2. help the student in organizing and sharpening his or her own critical responses to literature;
3. demonstrate how the reader communicates an informed esthetic evaluation by making convincing use of evidence;
4. broaden the range of approaches according to which the student makes esthetic judgments, and demonstrate the applicability of literary critical terms;
5. provide the student with a sense of the cultural, historical, and biographical contexts out of which a work has grown; identify the conventions within or against which the work operates.

Systems of Knowledge and Belief

Courses satisfying this requirement examine systems of human thought and belief, with emphasis upon matters of value and choice. Such a course must:

1. be devoted to one or more of the following: (a) the problems of defining and acting upon ethical concepts such as good, obligation, and justice; (b) the nature of knowledge or belief, including questions of evidence and validity; (c) ontological, cosmological, or theological considerations and their reflection in human action, perhaps including the relationship between culture and thought or belief;
2. concentrate on the beliefs themselves, relating them to their historical or social context as required to reveal the content and implications of beliefs;
3. require students to analyze critically the concepts and systems discussed, and the kinds of considerations relevant to their defense;
4. introduce students to the major figures, theories, and works associated with the system(s).

The appropriate focus of such a course should be upon systems of knowledge or belief which have continued to compel attention over extended periods of time.

Foreign Cultures

Courses satisfying this requirement should familiarize students with one important and distinctive foreign culture, a culture in which English is not the dominant language of use. Such a course should provide students with an appreciation of different customs, traditions, and values, and enable them to come to a deeper and richer understanding of their own culture. Courses that satisfy this requirement may be of two different types, each with its own criteria:

A. Courses on a foreign culture. In order to satisfy this requirement, a course must:

1. examine a single foreign culture or discrete cultural area in depth through a study of several of the following: the political system, the economic system, the social system, the arts, and the religion(s);
2. focus on the ways in which cultural values are manifested;

3. describe the nature of the culture under study within a theoretical or conceptual framework;

4. contrast the culture under consideration with cultural systems familiar to the student.

B. Courses in a foreign language and literature. Students may fulfill the foreign cultures requirement through a course in foreign language. A course satisfying this requirement must be beyond the first-year college level. Students will be placed in a course appropriate to their previous training. In order to satisfy this requirement, a course must also:

1. pay attention to the language's larger cultural tradition in order that the language may be viewed not in a literary isolation but as the central mode of expression of a people's life;

2. refer to and include readings in the most appropriate literary materials from the tradition of the language;

3. emphasize the development of skills in reading, writing, and conversation through the study of the language, its grammar, syntax, vocabulary, and idiom;

4. include comparisons with the English language, with respect to its usage and its reflection of culture.

Arts

Courses satisfying this requirement center on the making, criticism, theory, or history of the arts of dance, theater, music, sculpture, painting and graphic arts, or architecture and recognize the sensuous, unique character of the work of art, the value of which stands outside conventional ideas of utility. These courses must stress the peculiar value of the work as a form of knowledge and experience both expressive and intellectual. They must show how careful thought and systematic analysis can add to pleasure as well as to understanding. Attention must always be given to the choice and manipulation of texture, mass, color, line, form, rhythm, sign, and symbol—all the substantial materials proper to that art.

Arts courses satisfying this requirement must:

1. recognize that the work may have powerful intellectual content and be deeply rooted in a particular tradition and the history of ideas;
2. show that the work while subjective and occasionally inspired is nevertheless an artifact dependent upon reflection and fine craftsmanship;
3. study the work of art as a dynamic tension between spontaneity and convention or as a process in problem solving;
4. emphasize that while the process is of high value, the integrity of the process is to be found in the quality of the product, in the work itself.

Courses that satisfy the arts requirement may be of two general types: (A) The studio course where direct experience in making the work of art dominates. Studio courses are to be regarded as preparation for unspecified performance (not as performance itself, which is formal and public). In such a course there must be a historical/critical/theoretical extra dimension of sufficient extension and depth to alert the student to the manner in which a work may be studied and valued subsequent to its making. (B) The historical/critical/theoretical course where these concerns about art dominate. These academic studies will focus on those major figures whose work has helped to define an important movement or tradition that has gained classic status. In such a course there must be an extra dimension of direct experience such as making the work of art or, where appropriate, directly observing the process of its creation, or directly observing the work of art itself.

Chapter Six

Providing Support Through Administration, Finance, and Evaluation

A contemporary educational philosophy, a set of basic requirements, and well-taught courses cannot, in themselves, remedy
the problems that plague general education. To coordinate these
elements and form a coherent program of study, some campus
agency must administer and monitor the program, ensuring its
quality. Further, provision for financing its full development is
necessary. Finally, the program must be periodically evaluated.

Administration

The essential problem with the administration of general
education is that, at most institutions, no one has the responsibility and authority to act on behalf of the program as a whole.
At the institutional level, the chief academic officer is usually

assigned responsibility for general education, but it is far from a
top priority. Such officers are responsible for hiring faculty,
evaluating performance of faculty and administrators, preparing
budgets, operating adult education, overseeing the library, and
directing the graduate school, among other tasks; and general
education tends to get lost among all these other demands.
Similarly, although the curriculum committee ostensibly is the
faculty group responsible for general education, it possesses limited authority to approve or reject course proposals offered by
the schools, programs, and departments. Most committees
adopt a reactive mode, make short-term decisions, and tend to
maintain the political status quo: "Standing curriculum committees are the burying ground of educational reform; they and
other hurdles exist for the purpose of restricting academic
change so that the curriculum won't get out of hand" (Hefferlin, 1972, p. 6). Thus, despite appearances to the contrary, institutional responsibilities for general education are vague.

The malady is passed on to the departments, each of
which is responsible for contributing to the program, most commonly by offering courses to meet breadth requirements. But
the departments' dozens of more or less independent decisions
about the nature and content of courses cannot yield an integrated curriculum. Further, each department naturally places a
high value on its own priorities, which are recruiting majors and
offering advanced courses related to the special interests of faculty members. To general education go the time and attention
left over from these more highly prized purposes. In short, the
trouble with delegated departmental responsibility is that when
everybody is in charge, nobody is in charge.

When institutional and departmental responsibility are ill
defined, faculty responsibility can only be ambiguous. The academic culture places general education at the bottom of the
pecking order of priorities, and in some instances faculty members may act as though they work for the department, not the
institution. After all, they are hired and promoted primarily on
the recommendation of the department, and their duties are assigned by the department. Their role in general education, if
any, is most commonly to offer a course that satisfies the distri-

bution requirements for nonmajors. Since the faculty are oriented primarily to the department, their courses for nonmajors often consist of narrow treatments of the discipline that do not relate to other disciplines, the world beyond the campus, or the personal lives of students.

For these reasons, many institutions are taking steps to reestablish responsibility for general education and to create a centralized authority that can reclaim integrity for the core of the undergraduate curriculum. One of the most popular arrangements during former general education revivals was to create a separate college to provide the core learning experiences. Some schools created experimental colleges for small groups of students; others formed a separate lower-division college to provide general education for all students. Although examples of both approaches exist, neither is popular with today's reformers. An experimental college is expensive, does not provide the flexibility institutions need to cope with an uncertain future, and fails to reach the majority of the student body. Although several cluster colleges and other alternative colleges are still functioning effectively, very few new ones are being created.

The separate college of general studies is a time-honored structure. For instance, since the 1950s Western Michigan University has operated an autonomous College of General Studies designed to foster cross-disciplinary and innovative teaching to supplement the departmental offerings. The college has a separate faculty and budget to support its mission, and it offers instruction to a broad cross section of the student body. This form of organization allows an institution to assign specific responsibility for at least a portion, if not all, the general curriculum and to support it with a staff and budget. However, by locating responsibility in a separate unit, a university may risk the noninvolvement of its traditional departments in general education because members may perceive that it is done "over there." Further, separate units have a tendency to be whittled down and eventually occupy a second-class status. A respected college of general studies at one major university has operated since the 1930s. Originally designed for talented students who wanted broad-ranging courses, it now almost exclusively serves students unable to meet the admission requirements of other units of the university. Once, its faculty were recognized as outstanding teachers who held joint appointments in regular departments, but today it has its own faculty and graduate assistants, few of whom hold joint appointments. And funding is now a problem. When such developments occur, a separate college is politically vulnerable and its leaders spend much time and energy simply justifying and fighting for their unit's survival. (Recently, the highly regarded University College at Michigan State University was in fact abolished.) These drawbacks preclude most schools from establishing a separate college to provide general education.

General Education Committees. Instead of relying on these earlier structures, many institutions that are seriously concerned with reestablishing authority for general education are constituting institution-wide faculty committees solely to oversee the general curriculum. The tasks assigned to a general education committee are several. First, it determines criteria of general education courses (or, in some cases, accepts those that have been defined by the faculty as a whole), publicizes guidelines within all the relevant departments, and solicits proposals from faculty members for various portions of the program. Sometimes, a new component of the curriculum will elicit few course proposals, and the committee takes special measures to stimulate them.

A second task for the committee is to review courses submitted by the faculty or departments and select a suitable array of offerings. Although judging a course proposed by a faculty colleague or a department is always difficult, at large institutions the review process is complicated by logistics. To keep the paperwork moving, some large schools give subcommittees in each subject area authority to certify courses within it. This review must not be a rubber-stamp approval. The committee must have the courage to reject proposals that fall short of key goals in order to substantiate its authority as well as ensure that courses are consistent with the original purposes. By rejecting course proposals—even from eminent colleagues—the committee signals that it believes high-quality general education to be important.

A third task of the committee is to coordinate the program as a whole, to produce a comprehensive program from diverse components. The committee must help faculty members relate their teaching and work with students to the larger program. A committee may use written materials, reports in faculty meetings, periodic meetings of teaching faculty, campus workshops, and off-campus retreats for the purposes of sustaining the consensus that generated the program and developing an intellectual community that characterizes general education at its best.

A fourth important task is overseeing the implementation of the program as designed. The committee may need to recruit faculty members to teach certain kinds of courses, actively stimulate course proposals for neglected areas, discuss current problems, soothe disgruntled faculty members or administrators, and anticipate future needs. Although a committee may not have formal responsibility or specific budget authority for implementation activities, it can use its influence and moral authority to great advantage.

Monitoring the ongoing development of the program is a fifth task of the committee. A committee that recertifies courses every few years gathers various kinds of evaluative evidence and can thus assess the progress of the program. The committee also serves as a lightning rod for comments, suggestions, and criticisms from throughout the college community; as such, it should not only be able to foresee difficulties in the program's day-to-day operation but also take steps to keep the enterprise alive and vital.

The composition of a general education committee depends on an institution's size and structure. The committee should be large enough to assure a degree of representation from all relevant schools, divisions, or units; yet small enough to be efficient. It should include members to provide liaison with key committees or units; and it should have some members from the planning group to provide continuity from plan to operation. The committee at the University of Southern California provides a model of membership for a large school; it is composed of: three members of each division, elected by the

faculty; the university's coordinator of general education and
the committee's chair, both appointed by the dean of the College of Letters, Arts, and Sciences; two students selected by the
faculty senate; the director of the Freshman Writing Program,
chairperson of the Foreign Language Committee, and the director of the Mathematics Skill Level Program; a liaison with the
professional schools, appointed by the vice-president for academic affairs; and nonvoting ex-officio members (chair of the
Undergraduate Education Commission, chair of the University
Curriculum Committee, dean of advisement of the college, and
divisional assistant deans). This may appear to be a bulky committee, but a smaller committee would not honor the principles
of representation and liaison with relevant groups. Smaller colleges can, of course, create smaller committees.

General Education Directors. Committees, however valuable their contributions, are unable to provide day-to-day administration of the program. Therefore, institutions with such
committees also usually designate an administrator with special
responsibility for general education. This administrative appointment is often a part-time one, given to either a faculty
member, who continues to teach, typically in general education,
or to an associate dean or an assistant vice-president. Most such
directors of general education have previously served with distinction on the task force responsible for fashioning the new
curriculum. They also tend to be well known for their intellectual scope, their effectiveness as teachers, and their success in
teaching nonmajors. Almost uniformly, they are drawn from
the institution's faculty rather than from outside.

For a description of the job of a director of general education, we may turn to David Unumb, the newly appointed coordinator of general education at Northeastern Illinois University, a position the committee jokingly referred to as "Czar" of
general education. Unumb (1981, pp. 6–7) describes four primary roles: agent of change, facilitator, ombudsman, and advocate. As the agent of change, he and his committee are "the
locus of all concerns manifested about the implications of
change, resistances to change, and further suggestions for detail
in that change." Facilitator's skills are used to stimulate discus-

sion, ameliorate differences, and expedite agreements among the program's various constituencies. Although a director of general education may not control administrative decisions about staffing nor oversee faculty development programs on curricular design, he or she can initiate discussion of such issues and press toward their successful resolution.

The director also serves as ombudsman for the academic community, "acting as an amicus curiae for the general education program." Unumb observes that this role involves "not only the important cooperating and coordinating function with all academic and support services, including student advising, library services, and faculty welfare, but also represents special 'case pleading' whenever and wherever it proves necessary." Among the areas in which an ombudsman's conciliation skills prove valuable are student advising prior to their declaration of a major; determination of the general education program's commitment to interdisciplinary courses and shared instruction; and the creation of a reward system for faculty who contribute to general education.

Finally, Unumb holds that the director and the general education committee must serve as "preacher to the parish," that is, they must continue to persuade the faculty, administration, and students to continue the process of curricular reform, to keep the spirit of reform alive, and to prevent complacency from vanquishing that spirit.

Of course, the creation of the post of director, or that of a general education committee, may initially cause resentment or distrust. Other campus committees may fear losing part of their power, as may deans and department heads who previously operated as autonomous decision makers about general education courses. But ultimately the change in the balance of power results in centralized administration, which can be more supportive of general education. And although some disapprove of efforts to centralize the administration of general education, others question whether present reforms go far enough. For example, Maher (1982) criticizes the reforms at his alma mater: "I would argue that the university should give the director of liberal education the title of dean or associate provost and establish the position at this level. The incumbent should be paid a salary in the range of those currently paid to the academic deans and should be a member of any governing group to which deans belong."

But current developments do attempt to reclaim authority for general education. Institution-wide committees and special administrators in tandem provide ongoing institutional responsibility for general education. Their policies and actions establish an overall framework within which separate departments and other units can operate. Individual faculty members thereby gain a better sense of the program as a whole and of their own roles and responsibilities.

Finance

Many of the problems associated with general education are a reflection of financial practices. Large, mass-produced lecture courses for lower-division students serve to subsidize small-enrollment specialized courses for advanced students. General education, put simply, has been starved for funds. Its neglect is related to its lack of financial support as much as to its conceptual ambiguity and the abandonment of its philosophy. If there is to be a genuine reform of general education, it will have to be accompanied by a shift in its financial base. As Spitzberg (1980, p. 426) notes, "Too often, attempts at resurrection of general education have been made without any real economic transfer. The economic decisions must be recognized as real resource transfers away from the specialization of the upper divisions. . . ." If general education is valued as an educational goal, and if it is considered as essential to a college education as the major field of specialization, then it requires comparable financial support. Only then will it be a truly coequal portion that can be as meaningful and intellectually exciting as the major.

The costs of strengthening general education vary with the program, but a few representative expenses may be cited. Policies to enhance the quality of teaching in general education have economic repercussions. For example, if instructors must be regular faculty members, an institution can no longer use less-expensive part-time staff in introductory courses. Similarly, if senior faculty can be enticed to offer courses, the instructional budget for general education will be higher than if junior faculty teach. Limiting the size of courses also affects the budget. Various institutions have determined that small classes are needed to serve particular purposes, such as teaching writing skills, providing a more meaningful introduction to college, affecting attitudes toward other peoples, or integrating knowledge. If enrollments are limited, then more courses or sections are needed to serve the programs, and expenses increase.

The administration of general education programs also entails expenditures: the salary of an associate dean or a director, the necessary office support, the time of a faculty committee, and the time of the faculty to establish and follow the coordinated procedures. Likewise adjunct faculty development programs—to assist instructors in acquiring new skills and designing new courses—must be supported by the institution if faculty members are to be expected to carry out the intentions of new curriculums. Workshops, consultants, travel, and related costs must be calculated in such efforts.

Even in difficult economic times, most schools are hiring at least a few faculty members. Although few institutions are hiring simply to staff general education, many are considering new faculty as potential contributors to the core. This practice also shifts the balance of power as well as economic control away from departments. And faculty who contribute to the program must be rewarded for their efforts. Whereas most institutions reward service to the department, more are also rewarding service to general education.

Finally, as we will see in the next section, evaluation of new programs is necessary. Existing academic programs are seldom evaluated in any rigorous way, not because they are thought to be doing so well but because their operations are not seriously questioned. Any new program, however, must prove itself, and evaluation of some sort is vital.

But we must also note the important economies associated with new forms of general education. Fewer courses are needed for a more heavily prescribed program, and savings are realized from reversing course proliferation. Mandatory courses are more fully subscribed than most electives, which leads to further efficiency. Fuller utilization of faculty members also occurs when courses are required in currently less-popular liberal arts fields. And the faculty flexibility that results from their heightened sense of responsibility for general education as well as for various departmental purposes allows for additional flexibility in staffing. These advantages offer considerable economic leverage to an institution feeling the effects of retrenchment.

Then there are less-tangible, but potentially quite significant, benefits. For instance, can an attractive program of general education coupled with desirable majors be a useful marketing technique to recruit students, one more effective than reliance on specialization alone? What is the economic benefit of retaining students and their tuition dollars by virtue of a sound program of general studies? What is the ultimate payoff of offering a quality educational program that lives up to the expectations of various constituencies and gives a generation of students the basis for productive lives? Although such benefits cannot be forecast with any exactitude, general education would seem to produce several long-term real, if intangible, benefits.

In considering the funding of new general education programs, one must bear in mind that most of the increased costs do not represent actual expenditures, but rather a transfer of time, a reallocation of budget, and a realignment of priorities; large amounts of additional money are not needed. Of course, the burden of reallocation falls unevenly throughout an institution. For example, an extensive study of the new requirements at SUNY at Buffalo concludes that roughly one quarter of the total undergraduate instructional capacity of the university is needed to meet the commitments in general education (Task Force on Implementation of General Education, 1980). Further analysis shows expected decreases in student enrollment in the areas of social and behavioral sciences, foreign languages and cross-cultural studies, and art, and increases in historical and philosophical studies, physical and mathematical sciences, technology, life and health sciences, and literature. The area of literature is a particular problem, as the task force estimates that general education demand will be about 800 percent of capacity, assuming a continued serious commitment to basic skills and no reduction in advanced courses. Obviously, the differential effects mirror the nature of a school's new curriculum, and institutions would be wise to anticipate the resource shifts.

As with any national reform movement, funding agencies are heavily involved in general education. Government agencies, such as the Fund for the Improvement of Postsecondary Education and the National Endowment for the Humanities; private national foundations such as the Exxon Education and Andrew Mellon Foundations; and regional foundations, such as the Bush and Northwest Area Foundations—all have contributed to the climate of curricular reform. However, as valuable as such funding sources are, the great bulk of curricular change is taking place without benefit of external grants; the funds are coming from schools' regular operating budgets. Most institutions finance general education by crediting departments that offer courses counting toward general education with enrollments in those courses. Obviously, at institutions whose budgets are driven by student credit hour production, it is in the economic interest of a department to offer desirable courses, thereby increasing its budget.

A different approach is taken by schools that allocate funds directly to the general education program. Harvard, for instance, reimburses departments for the instructional time of faculty members who teach a course in general education. Although the general education director does not have the power of appointment, this budgeting technique gives him effective veto power over who teaches courses in this area. This arrangement keeps general education from becoming a dumping ground for ineffective teachers.

Whatever the budgetary mechanism, general education will continue to be a disaster area until it receives a fair share of the instructional budget. If it is viewed only as a way to support other courses, it will tend to have large classes and second-rate instruction. If budgeting formulas discriminate against lower-division instruction, faculty will respond to that signal by assigning less importance to general education than to other parts of the curriculum. By giving general education its proportionate share of the budget and revising budgetary formulas, an institution confirms that general education is as important as the major.

In concluding, we can step back and observe that the changes in funding, as well as in administration, are consequences of the hard times facing colleges and universities. During a time of growth and expansion, an organization must decentralize in order to generate rapid and effective growth. No central administration can possibly have the imagination and wisdom to develop new programs and hire competent faculty in all its far-flung units; imaginative growth must be driven by departments. But during times of contraction and retrenchment, the scale of operations must be reduced, and it is counterproductive for isolated units to make decisions that may jeopardize the welfare of the whole. Only some central authority with responsibility for the entire institution and with information about the parts is in a position to make decisions that benefit the institution as a whole. More centralized administration backed by more centralized funding is a natural institutional response, even though it flies in the face of earlier conventions.

Finally, one should note that many schools are tightening their requirements during a difficult financial period when they are competing more fiercely for students. Common sense would indicate that they would further reduce requirements and do whatever they could to make it easier for students of all sorts to enroll, attend classes, and get degrees. However, instead they are trying to gain a competitive edge, sometimes quite consciously, by upgrading the quality of their basic product. This is a classic response to hard times in a free-enterprise economy. Most schools are wagering that they will be better served by offering a better-quality education than by making college easier.

Evaluation

All the debate about general education, all the changes in the philosophy, curriculum, courses, teaching, governance, and financing—however persuasive the various cases may be and however promising the changes are, lead to a single question: Do they make a difference in the education of students? Therefore let us now turn our attention to evaluation—its rationale and practice.

Evaluation serves several purposes. For one, it shifts the grounds of the discussion about general education from a normative to an empirical basis. As we have seen, debates about general education and about various practices are conducted in a value-laden rhetorical framework. In a blistering attack on the liberal arts, Bird goes even further, claiming that: "The liberal arts are a religion, the established religion of the ruling class. The exalted language, the universalistic setting, the ultimate value, the inability to define, the appeal to personal witness . . . these are all the familiar modes of religious discourse" (1975, p. 109). Only evaluation, using scientific procedures, operational definitions, public data, and duplicable methods, can test such claims. Curricular reform can best proceed on the basis of empirical findings that elicit the credibility of all constituencies.

Second, evaluation, in the words of Gamson (1980), is an instrument "to further self-consciousness," the only way for individuals to know whether a program they champion is having the desired effects. While often seen as an arcane collection of specialized jargon and techniques in the hands of detached professionals and therefore resisted by innovators, evaluation is actually an aid to understanding. The idealism that characterizes innovation must be tempered by a realistic assessment of the consequences. Evaluation thus enables educators to become more aware of the consequences of various practices in their profession and their craft.

A third rationale for evaluation is to identify problems and remedies in a new program. *Formative evaluations* are designed and conducted primarily to yield information that can be used by program planners to adjust the program as it evolves. Formative evaluation asks students and faculty to describe the best and worst parts of the program, problems encountered, and suggestions for improvement. Although a formative evaluation may not yield a definitive verdict about the success of the program, it provides information that can help program planners maximize whatever strengths it possesses.

A fourth reason for evaluation is to gather information useful in making critical decisions about continuing the program. *Summative evaluations* are efforts to summarize the best available evidence for the purpose of making decisions about the success of the program, its cost effectiveness, and whether and how to continue it. Unless evaluative evidence is carefully gathered, such decisions can only be made on the basis of impressions, guesswork, and chance conversations. Reliable evidence neither removes all ambiguity nor eliminates the necessity of difficult value judgments, but it does provide accurate factual bases for some of the decisions.

A final reason for evaluation is to generate or retain political support. This purpose is very important, albeit sometimes not acknowledged. Faculty members, particularly, seem to overestimate the rationality of the change process. They reason that if a program is well designed and implemented, and if evidence of its effectiveness can be adduced, then it will, of course, be supported. But even the most favorable evaluation does not guarantee success; the results of the evaluation must be introduced into the political process. Indeed, the act of evaluation itself is a political act; as one person put it, "If *we* conduct an evaluation of our program, *they* won't be able to get us on that one." The politics of evaluation requires attention to the framing of questions, the kinds of methodology and measures used, the sample group, the presentation of the data, and above all, the utilization of the results. By widely publicizing achievements and making sure key decision makers grasp their significance, educational leaders may avoid the termination of even a successful program.

Institutions involved in curricular reform are quite interested in evaluation. Of schools responding to the AAC survey question about evaluation, 39 percent had specific plans for evaluation, and another 34 percent said they intended to evaluate but had no specific plan (see Appendix A). Thus schools are attentive to the need for evaluation and are entering this phase of the change process. Only 7 percent reported already having conducted an evaluation, a figure that probably reflects the fact that most of the institutions are still fashioning a structure, implementing new courses, or attending to similar tasks. Evaluation would be premature for such schools.

Research on the Effects of College. Although most new programs have not yet been rigorously evaluated, a great deal of research has been conducted on student development and the conditions affecting intellectual and personal growth of undergraduates. Unfortunately, this body of literature does not resolve the most salient questions about general education programs. No particular type of curriculum receives clear and overwhelming support, nor is there greater support for any one kind of general education program. But several consistent findings are reported by investigators studying various institutions with different methods. These findings yield principles that are critical in the assessment of general education.

Important summaries of this research are offered by Jacob (1957), Chickering (1969), Feldman and Newcomb (1969), Astin (1977), and Bowen (1977). Bowen's conclusions about the changes students experience while in college are representative:

> The evidence points to the conclusion that, on the average, higher education significantly raises the level of knowledge, the intellectual disposition, and the cognitive powers of students [p. 98].

> The structure of values, that is, the relative strength of different values, appears to shift during college, with substantial increases in theoretical and esthetic values, substantial decreases in religious values, minor increases in social values, and minor decreases in economic and political values [p. 132].

> Colleges and universities appear to be effective in helping students achieve personal identity— that is, to discover their talents, interests, values, and aspirations—and to assist them in making lifetime choices congruent with personal identity [p. 132].

> In its impact on the psychological well-being

of students, college appears to strengthen auton-
omy, nonauthoritarianism, and social maturity; to
increase self-assurance and confidence, to enhance
spontaneity and freedom; to lessen anxiety and ali-
enation; and to increase the sense of self-esteem
and control over one's destiny" [p. 132].

Of course, not all students are affected the same way nor to the
same extent; and some institutions are more effective in producing these changes than others. Still, these results document that,
by and large, college students do tend to develop intellectually
and personally in demonstrable ways.

A knowledge of the conditions that elicit change enables
us to draw implications for the practice of general education.
The effects of the academic program, the curriculum, faculty,
and teaching have been topics of research interest for some
time. Jacob (1957, p. 7) cites evidence that "quality of teaching
has relatively little effect upon the value-outcomes of general
education . . . so far as the great mass of students is concerned."
His added proviso that "some teachers do exert profound influence on some students" did little to modify the nature of his
conclusion. Feldman and Newcomb (1969), in a subsequent
review of a far more extensive body of research literature, reach
a similar conclusion: "Though faculty members are often indi-
vidually influential, particularly in respect to career decisions,
college faculties do not appear to be responsible for campus-
wide impact except in settings where the influence of student
peers and of faculty complement and reinforce one another" (p.
330). Feldman and Newcomb report the experience of going
away to college, the peer group, and the general atmosphere of
the campus to be more powerful in shaping the development of
students than their teachers, the curriculum, or their academic
experiences.

Regarding those conditions in which faculty members do
have the greatest influence on the lives of students, Jacob (1957)
observes: "Faculty influence appears more pronounced at institutions where association between faculty and students is normal and frequent, and students find teachers receptive to unhur-

ried and relaxed conversations out of class" (p. 8). Feldman and Newcomb (1969) put it this way: "The conditions for campus-wide impacts appear to have been most frequently provided in small, residential, four-year colleges. These conditions probably include relative homogeneity of both faculty and student body together with opportunity for continuing interaction, not exclusively formal, among students and between students and faculty" (p. 331).

A study of student-faculty relationships and their influence on the course of student development conducted by Wilson and others (1975) related information obtained from students in their freshman year in 1966 and again in their senior year in 1970 to information gathered from faculty at the same institutions. They found several aspects of academic life to be associated with the intellectual and personal growth of students. First, the faculty members who had the greatest impact on undergraduate students, whether defined by the testimony of seniors or nomination of colleagues, differed from other faculty in several ways. They were more interested in teaching than in research and in teaching undergraduates than graduate students, and they, more often than their colleagues, punctuated their classes with anecdotes, humorous stories, and tales of personal experience. Influential teachers were also much more likely to talk with students about a variety of issues important to young adults of that day, such as drugs, sex, alternative life-styles, the draft, and student protest. These faculty did not differ significantly from their colleagues in their views of these topics or in age, only in their willingness to explore these topics with students. And the single biggest difference between the influential faculty and their colleagues was the extent to which they interacted with students outside the classroom.

Second, students who showed the most intellectual and personal development were those who took special initiatives to expand their self-awareness. To a greater extent than other students, they became involved in a range of intellectual, artistic, and political activities, often of an unconventional nature, and they actively sought out faculty members for discussions of intellectual, social, and campus problems. In a disproportionate number, they studied the humanities and were influenced by literature reflecting strong personal and social values. In addition, they held an ideal of a college that involved working closely with teachers, provision for independent study, emphasis on a broad general education rather than narrowly specialized studies, and a rigorous set of academic standards. In short, their ideal—and to some extent their experience—was that of an active participant in an intellectual community.

Third, the conditions of teaching and learning that promote student development do not depend solely on the personal qualities of teachers and students, but also on the relationships by which they are joined. In the study, students were asked to describe the faculty member who had contributed the most to their educational or personal development, and faculty members described a student to whose educational or personal development they had contributed a great deal. Both sets of descriptions depicted relationships that were continuous (having been initiated early in the student's college career), casual, and personally engaging. Such relationships usually developed after the faculty and student were brought together in at least one course, more commonly two or more courses, and were continued outside the classroom. Both faculty and students reported that such relationships were characterized by a good deal of intellectual excitement, and conversations usually ranged beyond the narrow bounds of coursework. Thus conditions that increase the frequency, closeness, breadth, and duration of student-faculty relationships tend to enhance the development of students toward the ends of general education.

On the basis of such scholarship, one can draw several implications for effective general education programs. A program will foster the intellectual and personal goals of general education to the extent that the following conditions are present:

The rationale for the curriculum—its purposes, the reasons for specific requirements, and their particular educational contributions—is explained to students, and they are encouraged to pursue their own interests within the context of both the overall program and individual courses.

Instructors make a determined effort to interest, motivate, and stimulate students to learn their subject matter by showing them its significance for their lives. Teachers should not assume that students are necessarily interested, especially in required courses; any such assumption merely encourages students toward superficial compliance rather than self-motivated learning.

High academic standards are maintained, students are expected to master learning, and teachers give support to students and help them gain confidence that they can reach the goals. If expectations are clear and students are given to believe that they can meet them, a surprising amount of learning can occur. A good deal of research documents that students will learn as little, or as much, as teachers expect.

A high level of intellectual excitement is generated and maintained. New developments in a discipline, such as conceptual or theoretical breakthroughs, discoveries that force reinterpretation of prevailing ideas, or implications of knowledge for society or for individuals are particularly well suited to foster curiosity.

The curriculum is coherent and integrated. Connections among separate courses make learning additive and cumulative, and they reinforce single episodes that are otherwise likely to be forgotten.

Students are led to explore and to develop value positions that are intimately related to their factual knowledge and to examine the implications of their knowledge for their own behavior. Unless knowledge is related to values, students will not see its power to help them achieve the ends they prize, the very purpose of an education.

Active methods of learning are regularly employed. Only if students exhibit curiosity and seek answers to their own perplexing questions will they regard learning as a practical way for them to approach problems in their lives and work. Passive absorption of others' knowledge has a role in education, but students must appropriate such knowledge at a very early stage if it is to have enduring utility.

An open-ended approach to knowledge is adopted, and

students are inducted into the world view common to both science and humanities that Thomas (1982, p. 91) calls "bewilderment." Commenting on the belief in the fixity of knowledge, he declares, "Science, especially twentieth-century science, has provided us with a glimpse of something we never really knew before, the revelation of human ignorance." Students should be introduced to some of these mysteries and then invited to participate in the slow but persistent advance of knowledge, seeing their ideas as part of an evolving human drama.

Instruction is individualized as much as possible. The proper unit of learning is not the student body as a whole, or even the course, but the individual student. Each individual's concerns must be engaged, and individual biases, misunderstandings, and ineptitudes remedied. Of course, not all instruction can be one-to-one, but in effective programs teachers address the needs of individual students and their concrete circumstances, whether using a lecture, seminar, tutorial, or other method.

Higher-level thinking skills are stressed rather than a mastery of factual details or basic information. Students can easily obtain facts and details from textbooks and other documents, and research demonstrates that much factual information is forgotten soon after it is learned. Principles and generalizations, as well as mental processes, tend to remain with the learner and are therefore of greater significance.

Teaching and learning occur outside the classroom, as instructors engage their students' substantive social and personal concerns. The integration of students' lives inside and outside the classroom is one of the surest signs of a powerful educational program. The most influential schools have found ways to relate their academic program to the values, activities, and conversations of the student peer group so as to extend the range and power of the curriculum.

A close community of learners is cultivated. A sense of community encourages faculty and administrators, as well as students, to become active learners, and thus the whole of the college environment contributes to the learning of all.

Approaches to Evaluation. Just as there are different approaches to general education, so are there various approaches to its evaluation; these are summarized by Davis (1980). The most common approach may be called *goal-based evaluation* because it seeks to determine the extent to which a program's goals are accomplished. The essential tasks here seem simple enough: specify the goals with clarity and precision, translate the goals into indicators of accomplishment, and gather evidence about the indicators. But the complicated execution of these principles has given rise to a whole profession of evaluators. In regard to specifying goals, for instance, one finds that general education goals frequently are pious statements that are ambiguous and lacking precision; some goals may work at crosspurposes with others; and program goals are not static but evolving. Furthermore, their translation into measurable indicators is fraught with difficulty. For example, is the goal of having students develop a global perspective indicated by their having a cognitive understanding of another culture? knowledge of the main outlines of world history? mastery of another language? tolerance for different customs? or an understanding of the principles of international relations? And how many measures of any indicator are necessary to understand the outcomes, without being redundant and excessively costly? Despite these difficulties, the prevalence of goal-based evaluation testifies to the fact that purposes can be specified, indicators chosen, and measures devised, even if imperfectly.

A new curriculum sets in motion many forces, some of which may produce unintended as well as intended consequences. For this reason Scriven (1973) argues for *goal-free evaluation.* If evaluators are not limited to looking at the explicit purposes of a program, they may cast a wider net to determine other outcomes, perhaps ones generated unwittingly. Carnegie-Mellon University, for instance, developed a core curriculum in the College of Humanities and Social Sciences that met its educational objectives reasonably well, but initially there was a decrease in enrollment, which could have been attributable to the continued use of old promotional material. New materials describing the revised curriculum helped account for a 67 percent increase in enrollments in one year and a doubling of applications in two years. These consequences are significant but would have been missed in a goal-based evaluation.

A third approach, developed by Stufflebeam and Associates (1971), is *decision-oriented evaluation.* Here one attempts to gather evidence relevant to some specific set of decision makers. For example, the administration of the University of California, Berkeley approved the establishment of an innovative collegiate seminar program, Strawberry Creek College. The program was highly successful in meeting its goals for participating students and faculty, but the faculty senate's approval was needed to continue beyond the initial five-year period. The decision-oriented evaluation that was conducted gathered the kinds of information regarded as relevant by the faculty, which slighted the educational outcomes that had been central to the program's participants.

A fourth approach employs an *external criterion,* as is common in grading or reviewing manuscripts for publication, for instance, when instructors and referees evaluate the performance of students and authors. But, as Davis (1980, p. 122) observes: "One difficulty with the external-criterion model is that the criteria for assessing goodness are often not specified to those whose performance is being evaluated. This creates two problems: first, it is difficult for those who are being evaluated to improve without clear knowledge of what is expected; and secondly, this model can result in a great deal of resistance to change because the criteria of goodness are subject to disagreement." External criteria in the evaluation of general education are sometimes used by statewide systems. The Colorado State Board for Community Colleges and Occupational Education, for instance, was concerned about the quality of general education in the several schools under its jurisdiction; it devised a set of criteria involving skills, breadth, and integration of knowledge. But this proposal met resistance from campuses that naively regarded breadth alone as the essential ingredient of general education.

Portrayal evaluation, a newer method, seeks to describe the whole of a program, including its goal-directed activities and its broader outcomes as seen from a variety of viewpoints. Perhaps the best-known form is *illuminative evaluation,* developed by Parlett and Dearden (1977), which relies on qualitative information as much as or more than quantitative data. The evaluator using this approach seeks to interpret both the program as a whole and how various parts affect various constituencies, rather than documenting the extent to which certain outcomes were attributable to the program.

The debate on alternative models of evaluation includes a number of issues about which reasonable people differ. One is the utility of thinking about evaluation as a form of a scientific experiment; for example, making cross-group comparisons among similar groups of students who take different general education programs, and attributing differences in outcomes to the differential effects of the programs. Although experimental models have their advocates, others argue that students in two different colleges or even two different programs on the same campus will not be similar in all respects—they selected their schools for different reasons, and they often differ in backgrounds, abilities, and aspirations. The experimental variable, the general education program, is not easily varied because all programs are both like and unlike others. Further, any outcome measures may reflect factors other than the program, such as students' maturation or experiences outside the curriculum. As a result, the practical issue is whether to approximate the experimental model as best one can or to scuttle it in favor of an approach that better illuminates the natural setting and its dynamics. One group of evaluators opts for the quasi-experimental design, while another favors illuminating the particulars of a single case.

A related matter is whether to rely on quantitative or qualitative evidence. As with the preceding question, this issue elicits a host of ideological notions about human nature, for instance, whether it can or should be quantitatively measured. As a result, some evaluators rely on one type of evidence, while others use both so that each compensates for the other's limitations. Social science methodology is such that each method provides useful information, but none provides sufficient information; the use of various sources of information and different methods of gathering and analyzing it is probably the most prudent course.

A final issue concerns pilot testing. Clearly, if a university works for several years and finally inaugurates a new general education curriculum, it wants that program to be validated by the evaluation. The stakes involved are so high as to possibly prejudge the evaluation. But if an institution experiments with a particular portion, for instance, freshman seminars or a writing skills effort, it can gather data on this component, make some needed adjustments, and later incorporate that component into the regular program. The use of pilot testing is a central feature of the Project on Quality Undergraduate Education of the Council of Independent Colleges, in which sixty colleges are experimenting with various curricular changes and evaluating them before adopting them for the permanent program. Pilot tests, however, are relatively rare because most institutions reforming general education are convinced that their offerings are deficient and their revisions are improvements; they do not feel a need to wait for the results of a pilot test before making a major overhaul.

As is apparent from this cursory survey of various approaches to program evaluation, there is no one best way to evaluate. Each model contributes its part to an understanding of the complexities of undergraduate general education.

New Measures. Whatever approach to evaluation is taken, the results can only be as good as the evidence derived from the measures used. Although grades are the most common way to evaluate a student's accomplishments, they are inadequate measures for a program evaluation. Faculty are not trained to design, administer, or interpret tests, and thus their homemade tests are filled with what sophisticated experts in testing call measurement errors (Milton, 1976). Similarly, the combination of individual instructors' judgments, a student's cumulative grade-point average, generally is not markedly related to measures of achievement in other areas of life—except success in another academic setting (McClelland, 1973; Heath, 1977). Other kinds of measures are therefore needed to evaluate rigorously the effectiveness of a program of study.

Several sophisticated instruments developed for other purposes have been pressed into service to assess programs of general education. Some measures come from the psychological clinic, such as interest inventories, personality tests, and value preferences; other derive from college and graduate school admissions testing, such as the Scholastic Aptitude Test or Graduate Record Examination. Such measures have appeal—they are readily available, have known reliability and other desirable psychometric properties, provide quantitative data and norms for comparisons with other groups, and can be administered relatively easily and inexpensively. However, they are often at best only indirect measures of the intended outcomes of general education.

In recent years psychometricians and other professionals have sought to develop better measures of the outcomes of general or liberal education. Winter (1979, pp. 2-3) suggests five standards for a good measure of liberal arts competencies; it should "(1) seem to measure what it purports to measure; that is, it should have face validity; (2) be generic, applicable to different levels and across different fields; (3) be based on criteria that are public, so that different evaluators would make approximately the same assessments of the same student performance; (4) have educational validity; and (5) be demonstrably relevant to performance in later life." Although these criteria are easily stated, they constitute quite high standards that tax the creativity of researchers.

Winter, McClelland, and Stewart (1981) present a battery of tests that satisfy these criteria, including two nearly developed instruments. One of the main distinguishing characteristics of their tests is that they do not use the traditional multiple-choice format; rather, they elicit more elaborate and complex responses from each individual. They assess not simply a student's knowledge of facts but how he or she uses and processes knowledge. For example, in the Test of Thematic Analysis students are given two stories and instructed to formulate and describe the differences between them in whatever terms and at whatever level and length they wish. The responses are scored in ways that provide information about the precision, parallel structure, breadth of coverage, and emotional neutrality of comparisons of complex concepts—all aspects of critical thinking. In the test of Intellectual Flexibility in Analysis of Argument, students are told to argue both sides of a controversial issue. Other measures in the battery were adapted from more traditional measures of thought processes, including concept attainment, divergent thinking, sensitivity, and learning new material. Still other qualities are measured by using existing tests, such as achievement motivation, leadership motivation, fear of success, self-definition, maturity of adaptation, and self-ratings on a range of skills. These measures can be scored reliably and have produced promising results in early research. But they do have drawbacks—they take longer to administer, their scoring is more complicated and time consuming, and they are more costly to use than conventional paper-and-pencil tests. Nevertheless, they seem more effective as measures of general education outcomes than traditional tests.

A similar approach to assess certain generic intellectual skills has been devised by Jonathan Warren at the Educational Testing Service. Warren (1982), too, doubts that traditional multiple-choice tests can adequately assess the complex intellectual skills associated with general education. He defines four observable concepts relevant to most general education programs—communication, analysis, synthesis, and awareness. Warren asked faculty members from many fields of study and postsecondary institutions to formulate questions to measure each competence; the questions were refined and then used to assess student achievement. These items call for students to make free responses which are rated by trained scorers.

The Educational Testing Service also developed an instrument to assess global understanding. A traditional paper-and-pencil form with structured items, it contains sections that measure general background, scholastic ability, educational experiences, interests, attitudes and perceptions of world issues, language background, and knowledge of world affairs. Factor analysis reveals that these items cluster around three major foci —knowledge, affect, and language—each of which can be scored separately. The test's authors report: "The mean of 50 percent on the survey test indicates a considerable lack of knowledge—knowledge that the assessment committee thought critical to an understanding of today's world. In addition, patterns of responses to specific test questions indicate that important misconceptions exist and that these misconceptions are sometimes held by quite able students. The questions that correlate most highly with the total test score are, for the most part, those that cover issues and content characteristic of traditional fields of study. These facts may reflect the college curriculum, which addresses global affairs in a fragmented, discipline-bound way. Media reporting may be the primary source of knowledge structured by issues rather than disciplines" (Barrows, Clark, and Klein, 1981, p. 45).

Another paper-and-pencil test has been devised by the American College Testing Program. The College Outcome Measures Project (COMP) concentrates on six major areas of knowledge and skills regarded as important to effective functioning in adult society: communicating, solving problems, clarifying values, functioning with social institutions, using sciences and technology, and using the arts. Three forms have been developed, the most comprehensive of which is the Composite Examination. This test presents a series of stimulus items in the form of television documentaries, recent magazine articles, advertisements, newscasts, and the like, and students are asked to respond in a variety of ways: short and long written answers, oral answers, and multiple-choice answers. The test is divided into modules, so that only those portions relevant to a particular purpose need be used. The complete test takes four hours to administer, and a team of four faculty members can score the written and oral responses in about fifty minutes. A short version of the Composite Examination is entirely multiple choice, takes two hours to administer, and is machine scored. The results of the two tests are highly correlated, indicating that for most purposes the short version serves as well as the lengthier test. The third form is an Activity Inventory in which students report on the extent of their participation in out-of-class activities related to each of the outcomes. This inventory is not timed, but it requires about ninety minutes to complete; used with either of the other two instruments, it produces a more valid assessment than any one of the instruments alone.

Thus there now exist a series of new instruments to measure some key outcomes of general education. And, doubtless, research and development will continue to supply even more sophisticated instruments for assessing the outcomes of new campus programs.

Conclusion

No curriculum stands alone; a vital curriculum requires a solid foundation of related supports. Whatever a program's structure or content, general education needs firm administration, adequate financing, and rigorous evaluation. Many institutions are now reexamining their support structures. Specific responsibility for the general curriculum increasingly is vested with an administrator having institution-wide authority for overseeing the many facets of a sound general education program, and institution-wide committees are providing centralized faculty leadership over the common curriculum. Resources that traditionally have been under the control of many separate departments and other units—and typically weighted toward specialized interests—are flowing toward the general curriculum, which is coming to be recognized as central to every specialized program. Although few new programs have yet been formally evaluated—indeed, most have not been fully implemented—campus leaders indicate that evaluation is high on their agenda. Fortunately, several new instruments and a great deal of research on the effects of college on students can aid these efforts.

Chapter Seven

Implementing
Successful
Curricular Reforms

Listening to the debate about general education, college administrators and faculty members hear so many varied statements of purposes, analyses of problems, and proposals for change that they cannot easily decide how to approach the program at their institution. Many agree with Boyer and Levine that "in the end, each college and university faculty must clarify for itself the purposes of general education and shape a program to reflect its own unique values and traditions" (1981, p. 45). But the question remains: How to accomplish this, given the very different conceptions of general education, the forces that impede the realization of its purposes, and the disagreements among various interest groups on campus? In this chapter numerous specific recommendations on strategies and procedures are presented to help administrators and faculty review the curriculum and fashion improvements.

This chapter draws on a previously published article, "Avoiding the Potholes: Strategies for Reforming General Education." *Educational Record*, Fall 1980, pp. 50-59.

General Strategies

Reforming the curriculum is always difficult and fraught with perils. The task now facing curricular reformers is particularly difficult in that they must construct a curriculum, a much more complicated procedure than eliminating requirements, which was the primary goal of curricular change during the late 1960s and early 1970s. Furthermore, various sectors of the academic community each advance legitimate but conflicting claims. Often these special interests are voiced with an intensity and stridency that almost precludes compromise. In the absence of working agreements about the aims, content, or structure of general education, an institution simply cannot build a curriculum. Too, faculty members have become so isolated in their specialized pursuits that they cannot easily communicate with their colleagues about substantive intellectual or pedagogical matters.

Yet such dialogue—within and across disciplines—is essential if a new curriculum is to be instated and realized. For a curriculum is a social contract and curricular reform is a corporate activity. While individuals may develop widely acclaimed proposals for change, instituting curricular change requires the cooperation of the administration, faculty, and students. For example, Daniel Bell's *The Reforming of General Education* (1966) was an award-winning book, but his solo effort did not result in any changes in Columbia University's program. What is needed, instead, is a group working together to reach an agreement about the purposes of general education and to develop an appropriate program for their institution.

Because curricular change is an institution-wide social activity with which few campus leaders are experienced, they must devote special attention to strategies that can effect a working consensus concerning an acceptable curriculum. Academics tend to be attracted to substantive issues—the philosophy of general education or alternative curricular structures—and less interested in the strategies and procedures that bring about change. Feldman (1979) describes three general approaches to reform: the strengthening, replacement, and multiple-experiments models. In the strengthening model, the current program remains basically intact, but steps are taken to improve it; for example, a communication component, a series of integrative courses, or offerings on global understanding might be added. This is perhaps the easiest of the three approaches, since the basic curricular structure remains unchanged.

In the replacement model the current program is dismantled in favor of a new and presumably better program. Clearly, this approach is more ambitious and comprehensive, as it involves examining a variety of alternative curricular structures as well as individual components. Such change requires considerable time and effort; but if an institution's current program is blatantly ineffective, replacement is more likely to effect significant improvement in the quality of general education than strengthening the program.

The multiple-experiments model posits that no single program is likely to be equally effective for all students or attractive to all faculty. If an institution is sufficiently large and has sufficient resources, it may develop two or more programs; the distinctive curriculums of the Integrated Liberal Studies program at the University of Wisconsin, and the Residential College at the University of Michigan offer such alternatives in general education programs to members of their institutions. Although this may seem an easy divide-and-conquer strategy, in fact it is very difficult to maintain two or more equally respected programs on the same campus. This model may be the most sophisticated and difficult of the three, since each alternative program requires vision, energy, and support.

Another set of general approaches to reform is offered by Levine (1980b), who relates types of programs to college environments. A given college will have a negative, neutral, or positive attitude toward general education, depending on such factors as administrative leadership, faculty commitment, the reward system, and the like. Each type of environment is best served by particular strategies to improve general education. In the negative environment, reformers can establish an enclave, an alternative program with a champion, a few faculty members, and a small number of students. Because an enclave involves only a few voluntary participants at an institution, its designers can enact a more radically innovative program than reformers working within the mainstream. This was the basic approach used by Hutchins in creating the College at the University of Chicago as an entity with its own faculty, students, and rationale. More recently, under the leadership of Joseph Tussman and Charles Muscatine two enclaves were established at the University of California, Berkeley, which is among the least hospitable environments in the country for undergraduate general education (see Tussman, 1969; Muscatine, 1977). Each program was discontinued, although illustrious results were achieved—one of the ever-present risks of establishing an enclave in a hostile environment.

In an environment that is more neutral, Levine says, reformers can create an enclave, or they can engage in piecemeal change, making modest improvements in portions of the program. Advocates of values education, for instance, may be able to develop a new course, or a senior capstone course may be inaugurated to provide a measure of integration.

In a positive environment, comprehensive change in general education is possible, as well as piecemeal change or an enclave. Institutions that have strong administrative leadership, senior faculty who support general education, or a tradition of interdisciplinary and value-related courses stressing critical thinking can embark on holistic change. Comprehensive change may not be necessary, but at least it is possible in this context.

Preparation

Once a committee or task force is appointed to review general education, and before it leaps into the task of redesigning the curriculum, it should develop agreement about five separate issues. This preparatory work is essential to the task of curriculum development and some provisional agreement should be reached before specific recommendations are proposed and debated. These five topics are: (1) an understanding of the mission of the institution, (2) a definition of an educated person, (3) an assessment of the adequacy of the current program, (4) a con-

sideration of how to help the faculty make an informed decision, and (5) a statement of the philosophical basis of the curriculum. Let us briefly examine each of these topics.

The institution's mission provides the essential context
for general education, but a curricular review committee sometimes ignores this critical factor. For example, one committee
worked for years on a proposal that was defeated by the faculty. Part of the problem involved faculty members' radically
differing notions about whether the school was a small university (in which case defenders held that general education should
stress the departments, use a distribution scheme, and emphasize majors) or a large college (in which case it should transcend
departments, use a core, and emphasize general education). The
faculty was asked to support a curriculum before reaching
agreement on the nature of the institution; thus differences of
opinion scuttled the proposal. Task forces are wise to begin by
considering their institution's mission and its curricular implications. Once Spelman College, for instance, decided that its major purpose is to educate young black women in the Southeast,
its committee developed a curriculum tailored to this mission.

Often general education task forces work to create a curriculum without first determining the qualities with which they
wish to endow their students. Because a curriculum is only a
means, it is important to have some consensus about the ends
the curriculum is to serve. Without pursuing some ultimate criteria, such as working to develop the qualities of an educated
person in students, a committee can have no rational basis for
deciding among different curricular proposals. Furthermore,
this exercise attunes faculty to thinking about educational issues and helps prepare them for curricular change. Further,
most statements of educational ideals fall short of attainment in
practice, thus allowing reformers to make a case for the need
for improvement. Although this step may prolong the process
of curricular renewal, it produces long-term gains.

Once a task force is charged with conducting a review or
producing a new proposal, members tend to assume that the
present program is flawed. That may well be, but the larger
campus community often does not share that judgment and in-

evitably asks for evidence, or at least a case, for change. Shortly after the Rochester Institute of Technology decided to review its curriculum, the committee conducted a thorough study of the present curriculum by means of student and faculty surveys, administrator interviews, and alumni studies. Not until these data were fully analyzed did the task force consider curricular revisions. The analysis was used both to guide the revisions and to help the faculty decide that changes were needed; the new proposal was later approved handily. Although the extensive documentation of inadequacies in the current program took about a year to complete, this prior step saved time in the long run and gave enormous credibility to the new proposal.

Although professionals assume that their colleagues are capable and willing to act reasonably and knowledgeably, more than one curricular recommendation has been rejected because faculty were not sufficiently well informed. It is not that faculty are ignorant or self-centered; in fact, faculty typically are well read and knowledgeable about their specialities. However, they seldom have a sophisticated understanding of the issues, scholarship, and alternative practices relevant to the general education curriculum. The University of Tennessee, for example, engaged in an extensive educational campaign by creating a series of faculty study groups and providing participants with a few key texts to read and discuss. Only then were specific proposals for change offered to the faculty for a vote. Similarly, David Schramm, dean at California Lutheran College, distributed selected readings to the entire faculty and provided materials for members of the curricular task force so that all could competently discuss the issues.

Every curriculum is a statement of philosophy, but often committees rush to make decisions about content and structures before examining their philosophical assumptions and receiving the faculty's response to those basic principles. Since we have discussed curricular philosophies in Chapter Three, we need not say more here—except to note that it is easier to design a curriculum after the faculty reaches agreement on a rationale and a few basic principles than to proceed without such agreement.

Defining the Task

While the committee is conducting its preparatory discussions on the five issues just discussed, members usually begin to develop a general sense of the task before them and may even begin formulating specific approaches to this task. Their thoughts at this time often derive from common-sense approaches or methods used in their own scholarly practices. But many committees soon learn that common-sense approaches are too naive to be effective. For example, consider three common-sense notions that are in reality misconceptions about the task of curricular reform.

The first widespread misconception is that the committee need only find the correct program, developed at another institution, to import. For example, during the first workshop of Project GEM, many participants—task force members from member institutions—expected to be presented with an array of model programs from which they need only make their selections and then write a proposal and await the faculty's prompt approval. Instead, the staff urged the task force members to develop their own programs with the advice and support of the workshop and project staff. Some participants were angered and thought the staff members incompetent because they could not or would not provide easy solutions to their offer them a "quick fix" for their institutions' general education needs. However, experience proved the wisdom of the staff members' insistence on tailoring programs to a particular institution's mission and character. Within a year some of the Project GEM participants, acting as panel members at a professional meeting, were asked by audience members for program models to take back to their campuses; every presenter on the panel replied that a program of general education should be designed to meet each institution's character, the strengths and interests of its faculty, and the needs of its students.

A second misconception is that the task of a curricular reform committee is to fashion a comprehensive curricular program that will be introduced all at once to produce revolutionary change. Radical departures from established traditions are, in fact, rare in the history of American higher education. They have occurred, but usually only with the creation of a new institution (such as Empire State College and Evergreen State College in the 1960s) or as the result of a crisis—for instance, when Antioch College's curriculum was radically restructured in 1919 —or the action of a charismatic individual, such as Hutchins at the University of Chicago. But the overwhelming majority of changes are evolutionary, introduced in a piecemeal fashion, or developed over time (Hefferlin, 1969, pp. 22-32). Furthermore, the holistic approach is a high-risk strategy, for a comprehensive proposal takes a long time to fashion, yet a faculty can reject it in a single meeting. A proposal that retains some of the curriculum's existing features while changing others constitutes an evolutionary, modular approach that has a greater chance of gaining acceptance. Thus practical wisdom suggests that "Curricular reform of significance requires (1) overall thought but (2) piecemeal action" (Carnegie Foundation for the Advancement of Teaching, 1977, p. 16).

A third misconception is that the committee's task is merely to reinstate distribution requirements. Although this approach may indeed improve the general education of students at some institutions, it has major limitations, as noted in Chapters Two and Four. Theodore Lockwood, former president of Trinity College, thus summarizes present skepticism about distribution requirements: "The current trend at colleges of reviving distribution requirements does not convince me that we are improving the quality of education. Giving the curriculum more structure doesn't necessarily give it coherence. I am skeptical that meaningful educational reform can occur if it is not based on a new philosophy of education and shared assumptions by faculty members of what education should be in the last quarter of the twentieth century" (1978, p. 1).

For these reasons, a review committee should consider the reinstatement of distribution requirements as merely one option among others. Indeed, many committees have sought rather to develop a philosophy of education from which they can develop a contemporary program of general education that transcends distribution schemes and that provides a sound long-term basis for specific reforms.

Developing Procedures

Seven procedural errors often make the curricular review process more difficult and less effective.

The first error is to assume that the review or reform should be conducted by the school's standing curriculum committee. In fact, in most cases, it is better to appoint a special task force for the review. The principal reasons for this recommendation are three: a standing committee has its regular business to accomplish, but a task force can devote all its time to a single purpose; a standing committee regularly changes its membership, but a task force does not and thus it can become a cohesive working group that need not retrace steps for the benefit of new members; and curriculum committees tend to work in a reactive manner, either approving or vetoing proposals from faculty members or departments, whereas efforts to reform general education require a group that can initiate change by developing a proposal and actively garnering campus support for its ideas.

The second error is to adapt the common-sense approach that the best thinkers on the faculty should be assembled to prepare the best possible proposal. In practice, this approach may generate heady debate about high principles but little action. A good task force needs various kinds of talent—thinkers and doers, idealists and pragmatists, educational innovators and conservatives, campus politicians and faculty knowledgeable about national trends and resources. Failure to include a mix of talent may result in more progress reports like the one issued by Richard Clinton of Oregon State University: "When all is said and done, more is said than done." Furthermore, Project GEM task forces were required to include other persons in addition to faculty members: an academic administrator to provide institutional support and several students to remind all that *they* are the ultimate beneficiaries of the curriculum. Each of these constituencies has a legitimate interest in the quality of general education, and each has a role to play in the reform process.

The third error, made by a surprising number of committees, is to try to effect massive curriculum reform without adequate special support. This situation frequently occurs when the task is given to a standing committee, because regular committees seldom receive any special budget or other assistance. Two kinds of support are important: reduced teaching assignments to allow faculty members the time and energy for the curriculum revision (for example, a half-time reduction in teaching assignments for the chairperson and smaller reductions for other key task force members) and a modest fund for purchasing materials, holding retreats, attending conferences, visiting other institutions, inviting consultants to the campus, reproducing papers, and the like. Without adequate support, a task force or committee cannot be expected to provide creative and effective leadership for curriculum reform.

Fourth, many committee members assume that their work will be completed in only a few months. At Harvard University, for example, a group was first assembled in 1974 to discuss the quality of undergraduate education at that institution. A task force report on the core curriculum was issued in 1977, and the faculty approved it in principle. In 1978 a more detailed proposal was presented and approved. Subsequently, a standing committee to oversee this part of the curriculum was established, and specific course proposals were solicited from the faculty and negotiated. Not until 1982 was the program fully operational—eight years after the process began. General education reform committees would do well to keep in mind the dieter's dictum: Weight that took years to put on cannot be removed in a few days. The difficulties surrounding general education are so severe and deep-seated that they cannot be resolved overnight, and more time than anticipated is usually needed to rectify them.

A fifth error is having the committee work by itself to develop a proposal. True, the rationale for committees is that a small group can probe a subject in depth, issue a report, and then ask the larger group to make an informed decision. But committees that work in full isolation—surveying other college's programs, examining alternative forms of general education, and issuing a report to the faculty at large—often fail to win faculty approval for their proposals. The faculty frequently perceives such reports as coming out of the blue, accuses the committee of holding secret deliberations, and feels that its perogative to be actively involved in curriculum policy making has been ignored. This procedure was followed by a summer planning group of faculty at Eckerd College, and the rest of the faculty killed the report without its ever being submitted for a formal vote. A reconstituted committee spent a great deal of time at the outset working to involve the entire faculty through several college-wide activities, such as a monthly colloquium on general education and the involvement of academic units. The proposal that evolved from this effort won widespread support from the Eckerd faculty.

A sixth error is committed in issuing a sole final report. When writing a scholarly paper, one waits until one's ideas are fully developed and well expressed before submitting the paper for publication or critical scrutiny by colleagues. But applying this common-sense approach to the preparation of a curriculum proposal can be disastrous. For instance, a committee at one institution worked for two years to develop an elegant and comprehensive proposal. The document was lengthy and impressive in its philosophy of education, analysis of the institution, and number of recommendations. Unfortunately, it contained something for everyone to dislike and was defeated by a coalition of opposition. Successful results are more likely to be achieved if the committee issues a series of reports, holds discussions of each report, and seeks approval of portions of the reform proposal as it unfolds. For example, at Valparaiso University, a set of assumptions about general education was developed and debated before a specific program was developed; at the Community College of Denver, a framework for the curriculum was presented for discussion and approval before specific courses and details were determined. Such a procedure allows the faculty to accompany the committee as it progresses with the task.

The seventh and final procedural error is for the task force to become sidetracked by debating large and enduring issues, such as the plight of undergraduate education, lack of interest in teaching, or the absence of professional incentives for teaching general education courses. These are important and legitimate issues, and they deserve a portion of any group's time. But productive committees do not spend inordinate time worrying about matters over which they have little control. In contrast, they tend to take a practical stance and focus on issues they can control using their own resources. Such large-scale changes as the competency-based curriculums at Alverno College and Mars Hill College resulted from their leaders' maintaining a practical focus in their agenda.

Understanding General Education

In discussing the nature and purpose of general education, committee members are likely to encounter several broad misconceptions. One of the most basic of these is the belief that there is only one true meaning of general education. Committee members often vest their respective definitions with unmerited authority, which naturally leads to disagreement and conflict within the committee and the lament that the group cannot even agree on the meaning of general education, let alone on ways to strengthen it. Eventually the committee may realize that general education has several definitions and that each member has a legitimate claim to his or her view. The committee may then adopt a provisional definition, attempt to explore and elaborate its meaning as work progresses, and seek to understand the assumptions and values that underlie the various concepts of general education. Typically, committee members will have a richer understanding of the meaning of the term at the conclusion of their efforts than at the outset.

Another common misconception is that general education deals only with breadth of knowledge. Few would dispute the contention that breadth—the introduction to an array of academic disciplines—is part of general education; but as noted in Chapters Three and Four, skills and the integration of knowledge are equally important. Indeed, some thinkers (see Boyer and Kaplan, 1977) argue that a core curriculum that is based on common needs, concerns, and themes and that offers interdisciplinary courses is more productive than one stressing distribution requirements.

Many committees begin with the idea that general education is only cognitive in character. The starting point for many faculty members is a perfectly reasonable question: "What knowledge should a generally educated person have?" However, this approach generally leads to a consideration of which disciplines to emphasize, which in turn prompts interdepartmental battles. Some committees have avoided these difficulties by seeking to identify the qualities, not just the knowledge, that mark the generally educated person. Northeastern Illinois University, for example, developed a list of these desired qualities, including effective communication skills, critical thinking abilities, problem-defining and problem-solving skills, human relations competencies, and commitment to ideals such as truth and social justice. Thus, many affective qualities, attitudes, values, and skills can be goals of general education and important complements to cognitive knowledge. Clearly, too, many departments can provide valuable training in these areas.

Obviously, then, a program of general education is not merely curricular. Whereas the question of what knowledge a student should possess leads to a discussion of how many courses to require in each subject area, the question of the qualities of an educated person leads to a discussion of how best to encourage students to develop these traits. This approach allows the committee to consider both what can be taught directly through the curriculum and what attitudes toward knowledge, relationships with others, and awareness of values may be better taught through the college community, dormitory life, informal relationships with faculty and students outside class, and off-campus experiences.

Another common myth is that liberal arts faculties are the beleaguered defenders of culture and general education against the infidels in professional and vocational programs. At Valparaiso University, for example, the general education task force encountered some initial opposition from the professional schools to its proposals. On closer inspection the task force found that, at least in some departments, the concern did not stem merely from narrow specialization. The nursing department's requirements, for instance, include relatively few nursing courses but a number of cognate courses, such as courses in biology and chemistry. Furthermore, the national accrediting association ensures that baccalaureate nursing students get a general education by requiring several liberal arts courses. The nursing department's opposition to the task force's proposal was thus not a rejection of general education per se but an objection to the extra course load it would place on nursing students. Committees at other institutions, however, have received greater support for their proposals from professional schools than from the supposedly amenable liberal arts departments.

A related myth is that the humanists are the defenders of general education and the scientists are the opposition. A survey of the General Education Committee at the State University of New York at Buffalo (1978, p. 3) suggests the inadequacy of such generalizations: "Overspecialization is a fault usually associated with the rigorous requirements of vocational or preprofessional majors, and the decline of general education is presumed to relate to the increasing proportions of students seeking such majors. . . . [But] in the fall of 1977, [our] English majors . . . took only 3.5 percent of their courses in natural sciences, mathematics, health sciences, or engineering. This matches, almost exactly, the proportion of engineering students taking courses in arts and letters and is significantly less than the comparable figures for students in health science and management majors." Rather than polarizing the faculty by pointing to "good guys" and "bad guys," task forces have found it more productive to assume that general education is a problem in all fields of study and for all types of students. They may then consider how faculty from all areas can improve course offerings.

Finally, while nearly everyone agrees that students should not merely master discrete bits of knowledge but integrate them, some faculty members are content to leave the full responsibility for integration to students. But as Jonathan Smith, former dean of the College at the University of Chicago, declares: "Students shall not be expected to integrate anything the faculty can't or won't." Students are most unlikely to acquire an integrated sense of knowledge if integration is not a planned and structured part of their academic program. Thus to achieve this goal faculty members from different academic disciplines must come together to discuss substantive issues and build an academic community that will sustain their general education program.

Program Planning

Strengthening an existing program or devising a new one are lengthy and complex processes. Here again, common-sense approaches may impede progress; among the more widespread misconceptions are the following set.

Change by addition: A misconception that is a legacy of recent decades, during which academic change was accomplished largely by adding new programs, securing larger budgets, recruiting more students, and hiring more instructors. Today most institutions can introduce new programs only by shifting priorities, reallocating resources, reassigning faculty members, and developing the professional competence of current personnel.

Keep the debate internal to the campus: A mistaken approach that leads many committees to begin their deliberations by having members share their best thinking and offer their ideas for improving general education. But this approach often yields uninformed opinions and half-truths, and it frequently results in premature polarization of the group. Other task forces have first researched the topic, consciously cultivating a spirit of inquiry so that each member expands, refines, and enriches his or her initial ideas. Such research may include reading, discussions with consultants, attendance at conferences or workshops, or visits to other institutions. A useful guide to ideas, programs, and literature for task force members is *General Education: Issues and Resources* (Project on General Education Models, 1980).

Write autobiographical proposals: Although valuable proposals may come from personal experience, task force members should not merely prescribe for today's students the same general education program they once received. Groups that encourage members to transcend their personal experiences, particularly by trying to anticipate future conditions that their students may face in their lifetimes, are more likely to design programs that are responsive to students' current interests and to their future needs.

Assume the committee knows the experiences and views of relevant constituencies: This faulty assumption often precludes committees from surveying faculty and student opinion to test committee members' preconceived ideas. But surveys of students, faculty members, and alumni can yield results valuable to planning. To assess the two key constituencies of students and faculty, Project GEM conducted a survey of students (Gaff and Davis, 1981) and developed a faculty interview schedule (Van Haitsma, 1980); other research instruments are discussed in Chapter Six.

Plan rationally: Virtually all rational planning models call for planners to specify goals, assess needs, determine alternatives, design and implement a program, and evaluate outcomes. Although such models are useful, effective programs are actually fashioned in many different ways. For example, Columbia University created a series of "teaching companies," upper-division interdisciplinary study groups, by having faculty members identify common interests that transcend their disciplines and by offering courses on such topics (Belknap and Kuhns, 1977). Thus Columbia is building this part of the program around faculty rather than the usual practice of recruiting faculty to staff a predetermined program.

Use *either-or* thinking: In preliminary conversations, committee members often pit one pet idea against another; such *either-or* thinking is inadequate for the resolution of complex problems. Some committees have discovered that *both-and* thinking allows the consideration of various ideas and avoids the political polarization caused by exclusionary thinking. For example, the Community College of Denver adopted a program that calls for all degree students to take four skills courses—communication, critical thinking, computation, and interpersonal skills—*and* for students seeking an associate degree to take five additional disciplinary courses *and* an interdisciplinary course. This scheme incorporates the desires of those faculty members who demand attention to basic skills, those who favor studies of academic disciplines, and those who prefer some interdisciplinary mode of integration. Both-and thinking thus enables a committee to develop a sophisticated program and garner the necessary political support.

Search for the one best program: This fallacious assumption reflects many American educators' penchant for standardized answers to all problems (Hechinger and Hechinger, 1975). The search for the one best way is largely responsible for education fads that range from one extreme to another. Simple human diversity suggests that any single program is likely to be a Procrustean bed, that students and faculty need to be given choices among a structured set of alternatives. For example, Harvard certifies a limited number of courses for each required area of study, from which students make selections, and Syracuse University offers a series of interdisciplinary and thematic clusters of courses. More radical approaches include the creation of a series of federated learning communities with thematic topics at SUNY-Stony Brook, and an alternative Paracollege at St. Olaf. Each approach is based on a respect for common standards as well as an aversion to standardized solutions.

Neglect personal biases and politics: This fallacy leads some committees, such as that at Southern Illinois University, to seek to avoid partisanship by stipulating that members keep their personal biases out of the discussions. This technique is intended to help prevent partisan political issues from arising within the committee and spreading throughout the campus. Other committees strive to uncover the biases of various members and various campus constituencies so that those views can be explicitly incorporated into proposals. This strategy involves consciously building coalitions and showing how the self-interests of various departments and other campus groups are served by a proposal.

Couch proposals in the language of innovation: This error is based on the assumption that because the committee is engaged in innovation or reform, it should use such language in reports and other written materials. But such rhetoric may only produce resistance to change, whereas more moderate language may foster consensus. This lesson is summarized by A. Lawrence Lowell in *What a University President Has Learned*: "If he desires to innovate he will be greatly helped by having the reputation of being conservative, because the radicals who want a change are little offended by the fact of change, while the conservatives will be likely to follow him because they look on him as sharing their temperament and point of view" (1938). Proposals that seem to advocate a return to fundamental purposes and procedures rather than a radical departure from present practices may draw support from both liberal and conservative campus groups.

Consider planning to be the final task: Because the process is demanding, even exhausting, committees are only too eager to complete the planning so they can turn the responsibility for the subsequent approval and implementation of the program over to someone else. But as James Q. Wilson, who chaired Harvard's task force, said after the faculty approved the new core curriculum, "To paraphrase Churchill, we are not at the end, or at the beginning of the end, but at the end of the beginning" ("The Core Curriculum . . . ," 1978, p. 7). A responsible task force must work to secure approval of its proposals and see them through to implementation.

Securing Faculty Approval

Obviously, the task force's planning will be for naught if the faculty votes down the reform proposals. The following are the most frequent misconceptions and erroneous procedures in seeking approval.

Some committees adopt the scholarly convention of publishing their best thinking and awaiting the reviews and critiques from their professional colleagues so as to allow the faculty a full and fair debate on the issues. Other task forces, however, have learned that they must take an active part in the debate and orchestrate the approval process if their proposals are to have any chance of passing. The role of the committee may shift from that of a deliberative body to that of an advocate for the proposals, for if the committee members do not speak for their own recommendations, who will? The faculty has only a few months to consider all the issues, problems, recommendations, and rationales that the committee grappled with for perhaps years. Committee members can greatly aid the approval process by initiating conversations with such key people as committee chairpersons, faculty leaders, and deans; discussing the proposals with academic departments; or holding open hearings.

An open hearing, however, may not be the best forum in which to first present a proposal to the faculty. GEM task force members at Northeastern Illinois University held a productive two-day retreat during which they developed a set of goals, brainstormed possible model curriculums, and planned strategy. Toward the end of the retreat, one member suggested that the committee hold an open hearing on campus for interested faculty members and present its best thinking to colleagues for a critique; it was feared, however, that an open hearing would provide a negative atmosphere in which faculty members would merely criticize the task force's best efforts. The committee thus decided to try to recapture the constructive atmosphere of the retreat by holding several small-group meetings before attempting an open hearing. Although time-consuming, this technique succeeded in engaging people in constructive and cooperative thinking about how to enhance the quality of general education, and it laid the groundwork for the subsequent approval of a revised curriculum.

A comprehensive proposal can generate a coalition of opposition, but at least some of its recommendations may be accepted if it has several distinct features that can be debated and acted on separately. For example, at the College of Brockport in the SUNY system, a college-wide committee on general education was created before the nature of the general education program itself was voted on. This procedure helped resolve some of the political ambiguities of who would be in control of the program before the actual program was discussed. Other schools break down a comprehensive proposal into portions that are brought before the faculty separately.

As the task force prepares to put its recommendation to a vote, it is natural for members to try to gauge the amount of faculty support they can count on and which aspects of the proposal will be best received. Sometimes the members pool their opinions about each faculty member or all members of a particularly important department to tally likely votes. But this effort is largely a matter of hunches and guesses; more than one group has worked for many months or even years on a proposal only to be surprised by the lack of support when the final votes were counted. One task force used a nonbinding straw poll to gauge faculty sentiment about each portion of its proposal. The members then reworked the draft on the basis of the survey results. A subsequent poll on the final draft found virtually every item accepted by a strong majority of the faculty. This polling technique played an important role in shaping the final positive vote by the senate.

Most committees eventually ask the question, "How can *we* get *them* to approve *our* recommendations?" Thusly posed, the question is difficult to answer, because faculty members will not vote for something they see as undesirable or contrary to their best interests. The most reliable strategy is to make sure the proposal contains portions that represent the ideas and values of those who must approve it; thus the committee can assure faculty that the entire proposal represents their best interests while highlighting particular portions of the proposal that address individual departments' or disciplines' special interests.

Any proposal will have its critics. Because avoiding persons with whom one disagrees is a characteristic of human nature, critics are often isolated and ignored. Ignoring them will not make them go away; indeed, they may become even more persistent and vocal. Some committees have deputized members or small delegations to meet quietly with these critics, hear their concerns, and either incorporate their suggestions into the proposals or explain why that cannot be done. This procedure may actually improve the proposal as well as win over some of the opposition. Similarly, many potential supporters of the proposal may have legitimate concerns or doubts. Therefore, some groups go out of their way to reassure these faculty members that the proposals to strengthen undergraduate general education are not, for example, antithetical to specialization, a threat to graduate education, contrary to the interests of specific departments, or a stalking horse for retrenching some faculty members. Some committee reports explain that not all faculty members will be involved in teaching new courses or describe resources that will be available to assist faculty members in developing new courses for the program.

It is not always prudent for a committee to assume that faculty members understand its proposals. Written reports and discussions may not be sufficient for educating faculty members about a proposed program; rare is the vote that takes place without at least some misunderstanding of portions of the proposal. Some opposition comes from simple misinformation about the current situation, the proposed improvement, the implications for other parts of the institution, and the like; committee members may wish to talk with known opponents to make sure that they are genuinely in disagreement rather than merely misinformed.

Three final issues arise as the time for a faculty vote nears. First, many schools, realizing that curriculum reform is not amenable to the business-as-usual approach, create special procedures for the vote. At the University of the Pacific, the voting procedure was determined by the Academic Council of the university. This group ruled that an abstention would be treated as a vote against the proposal; thus task force members had to persuade the faculty of the merits of their proposal and also, as in any political campaign, they had to get out the vote. The University of Tennessee adopted its current curriculum by a mailed secret ballot to minimize the oratorical influence of opponents in open faculty meetings and the undue influence that some persons might yield over others in a public vote. And because any curriculum should ideally have widespread faculty support, some institutions require a majority that is greater than the usual 51 percent for passage of a curriculum reform proposal.

The second issue is when to hold the vote. After a task force has spent years working on a proposal and held extended discussions with the faculty, it would be foolish to schedule a definitive vote if the outcome is in doubt. Further discussion and negotiation can keep the proposal alive and perhaps win a few more advocates. The committee's Machiavellian instincts dictate that the proper time to put the proposal to a vote is when the votes are assured.

Third, committee members need not assume that a negative vote is final. For instance, the committee at the University of the Pacific found that its proposal was narrowly defeated in the college of liberal arts, where it was first acted upon. Instead of abandoning the proposal, the committee immediately activated a contingency plan in three steps. First, the dean asked every department to state in writing specific problems with the proposal and specific modifications that would meet its objections. Second, additional committee members were recruited from the professional schools, in which there was strong support for the committee's recommendations. Third, once the departments' criticisms had been addressed, the revised proposal was resubmitted for faculty approval. This plan eventually resulted in passage of the committee's proposal.

Typically, when a faculty committee issues a report and its recommendations are accepted, an administrator is given responsibility for implementing the new policies. Curriculum revisions, however, require some continuity, and at least some members of the planning committee often play central roles in implementing the program. For example, Eva Wanton, the chairperson of the GEM task force at Florida A & M University, was asked to serve as director of general education to help implement the new program her group developed. Furthermore, committee members frequently teach courses in the new program and help secure colleagues to teach with them. Usually, a new program is best served by its planners taking an active part in its implementation.

Recruiting faculty to teach in the new program is one of the greatest challenges of implementation. Although the faculty as a collective approves a new program, individuals must be attracted to teach in it. In general, some rewards are necessary to attract and retain faculty. Often the opportunities to learn a new subject, to teach in a new context, to work with stimulating new colleagues, to engage in professional growth and renewal are sufficient to lure faculty members. But sometimes material rewards are necessary, or, at the very least, assurances that teaching general education courses will not be held against faculty members in decisions about salary, retention, and promotion. Prospective instructors can also be encouraged to participate if professional development workshops and other forms of support are available. Team-teaching and periodic faculty meetings can also aid instructors who are interested in the program but uncertain of their skills.

Implementation is usually less difficult if elements of the new program are gradually phased in rather than instituted all at once. For example, Ohio University is phasing in its new program with positive results. According to Dean William Dorrill, phasing in the new program makes securing the necessary personnel easier, is less disruptive to the rest of the instructional program, and helps the implementation team identify problems before the entire program is in place. Other schools, such as those in the Project on Quality Undergraduate Education, are attempting to run a pilot program involving a few faculty members and students before a course or an entire program is fully implemented. The first offering of a new course, program, or service will inevitably encounter some difficulties. Personnel problems, misunderstandings, personality conflicts, logistics, and other difficulties cannot all be avoided, even with the best advanced planning. The implementation team should regard the first run as a guide to improving the operation of succeeding trials.

After the first run and throughout the program's life, evaluation is critical. A careful assessment of the program, the reaction of students, faculty teaching effectiveness, and the like —particularly if focused on identifying problems that can be corrected during subsequent terms—can significantly aid program implementation. (See Chapter Six for a discussion of evaluation methodology.)

Conclusion

Reconstructing the general education program of a college or university is difficult and complicated. No curriculum review committee will flawlessly execute every step of the process, but errors need not deter them. By using variations of the strategies presented in this chapter, many institutions are fashioning new curriculums that are responsive to the various interests found on their campuses. The results often gain faculty approval not for their philosophical or conceptual elegance but because faculty agree that the proposals represent an improvement over the current hodge-podge that passes for general education. Reform proposals represent, quite simply, the best a college can do, if not the best to which individuals can aspire.

Chapter Eight

Epilogue: Assessing Current Progress and Future Needs

A genuine revival of general education is now taking place as new life is being breathed into the ideal of general education, and a recognizable configuration of institutional reforms is translating that ideal into practice. Cynics tend to dismiss the significance of the movement, regarding it as simply cosmetic, a "patina of reform." But the movement is too widespread and reform too extensive to be thus dismissed. Some charge that the interest in general education is self-serving, and they disparage the renewed emphasis on the liberal arts as simply a way for faculty to hold onto jobs. But, like any reform that has staying power, the general education movement serves personal interests and is motivated by varying amounts of idealism. Others portray it as another of the fads that occasionally sweep across the landscape of higher education. But every reform movement leaves marks on the academy; today's curriculum testifies to earlier reforms concerning career education, individualized studies, alternative programs, honors colleges, and the like. Another group of critics asserts that the reform movement is merely nostalgia, a wish to return to an imagined golden age when a limited body of knowledge was shared by all educated persons. Although some reformers may have such yearnings, this description is an inadequate caricature of what is happening in institutions. It would be at least as difficult for a college faculty to agree upon a philosophy of history—and far less useful—as to arrive at an operational philosophy of education; that is why none has attempted such an exercise.

The naysayers are wrong. Even a cursory glance, let alone a careful study, of the scope and depth of the current reform movement reveals that it represents a serious effort to define the nature of education at its higher levels and to reemphasize much of what is best in undergraduate education. Colleges are returning to the ideal of a broad general education for all students. When measured against this vision, most current general education programs are wanting, and colleges now seek to bring the reality closer to the ideal.

This effort poses enormous difficulties: there is no consensus about the aims, structure, and outcomes of a college education; and there are no generally accepted standards by which to evaluate either the general education of students or an institution's general education program. New student clienteles challenge those searching for connectedness and commonality: General education has been so neglected in the recent past that even some of its advocates are skeptical that the ideal can be salvaged; the spirit of retrenchment works against imaginative proposals and drains optimism from attempts to make improvements; and general education is held in low esteem, especially in the professional fields that have achieved dominance in many institutions during recent years. Given these impediments, it is rather surprising that a serious examination and any kind of reform have been made. But substantial accomplishments have been and are being achieved:

1. Institutions of all types, sizes, and locations have launched comprehensive institution-wide reviews of their programs. Countless others are dealing with important components of the curriculum, such as writing, global studies, and values.

2. Faculty members are once again discussing the purposes of general education, the qualities of an educated person, and the kinds of curriculums appropriate for achieving those goals. Agreement on such fundamental issues is hard to come by, but the fact that such basic questions are being pressed is a constructive sign.

3. There is a growing reaffirmation of the values of general education. A number of basic philosophical shifts can be observed in schools that are reviewing their curriculums, including increasing the amount of required general education and raising academic standards. Such commitments may be uneven throughout institutions and their strength uncertain, but general education values are definitely gaining increasing support and attention.

4. Action is being taken to see that the curriculum carries out an institution's educational philosophy; interdisciplinary core courses, limited distribution requirements, and required disciplinary courses are favored mechanisms. Colleges also are incorporating into their curriculums more liberal arts subject matter, attending to both basic and advanced cognitive skills, and fostering the integration of knowledge, and they are extending these concerns throughout all four years. Of course, structure is not synonymous with coherence or quality, and requiring courses does not guarantee that students will absorb their substance; but consistency between an institution's stated purpose and its curriculum helps promote learning and restore integrity to the academic program.

5. New courses are being devised and old ones are being altered in accordance with the purposes of new general curriculums. In the most thorough revisions, these courses address the specific needs of nonmajor students and meet carefully specified criteria, such as including substantial amounts of

writing. The current trend is toward introducing overarching purposes into individual courses and thus endeavoring to reduce fragmentation.

6. An active pedagogy is being sought that will give students more responsibility for their own learning and complement the lecture method that currently pervades all areas of the curriculum.

7. Stronger and more centralized administration is providing greater coordination for the general education portion of the curriculum, and there is a corresponding shift of resources toward general education. It remains to be seen, however, whether these leaders and resources can effectively invigorate general education or whether their efforts will be deflected by the forces of specialization and separatism.

8. Evaluations of the new programs are being planned, although few have yet been completed; it remains to be seen whether the good intentions of curricular reform are being realized and whether the results validate the changes that have been adopted.

9. A number of effective strategies for curricular change have been developed and can thus be used as guidelines in developing a quality curriculum. Learning in advance about the misconceptions and mistakes of curricular reform pioneers can help those who follow avoid some of the most serious difficulties.

These accomplishments are particularly impressive because they involve altering entrenched institutional interests. But concerned educators should not become too sanguine about these advances. General education reform is far from universal. Further, most gains are fragile, having not yet been fully implemented or incorporated into the regular ongoing academic life of institutions. And the actual results in the education of students are uncertain; in all probability they will yield both expected and unanticipated consequences, each of which will have to be addressed during this decade. But together these accomplishments represent a major reversal of the mindless drift of the curriculum and a serious attempt to provide students with a more considered program of general education.

That so many institutions are inaugurating reforms is also remarkable because reform is such a lengthy process. Consider that only some of the criticism leveled against the quality of education in general and the curriculum in particular leads to formal institutional reviews; that only some reviews produce specific proposals for change; that only some proposals are approved, sometimes in watered-down form; that only some approved changes are implemented; that only some implemented programs are successful; that only some successful programs are incorporated into the ongoing curriculum; and that, finally, only some institutionalized programs are able to maintain their original vision and vitality. Given this perspective, it is remarkable that general education reforms have progressed as far as they have at so many institutions—especially since, as Guardo (1982) reminds us, "As recently as 1977 general education was called a 'disaster area.'"

Much has been accomplished, but much more remains to be done if the reform movement is to fully realize its potential. Institutions are now at four quite different stages concerning the strengthening of general education curriculums, each of which is associated with a distinctive set of needs. At the first stage are those institutions whose leaders are yet unaware of the ferment surrounding general education. They need information about the inadequacies of programs, reforms underway at other institutions, and the like. Although all types of postsecondary institutions are involved in efforts to strengthen their programs, the movement is led by campuses that have a strong liberal tradition. Now other schools within the liberal tradition and other kinds of schools need to become involved.

The leaders of professional schools and programs, for instance, are recognizing that a broad general education is essential to the successful practice of their professions, that professionals need not only technical proficiency in their specializations, but also sensitivity to clients, understanding of society, familiarity with the spectrum of knowledge, sophistication about values, clarity of expression, and other qualities associated with a general education. The special problems in providing general education in a professional context include determining the liberal arts courses that will best complement heavily prescribed specialized curriculums and adapting their content to the practical needs of various professions, as in applied ethics.

Similarly, many two-year colleges that serve diverse populations remain outside the mainstream of reform; for example, the California Postsecondary Education Commission (1981, p. 26) observes, "The California community colleges, as a segment, do not appear to have effected any significant general education reform to date." Promising directions for general education improvements in community colleges include stressing literacy, particularly in an integrated manner across the curriculum, devising liberal arts courses for an adult clientele, and integrating humanities and social science perspectives in vocational courses. Sustained efforts to extend the concern for general education and its improvement to other settings will enhance its practice and enrich the understanding of it.

At a second stage are those schools actively involved in the review of their programs, typically through task forces appointed for this purpose. They are assessing their offerings, researching approaches used at other schools, developing imaginative and effective proposals, and working to convince faculty of the need for reform. Leaders of institutions at this stage need to share materials and experiences that will enhance the quality of their proposals and subsequently secure faculty approval. Such materials include definitions of generally educated men and women, assessment instruments, useful bibliographies, exemplary programs, new governance arrangements, criteria for courses, and strategies for curricular change. The sharing, selective utilization, and adaptation of these materials and ideas among institutions can deepen understanding of the range and varieties of purposes, contexts, programs, and techniques of general education. (See Appendix B).

At the third stage are those schools in the throes of implementing new programs. They need to develop some new courses and modify existing ones to carry out the purposes of their new curriculums. Their faculty members must learn to range beyond their familiar teaching practices and acquire new skills and knowledge in order to teach, for instance, interdisciplinary or value-oriented courses. Curriculum planners have to shift their attention from designing a program to implementing one. Evaluations of the new programs' effects on students, faculty members, and institutions need to be designed and carried out. In short, greater penetration, broader involvement, deeper commitment, and greater competence are needed to realize the adopted reforms.

At a fourth stage are schools working to maintain a newly implemented program. Some programs retain their vitality, while others soon lose their vigor. To keep a program alive and vital requires that the program's commitment to its ideal be constantly renewed, its rationale articulated, and its first principles recalled whenever new policy decisions are made. A corps of committed faculty must be retained, and faculty recruitment, evaluation, and development must deliberately cultivate faculty leadership and cohesiveness. The reward system must recognize the contributions of individuals to teaching general education courses and to the program as a whole. Resources, including administrative leadership, must be sufficient to permit the continual development and renewal of the program. Further, each successive generation of students must understand the purposes and rationale of the program, how it contributes to their present growth and potential successes, and how it engages them in actively learning about issues that affect their lives.

Looking beyond the efforts of individual institutions to the history of general education reform, one can see that general education periodically becomes the center of attention and then recedes to the periphery, only to burst forth again years later. Boyer and Levine (1981) offer a theory to account for this swing of the pendulum: General education emerges to forge common bonds among people after periods that tend to pull them apart (for example, after the two world wars or the radical individualism of the 1960s and 1970s). But the pendulum metaphor is misleading; undergraduate general education is better understood as a polar—a guiding—star, an enduring vision that provides a common point of reference for many different people traveling to many different destinations. The vision may be ignored, but usually with unfortunate results.

The current revival can be traced to the mid 1950s, when the reforms of the post–World War II revival were being institutionalized. Many then thought that the core of the curriculum was in good shape, and their attention was diverted elsewhere. Subsequently, enormous federal spending for research and development in the post-Sputnik era upset the balance of priorities. Faculty members, lured into research and specialized training, abandoned general education; they were encouraged to do so by administrators eager to advance their careers through larger budgets, additional programs, and institutional growth, especially in the prestigious areas of research and graduate education. By the 1960s, the decay of general education led to irrelevant courses taught by poorly prepared teaching assistants or low-status instructors. Faculties, for the most part, were only too willing to surrender their obligations to teach required courses in the general education program. Emboldened by their large population and their moral victories for civil rights—and, later, the Vietnam War—students rightly rebelled against such ineffective courses. During the 1970s, the rapid expansion of career fields and the enrollment of students unprepared for traditional college-level work further undermined the practice of general education. By this time, general education was in trouble not only because of student protest or vocationalism and not just because of demography or retrenchment, but because faculty members and administrators had allowed it to degenerate.

But the ideal of generally educated men and women continued to shine, however faintly, and in the late 1970s it again gained attention; today's revival of general education is a sign that colleges and universities are getting their directions straight. But is there any basis for optimism that current reforms will be any more long-lived than earlier ones? The answer is yes, for three reasons: First, the changes are taking place in the mainstream of colleges and universities. One might assert that the modern university, with its emphasis on research to the neglect of teaching, its stress on graduate and professional training rather than undergraduates, and its commitment to specialization at the expense of general education, is not a hospitable setting for reform. Proponents of this position advocate designing an enclave to advance general education, but few institutions are currently doing so. Although mainstream revisions are more difficult to orchestrate, are less pure in concept, and must concede to many more compromises, they are more likely to become permanent than are enclaves or experimental programs. Precisely because changing a curriculum is so difficult, the changes now being made are likely to remain in place for some time.

A second reason for optimism is that, in the face of declining enrollments, colleges and universities are now competing for students by improving the quality of their programs. This approach might appear contradictory, as the wooing of students might seem more easily accomplished by offering easier and more convenient educations. But, in fact, current thinking leans toward offering an excellent education as preparation for a productive and fulfilling life; schools are competing—some even staking their very survival—on the basis of educational quality. Because the pressures of the marketplace are unlikely to subside in the near future, there is every reason to expect institutions to remain concerned about the effectiveness of their general education programs. In this sense, current optimism is based on the hardheaded economic realities facing higher education, not simply on preferred educational philosophies.

The third reason for optimism is that a new generation of leaders is speaking out for general education. Faculty members, administrators, and students have become much more knowledgeable about general education concepts, the perspectives of various interest groups, strategies for change, and the resources needed for general education and its improvement. As they continue their learning, these leaders will surely advocate the sophisticated practice of general education for years to come. The creation of administrative offices for general education gives these proponents a home base around which to rally.

Mainstream structures, motivation to compete through quality, and the commitment of knowledgeable leaders are basic to current reforms, but neither these nor any other developments can guarantee the long-term survival of today's curricular changes. Social institutions must be reinvented and sustained by each succeeding generation; only continuing vigilence will help general education remain a vital force in undergraduate education. It is impossible to predict how much change will actually result from this revival, how deeply it will penetrate the academy, or how long it will endure. But the nature of current reforms ensures that the curriculum of the future will be different from that of today. Today's institutions are acting to restore undergraduate general education to its proper place, creating conditions for the liberal education of at least another generation of American youth. The guiding star, the ideal of general education, is once again pointing the direction for many who have lost their way.

Appendix A

Association of American Colleges Survey

The Association of American Colleges (AAC) conducted a survey in the winter of 1981 to learn about the breadth and character of the revival of general education. The survey had three specific purposes: to discern the nature of the current program changes; to learn about some of the factors aiding and inhibiting curricular change; and to determine how both individual campuses and national associations can further additional reforms.

The sample consisted of 272 colleges and universities thought to be conducting serious reviews of their undergraduate general education curriculums. These institutions were chosen from an earlier version of the directory that appears in Appendix B. They included institutions of all types—large and small, public and private, two-year and four-year. Completed questionnaires were received from 139 schools, resulting in a 51 percent response rate.

The questionnaire sought responses in three areas: demographic information and attitudes toward general education (completed by all respondents); the process of curricular change (answered by individuals from schools undertaking a formal review or revision); and the nature of these curricular changes (answered by individuals from institutions with new programs or specific proposals for change). The person most directly responsible for administering the program or conducting the review was asked to complete the form.

The results were summarized in *Reforming General Education: A Survey* (Klein and Gaff, 1982). That report is available from AAC for $3.00 prepaid. The questionnaire, with percentage responses indicated, is reproduced on the following pages. Because of rounding, percentages may not total 100.

General Education Questionnaire

For purposes of this questionnaire, general education is regarded as the part of the curriculum required of all students. It is often referred to as the "breadth" component, to differentiate it from the "depth" major and from free electives. It is sometimes called the "core," sometimes "distribution requirements."

Part I: *Your Institution* (To be completed by all institutions)

1. Name of institution: _____

2. Control: 58%   1. Private
              42   2. Public
              0   3. Other: _____

3. Size: 34%   1. Under 1,500 students
              30   2. 1,500–5,000 students
              14   3. 5,000–10,000 students
              22   4. Over 10,000 students

4. Type: 14%   1. Two-year college
              58   2. Four-year college, predominately undergraduate
              28   3. University with several graduate programs

5. Selectivity:
              35%   1. Low—open admissions
              50   2. Moderate
              15   3. High

6. How would you say attitudes regarding general education have changed over the last three years for each of the following?

	Less Favorable	Not Much Change	More Favorable
1. Students	5%	63%	32%
2. Faculty	4	25	71
3. Administration	3	19	78
4. The overall academic climate	3	25	71

Briefly state major reasons for changes:

7. We are interested in learning about institutions actively working on general education. This includes schools reviewing or revising their programs as well as those implementing or evaluating recent program changes. Is your institution involved in any of these forms of general education changes?

              11%   1. No
              88   2. Yes

If your answer is no, this is the end of the questionnaire. If yes, please complete Part II.

Part II. *Curricular Change* (To be completed by institutions engaged in reviewing or revising their curriculums)

1. At what stage in the review-revision process is your institution?

    __2%__ 1. Talking stage—we have not established a committee or formally launched the effort.

    __22__ 2. Early planning stage—a committee has been established and is working toward a proposal.

    __14__ 3. Advanced planning stage—a committee has been established and has a specific proposal.

    __9__ 4. Approval stage—the committee is working to secure approval.

    __31__ 5. Implementation stage—a revised program has been approved and is being carried out.

    __18__ 6. Evaluation stage—the program is being assessed.

    __5__ 7. Other (explain): _____

2. If your institution is beyond the talking stage, name of committee or group responsible for the review or revision: _____

    Name and title of person chairing the group or administering the program: _____

    (This information will be used for future mailings.)

3. Is the review or revision institution-wide?

    __20%__ 1. No. Name of unit in which review is located: _____

    __80__ 2. Yes

4. What have been the major obstacles to the improvement of general education? (Check the *two* most important)

    __4%__ 1. Little faculty interest in general education

    __40__ 2. Faculty resistance to change

    __2__ 3. Little administrative support

    __58__ 4. Department "turfism"

    __30__ 5. Competition from department majors and specializations

    __18__ 6. Competition from vocational interests

    __13__ 7. Lack of funds

    __21__ 8. Other: _____

5. What major factors have helped the most in your efforts to reform general education? (Check the *two* most important)

    __46%__ 1. Support of key faculty members

    __62__ 2. Support of key administrators

    __37__ 3. Work of the general education committee

    __24__ 4. Widespread involvement of the faculty

    __5__ 5. Initiatives of certain departments

    __12__ 6. External resources (please identify: _____)

    __7__ 7. Other: _____

6. On the basis of your experience, what advice would you give others who may be starting a curricular reform effort?

7. Which ideas, writings, persons, meetings or other external resources have been of greatest help in strengthening general education?

8. Can you think of additional external resources—such as might be provided by AAC's Center for General Education—that would be of assistance to your reform efforts?

    __32%__ 1. No
    __68__   2. Yes

    If yes, please explain: _____

9. Below are several possible activities of the Center for General Education. For each indicate whether your institution would utilize it, assuming modest charges would be made for materials, workshops, and the like.

	Probably Not	Probably Yes	Definitely Yes
1. Publish a newsletter with substantive articles, program examples, information about upcoming events, and the like	7%	48%	44%
2. Operate a clearinghouse responsive to inquiries about aspects of general education	24	50	26
3. Provide campus consultation on a cost-sharing basis	41	43	16
4. Offer advice about possible consultants	31	47	22
5. Plan and organize conferences or workshops on various topics	18	65	17
6. Assemble a temporary consortium of schools to share their experiences regarding reforms	36	49	15
7. Organize an interest group as a continuing organization within AAC	33	51	16
8. Arrange panels to make presentations at professional conferences	29	52	19
9. Circulate reports, papers, and curricular materials from campuses	10	52	37
10. Conduct focused studies (such as this survey)	10	51	32

	Prob- ably Not	Prob- ably Yes	Defi- nitely Yes
11. Serve as a national advocate of the importance of general education	13%	34%	53%
12. Other:	67	0	33

If you have a recently revised program or a specific program before the
faculty, go on to Part III. If not, this is the end of the questionnaire.

Part III. Characteristics of New Programs

In this section we are interested in the characteristics of new general education programs. Please answer the following questions in terms of
the revised program you recently adopted or the specific proposal most
likely to be adopted. Since general education requirements may vary for
different degrees and major fields of study, answer the questionnaire in
terms of the most generic program at your institution. For two-year
schools, this may mean the Associate of Arts degree and for four-year
schools, the program for the Bachelor of Arts.

1. Indicate the number of credit hours required in your new general
   education program and the total number of hours required for graduation.

   1. Required in general education: __44 semester hours (four-
      year schools) 31 semester hours (two-year schools)__ (means)
   2. Required for graduation: __124 semester hours (four-year
      schools) 60 semester hours (two-year schools)__ (means)
   3. Is this based on a: __15%__ 1. Quarter or __85%__ 2. Semester
      system?
   4. Is the number of hours in your new general education pro-
      gram fewer, the same, or more than in the previous one?

      __5%__ 1. Fewer
      __36__ 2. Same
      __59__ 3. More

2. For each of the following academic areas, indicate the number of
   credit hours (either quarter or semester) required, and whether these
   are less, the same, or more than were required previously.

	Credits Quarter or Semester	Less	Same	More
1. English Composition	5	3%	53%	44%
2. Mathematics	4	2	47	52
3. Foreign Languages	8	8	61	31
4. Humanities	9	5	48	47
5. The Arts	4	0	58	42

	Credits Quarter or Semester	Less	Same	More
6. Social Sciences	7	16%	52%	32%
7. Natural Sciences	7	9	57	33
8. Physical Education	3	7	87	6

3. In addition to exposing students to various subject matter areas, some general education programs are designed to expose students to various "modes of thought" (such as moral, esthetic, logical). How much emphasis on modes of thought would you say characterizes your new program?

    _10%_ 1. Very little
    _49_ 2. Somewhat
    _41_ 3. A great deal

4. Are the following modes of thought an *explicit* part (for example, a required course or competency) of your new program?

	Not an explicit part	Yes, a minor part	Yes, a major part
1. Esthetic (cultivate taste, imagination, creativity)	16%	46%	37%
2. Moral (develop ethical sensitivity, examine value implications)	21	30	48
3. Analytical (examine arguments, reason logically and critically)	12	25	62
4. Synthetic (make connections between separate items, think holistically)	19	28	53
5. Empirical (test hypotheses, study scientific methods)	19	39	42

5. Some general education programs are designed to develop various skills. For each of the following skills, check whether its development is or is not an explicit part of your new program. Also, indicate whether the new program gives less, the same, or more attention to each than the previous one.

	Skills? No	Yes	Less	Same	More
1. Writing	1%	99%	0%	29%	71%
2. Speaking	39	61	6	48	45
3. Mathematics	18	82	0	33	67
4. Computer literacy	55	45	0	47	53
5. Critical thinking	20	79	0	41	59
6. Problem solving	28	72	0	52	48

	Skills?				
	No	Yes	Less	Same	More
7. Research/library	37%	63%	1%	57%	42%
8. Interpersonal relations	66	34	5	73	21
9. Foreign language	43	57	5	60	34
10. Other _____	0	100	14	14	71

6. Writing is one skill that seems to be receiving a lot of attention these days.

    a. Does your new program have a required writing component?

        __2%__ 1. No
        __98__ 2. Yes

    b. If yes, in this component:

	No	Yes
1. Is there a required course on expository writing?	16%	84%
2. Is there a designated amount of writing?	28	72
3. Is student writing read critically by instructors?	2	97
4. Is a proficiency examination required?	45	55
5. Is writing explicitly taught in courses other than English?	22	78

7. How is the general education or breadth requirement structured? For each of the following, please indicate whether it is part of your new program and whether its role is less, the same or more than in the previous one.

	Is Not Part	Is A Part	Less	Same	More
1. Students must take interdisciplinary core courses	45%	55%	3%	37%	60%
2. Students must take *specified* courses (European History, American Literature)	53	47	4	51	43
3. Students *choose* from a *limited* range of courses to meet area requirements (humanities, sciences, social sciences)	12	88	6	26	68

	Is Not Part	Is A Part	Less	Same	More
4. Students may choose from a virtually *unlimited* range of courses to meet area requirements	85%	15%	56%	41%	3%
5. Students choose from totally free electives with no regard for areas	93	7	45	54	0

8. Which of the following curriculum models most closely conveys the overall character of your new general education program? (Check up to *three* that come the closest.)

    __80%__ 1. Discipline-based: students take a number of courses in a variety of disciplines, from groups like the humanities, sciences and social sciences.

    __25__ 2. Heritage-based: students study about their own cultural and historical backgrounds.

    __30__ 3. Theme-based: A specific problem or issue is studied in a way that encompasses a variety of academic disciplines.

    __23__ 4. Competency-based: A set of competencies which a student is to acquire or demonstrate is identified and guides the curriculum.

    __14__ 5. Methods-based: Modes of thought used in various academic fields are analyzed.

    __58__ 6. Skills-based: Students are taught a number of basic and advanced intellectual skills, such as communications and critical thinking.

    __4__ 7. Student-based: Students are given a significant role in determining the content, methodology and evaluation of their learning.

    __21__ 8. Value-based: Students are taught to clarify and expand their own values.

    __6__ 9. Other: _____

9. Does your new general education program contain requirements for interdisciplinary or other integrative study?

    __31%__ 1. No
    __69__ 2. Yes, briefly describe: _____

10. Are students required to study some foreign cultures?

    __45%__ 1. No
    __30__ 2. Yes, but it can be a Western one
    __24__ 3. Yes, and it must be a non-Western one

11.   (For four-year schools only) Are students expected to take general
      education courses over their entire baccalaurate experience?

      _41%_ 1. No
      _59_   2. Yes. Briefly describe upper-level requirements:

12.   Do the courses offered by departments as introductions for their ma-
      jors also serve as general education for nonmajors?

      _31%_ 1. Not in most cases
      _69_   2. Yes, in most cases

13.   General education courses often are taught by lectures to large num-
      bers of students. Are nonlecture methods of instruction a part of
      your new program?

      _14%_ 1. No
      _86_   2. Yes. Please describe what is done to encourage alterna-
             tives to lectures:

14.   Overall, how much change would you say the new curriculum repre-
      sents compared to the previous one?

      _2%_   1. We made very little change
      _39_   2. We changed some component(s)
      _58_   3. We made a comprehensive change

15.   What are you doing about evaluating your new program?

      _15%_ 1. We haven't talked about it much
      _34_   2. We intend to evaluate it but have no specific plan
      _39_   3. We have specific plans for evaluation
      _7_   4. We already have conducted an evaluation
      _5_   5. Other: _____

16.   Looking ahead, what are the major needs you anticipate during the
      coming months?

Appendix B

Directory of
Institutions Reviewing
General Education

The following directory of colleges and universities that are now reviewing their general education programs provides a perspective on the scope of contemporary interest in this topic and will enable individuals to share materials and information with their colleagues at other institutions. The list includes institutions of all sizes and types in all regions of the country. It is extensive but not exhaustive; doubtless other schools could be added. But it represents those institutions with which we have been in contact since 1978 that are taking concrete steps to strengthen their general education programs.

The efforts under way at these institutions cover a wide range of approaches, programs, and projects. Some are holistic in nature and apply to the entire student body, and others constitute only a portion of the total general education program or apply only to certain students. Some of the schools are involved in the early stages of a curricular review, and others have been working several years and are implementing new programs. Together, these efforts add up to an impressive number of separate attempts to strengthen the core of undergraduate education.

Alabama

Birmingham Southern College
Birmingham, AL 35204

University of Montevallo
Montevallo, AL 35115

Arizona

Maricopa Community College
District
Phoenix, AZ 85034

Western International
University
Phoenix, AZ 85021

Arkansas

Hendrix College
Conway, AR 27032

John Brown University
Siloam Springs, AR 72761

University of Arkansas at
Monticello
Monticello, AR 71655

California

California Lutheran College
Thousand Oaks, CA 91360

California State University and
Colleges
Long Beach, CA 90802

Chapman College
Orange, CA 92666

Dominican College
San Rafael, CA 94901

Los Medanos College
Pittsburg, CA 94575

Monterey Peninsula College
Monterey, CA 93940

Pacific Christian College
Fullerton, CA 92631

San Diego State University
San Diego, CA 92182

Stanford University
Stanford, CA 94305

University of California
Davis, CA 95616

University of California
Riverside, CA 92521

University of California
Santa Cruz, CA 95064

University of the Pacific
Stockton, CA 95211

University of San Diego
San Diego, CA 92110

University of Santa Clara
Santa Clara, CA 95053

University of Southern
    California
Los Angeles, CA 90007

Colorado

Colorado College
Colorado Springs, CO 80903

Colorado School of Mines
Golden, CO 80401

Community College of Denver
Denver, CO 80203

Loretto Heights College
Denver, CO 80236

Metropolitan State College
Denver, CO 80204

Rockmont College
Denver, CO 80226

University of Colorado at
    Boulder
Boulder, CO 80309

University of Northern
    Colorado
Greeley, CO 80639

Western State College of
    Colorado
Gunnison, CO 81230

Connecticut

Eastern Connecticut State
    College
Willimantic, CT 06226

Saint Joseph College
West Hartford, CT 06117

University of Bridgeport
Bridgeport, CT 06602

University of Hartford
West Hartford, CT 06117

District of Columbia

American University
Washington, DC 20016

Florida

Bethune-Cookman College
Daytona Beach, FL 32015

Daytona Beach Community
    College
Daytona Beach, FL 32015

Eckerd College
Saint Petersburg, FL 33733

Florida Agricultural & Mechan-
    ical University
Tallahassee, FL 32307

Miami-Dade Community
    College
Miami, FL 33176

North Florida Junior College
Madison, FL 32340

Santa Fe Community College
Gainesville, FL 32601

University of Central Florida
Orlando, FL 32816

University of Florida
Gainesville, FL 32611

Valencia Community College
Orlando, FL 32802

Georgia

Clark College
Atlanta, GA 30314

Clayton Junior College
Morrow, GA 30260

Mercer University
Macon, GA 31207

Spelman College
Atlanta, GA 30314

Idaho

Northwest Nazarene College
Nampa, ID 83651

Ricks College
Rexburg, ID 83440

Illinois

Barat College
Lake Forest, IL 60045

Bell & Howell Educational
   Group, Inc.
Evanston, IL 60202

City College of Chicago
Chicago, IL 60601

College of Lake County
Grayslake, IL 60030

College of Saint Francis
Joliet, IL 60435

DePaul University
Chicago, IL 60614

Governors State University
Park Forest South, IL 60466

Illinois Central College
East Peoria, IL 61635

Illinois State University
Normal, IL 61701

Milliken University
Decatur, IL 62522

Northeastern Illinois
   University
Chicago, IL 60625

Northwestern University
Evanston, IL 60201

Southern Illinois University
Edwardsville, IL 62026

Western Illinois University
Macomb, IL 61455

Indiana

DePauw University
Greencastle, IN 46135

Earlham College
Richmond, IN 47374

Indiana State University
Terre Haute, IN 47809

Indiana University at South
   Bend
South Bend, IN 46634

Marian College
Indianapolis, IN 46222

Marion College
Marion, IN 46952

Oakland City College
Oakland City, IN 47660

Purdue University Calumet
Hammond, IN 46323

Saint Joseph's College
Rensselaer, IN 47978

St. Meinrad Archabbey
St. Meinrad, IN 47577

Taylor University
Upland, IN 46989

University of Evansville
Evansville, IN 47702

Valparaiso University
Valparaiso, IN 46383

Iowa

Drake University
Des Moines, IA 50311

Graceland College
Lamoni, IA 50140

Grinnell College
Grinnell, IA 50112

Iowa Wesleyan College
Mt. Pleasant, IA 52691

Marycrest College
Davenport, IA 52804

Northwestern College
Orange City, IA 51041

Simpson College
Indianola, IA 50125

Wartburg College
Waverly, IA 50671

Westmar College
Le Mars, IA 51031

Kansas

Baker University
Baldwin City, KS 66006

Fort Hays State University
Hays, KS 67601

Johnson County Community
   College
Overland Park, KS 66210

Kansas Wesleyan College
Salina, KS 67401

Pittsburg State University
Pittsburg, KS 66762

St. Mary College
Leavenworth, KS 66048

Wichita State University
Wichita, KS 67208

Kentucky

Berea College
Berea, KY 40404

Centre College
Danville, KY 40422

Murray State University
Murray, KY 42071

University of Kentucky
Lexington, KY 46506

University of Louisville
Louisville, KY 40208

Louisiana

Centenary College of
Louisiana
Shreveport, LA 71104

Loyola University
New Orleans, LA 70118

St. Mary's Dominican College
New Orleans, LA 70118

Tulane University
New Orleans, LA 79118

University of Southern
Louisiana
Lafayette, LA 70504

Maine

Thomas College
Waterville, ME 04901

University of Southern Maine
Portland, ME 04103

Maryland

Catonsville Community
College
Catonsville, MD 21228

College of Notre Dame of
Maryland
Baltimore, MD 21210

Community College of
Baltimore
Baltimore, MD 21215

Frostburg State College
Frostburg, MD 21532

Hood College
Frederick, MD 21701

Montgomery College
Rockville, MD 20850

Towson State University
Towson, MD 21204

University of Maryland at
College Park
College Park, MD 20742

Massachusetts

Amherst College
Amherst, MA 01002

Assumption College
Worcester, MA 01609

Babson College
Babson Park, MA 02157

Boston University
Boston, MA 02215

College of the Holy Cross
Worcester, MA 01610

Fitchburg State College
Fitchburg, MA 01420

Harvard University
Cambridge, MA 02138

Northeastern University
Boston, MA 02115

Simmons College
Boston, MA 02115

Southeastern Massachusetts
    University
North Dartmouth, MA 02747

Springfield Technical Commu-
    nity College
Springfield, MA 01105

Tufts University
Medford, MA 02155

University of Massachusetts
Amherst, MA 01003

Michigan

Albion College
Albion, MI 49224

Aquinas College
Grand Rapids, MI 49506

Eastern Michigan University
Ypsilanti, MI 48197

Mercy College of Detroit
Detroit, MI 48219

Michigan State University
East Lansing, MI 48824

Nazareth College
Nazareth, MI 49074

Oakland University
Rochester, MI 48063

Olivet College
Olivet, MI 49976

Shaw College at Detroit
Detroit, MI 48202

Siena Heights College
Adrian, MI 49221

University of Michigan
Ann Arbor, MI 48109

Western Michigan University
Kalamazoo, MI 49008

Minnesota

Bethel College
St. Paul, MN 55112

Carleton College
Northfield, MN 55057

College of St. Teresa
Winsona, MN 55987

Gustavus Adolphus College
St. Peter, MN 56082

Macalester College
St. Paul, MN 55105

Moorhead State College
Moorhead, MN 56560

St. John's University
Collegeville, MN 56321

St. Olaf College
Northfield, MN 55057

Southwest State University
Marshall, MN 56258

Mississippi

Mississippi Industrial College
Holly Springs, MS 38635

Missouri

Stephens College
Columbia, MO 65201

William Jewel College
Liberty, MO 64068

Montana

Carroll College
Helena, MT 59601

Eastern Montana College
Billings, MT 59101

Montana College of Mineral
Science and Technology
Butte, MT 59701

Montana State University
Bozeman, MT 59717

Nebraska

Doane College
Crete, NB 68333

University of Nebraska at
Lincoln
Lincoln, NB 68588

New Hampshire

Franklin Pierce College
Rindge, NH 03461

Keene State College
Keene, NH 03431

Saint Anselm's College
Manchester, NH 03102

New Jersey

Bloomfield College
Bloomfield, NJ 07003

Drew University
Madison, NJ 07940

Kean College of New Jersey
Union, NJ 07083

Mercer County Community
College
Trenton, NJ 08690

Middlesex County College
Edison, NJ 08817

Monmouth College
West Long Branch, NJ 07764

William Patterson College of
New Jersey
Wayne, NJ 07470

Rider College
Lawrenceville, NJ 08648

Rutgers University
New Brunswick, NJ 08904

Seton Hall University
So. Orange, NJ 07079

Somerset County College
Somerville, NJ 08896

New York

Bard College
Annandale-on-Hudson, NY
    12504

Brooklyn College
City University of New York
Brooklyn, NY 11210

Colgate University
Hamilton, NY 13346

Cornell University
Ithaca, NY 14853

Dominican College
Orangeburg, NY 10962

Dutchess Community College
Poughkeepsie, NY 12601

Eisenhower College
Rochester Institute of
    Technology
Seneca Falls, NY 13148

Erie Community College
Buffalo, NY 14221

Fordham University
Bronx, NY 10458

Hobart and William Smith
    Colleges
Geneva, NY 14456

Iona College
New Rochelle, NY 10801

Keuka College
Keuka Park, NY 14478

La Guardia Community
    College
Long Island City, NY 11101

Marist College
Poughkeepsie, NY 12601

Marymount Manhattan
    College
New York, NY 10021

Mohawk Valley Community
    College
Utica, NY 13501

Niagara County Community
    College
Sanborn, NY 14132

Rochester Institute of
    Technology
Rochester, NY 14132

Rochester Institute of
    Technology
National Technical Institute
    for the Deaf
Rochester, NY 14623

Russell Sage College
Troy, NY 12180

State University of New York
    (SUNY) at Binghamton
Binghamton, NY 13901

SUNY Agricultural and Technical College of Alfred
Alfred, NY 14802

SUNY at Brockport
Brockport, NY 14420

SUNY at Buffalo
Buffalo, NY 14620

SUNY at Fredonia
Fredonia, NY 14063

SUNY at New Paltz
New Paltz, NY 12561

SUNY at Old Westbury
Old Westbury, NY 11568

SUNY at Oswego
Oswego, NY 13126

SUNY at Plattsburgh
Plattsburgh, NY 12901

SUNY at Potsdam
Potsdam, NY 13676

SUNY at Stony Brook
Stony Brook, NY 11794

Syracuse University
Syracuse, NY 13210

Touro College
New York, NY 10036

Vassar College
Poughkeepsie, NY 12601

Wagner College
Staten Island, NY 10301

North Carolina

Appalachian State University
Boone, NC 28608

Atlantic Christian College
Wilson, NC 27893

Davidson College
Davidson, NC 28036

Duke University
Durham, NC 27706

East Carolina University
Greenville, NC 27834

Elon College
Elon, NC 27244

Gardner-Webb College
Boiling Springs, NC 28017

Johnson C. Smith University
Charlotte, NC 28216

Meredith College
Raleigh, NC 27611

Pembroke State University
Pembroke, NC 28372

Saint Andrew's Presbyterian College
Laurinburg, NC 28352

UNC at Asheville
Asheville, NC 28804

UNC at Chapel Hill
Chapel Hill, NC 27514

UNC at Charlotte
Charlotte, NC 28223

UNC at Wilmington
Wilmington, NC 28406

Western Carolina University
Cullowhee, NC 28723

North Dakota

Jamestown College
Jamestown, ND 58401

Maryville State College
Maryville, ND 58257

North Dakota State University
Fargo, ND 59102

University of North Dakota
Grand Forks, ND 58202

Valley City State College
Valley City, ND 58072

Ohio

Antioch College
Yellow Springs, OH 45387

Bowling Green State
University
Bowling Green, OH 43403

Case Western Reserve
University
Cleveland, OH 44106

Central State University
Wilberforce, OH 45384

College of Mount St. Joseph
Mount St. Joseph, OH 45051

Hiram College
Hiram, OH 44234

Kenyon College
Gambier, OH 43022

Notre Dame College of Ohio
Cleveland, OH 44121

Ohio Dominican University
Columbus, OH 43219

Ohio University
Athens, OH 45701

Ohio Wesleyan University
Delaware, OH 43015

University of Dayton
Dayton, OH 45469

Oklahoma

Flaming Rainbow University
Tahlequah, OK 74464

Oregon

Chemeketa Community
    College
Salem, OR 97309

Columbia Christian College
Portland, OR 97220

Lewis and Clark College
Portland, OR 97219

Oregon State University
Corvallis, OR 97331

Portland State University
Portland, OR 97207

Warner Pacific College
Portland, OR 97215

York College of Pennsylvania
York, PA 17405

Pennsylvania

Allentown College
Center Valley, PA 18034

Beaver College
Glenside, PA 19038

Bucknell University
Lewisburg, PA 17837

Carnegie-Mellon University
Pittsburgh, PA 15213

Franklin and Marshall College
Lancaster, PA 17604

Gettysburg College
Gettysburg, PA 17325

Gwynedd-Mercy College
Gwynedd-Mercy, PA 19437

Indiana University of
   Pennsylvania
Indiana, PA 15705

Lafayette College
Easton, PA 18042

Pennsylvania State University
University Park, PA 16802

Thiel College
Greenville, PA 16125

University of Pennsylvania
Philadelphia, PA 19104

Widener College
Chester, PA 19013

Puerto Rico

Inter-American University of
   Puerto Rico
Barranquitas, PR 00615

University of Puerto Rico
Rio Piedras, PR 00931

Rhode Island

University of Rhode Island
Kingston, RI 02881

South Carolina

Central Wesleyan College
Central, SC 29630

Citadel Military College of
   South Carolina
Charleston, SC 29409

Morris College
Sumter, SC 29150

Winthrop College
Rock Hill, SC 29733

South Dakota

Dakota Wesleyan University
Mitchell, SD 57301

Mount Marty College
Yankton, SD 57078

Sinte Gleska College
Rosebud, SD 57570

Yankton College
Yankton, SD 57078

Tennessee

David Lipscomb College
Nashville, TN 37203

Maryville College
Maryville, TN 37801

University of Tennessee at
   Chattanooga
Chattanooga, TN 37401

University of Tennessee at
   Knoxville
Knoxville, TN 37916

University of Tennessee at
   Martin
Martin, TN 38238

Vanderbilt University
Nashville, TN 37240

Texas

Cedar Valley College
Lancaster, TX 75134

Dallas County Community
   College District
Dallas, TX 75202

East Texas State University
Commerce, TX 75428

North Texas State University
Denton, TX 76203

Southwest Texas State
   University
San Marcos, TX 78666

Texas A & M University
College Station, TX 77843

Texas Tech University
Lubbock, TX 79409

University of Houston
Houston, TX 77004

University of Texas at
   Arlington
Arlington, TX 76019

Utah

Brigham Young University
Provo, UT 84602

Southern Utah State
   University
Cedar City, UT 14720

Utah State University
Logan, UT 84322

Weber State College
Ogden, UT 84107

Vermont

Trinity College
Burlington, VT 05405

University of Vermont
Burlington, VT 05405

Virginia

College of William and Mary
Williamsburg, VA 23185

Eastern Mennonite College
Harrisonburg, VA 82280

George Mason University
Fairfax, VA 22030

James Madison University
Harrisonburg, VA 22807

Lord Fairfax Community
College
Middletown, VA 22645

Lynchburg College
Lynchburg, VA 24501

Mary Washington College
Fredericksburg, VA 22401

Richard Bland College of the
College of William and Mary
Petersburg VA 23803

University of Virginia
Charlottesville, VA 22903

Virginia Commonwealth
University
Richmond, VA 23284

Virginia Polytechnic Institute
and State University
Blacksburg, VA 24061

Washington and Lee University
Lexington, VA 24450

Washington

Pacific Lutheran University
Tacoma, WA 98447

Tacoma Community College
Tacoma, WA 98465

University of Puget Sound
Tacoma, WA 98416

University of Washington
Seattle, WA 98195

Washington State University
Pullman, WA 99163

West Virginia

Davis and Elkins College
Elkins, WV 26241

University of West Virginia
Morgantown, WV 26506

Wisconsin

Carroll College
Waukesha, WI 53186

Lakeland College
Sheboygan, WI 53081

Marian College of Fond Du Lac
Fond Du Lac, WI 54935

University of Wisconsin-
Parkside
Kenosha, WI 53141

University of Wisconsin-
Platteville
Platteville, WI 52818

Wyoming

Casper College
Casper, WY 82601

Northwest Community College
Powell, WY 82435

Western Wyoming College
Rock Springs, WY 82901

References

American University. *Report of the University Undergraduate Studies Committee.* Washington, D.C.: American University, 1980.

Antioch College. "A General Education Program for the Eighties." Antioch College, n.d.

Armstrong, F. H. Remarks made at session on "Faculty Renewal: The Case for Interdisciplinary Approaches." National Conference of the American Association for Higher Education, Washington, D.C., Apr. 1979.

Arons, A. B. "Using the Substance of Science to the Purpose of Liberal Learning." *Journal of College Science Teaching,* Nov. 1980, pp. 81–87.

Ashby, E. *Technology and the Academics.* London: Macmillan, 1958.

Astin, A. *Four Critical Years: Effects of College on Beliefs, Attitudes, and Knowledge.* San Francisco: Jossey-Bass, 1977.

Bailey, S. K. *The Purposes of Education.* Bloomington, Ind.: Phi Delta Kappa Education Foundation, 1976.

Bailey, S. K. "Needed Changes in Liberal Education." *Educational Record,* Summer 1977, pp. 250–258.

Barrows, T. S., Clark, J. L., and Klein, S. F. "What Students Know About Their World." *Change,* May–June 1980, pp. 10-17.

Barrows, T. S., Clark, J. L., and Klein, S. F. *How College Seniors Perceive Their World.* Research Report. Princeton, N.J.: Educational Testing Service, 1981.

Beck, R. E. *Career Patterns: The Liberal Arts Major in Bell System Management.* Washington, D.C.: Association of American Colleges, 1981.

Belknap, R., and Kuhns, R. *Tradition and Innovation.* New York: Columbia University Press, 1977.

Bell, D. *The Reforming of General Education.* New York: Columbia University Press, 1966.

Bergquist, W. H., and Phillips, S. R. "Components of an Effective Faculty Development Program." *Journal of Higher Education,* 1975, *46,* 177-211.

Bergquist, W. H., Phillips, S. R., and Quehl, G. *Handbook for Faculty Development,* Vols. 1-3. Washington, D.C.: Council of Independent Colleges, 1975-81.

Bernstein, A. "The New Humanities." *AAHE Bulletin* [American Association for Higher Education], Nov. 1980, pp. 8-9.

Berry, D. "The Liberal Arts as Attitude." *Journal of General Education,* Fall 1977, pp. 228-234.

Bird, C. *The Case Against College.* New York: McKay, 1975.

Birnbaum, N. Presentation at the conference "What Ought to Be Taught?" Bard College, Jan. 1979.

Blackburn, R., and others. *Changing Practices in Undergraduate Education.* Berkeley, Calif.: Carnegie Council for Policy Studies in Higher Education, 1976.

Blake, J. H. "The Social Context of Liberal Education." Presentation at the annual meeting of the Society for Values in Higher Education, Poughkeepsie, N.Y., Aug. 1981.

Bloom, B. S. "Mastery Learning." In J. H. Block (Ed.), *Mastery Learning: Theory and Practice.* New York: Holt, Rinehart and Winston, 1971.

Bonham, G. "Toward One Human Experience." *The Great Core Curriculum Debate.* New Rochelle, N.Y.: Change Magazine Press, 1979, pp. 1-4.

Bonham, G. "Education and the World View." *Humanities,* Aug. 1981, pp. 1-2.

Botstein, L. "Liberal Arts and the Core Curriculum: A Debate in the Dark." *Chronicle of Higher Education,* 9 July 1979a, p. 18.

Botstein, L. "A Proper Education." *Harper's,* Sept. 1979b, pp. 33-37.

Bowen, H. R. *Investment in Learning: The Individual and Social Value of American Higher Education.* San Francisco: Jossey-Bass, 1977.

Boyer, E. L. "Quality and the Campus: The High School–College Connection." *Current Issues in Higher Education,* 1980, no. 4, pp. 6-12.

Boyer, E. L., and Hechinger, F. M. *Higher Learning in the Nation's Service.* Washington, D.C.: Carnegie Foundation for the Advancement of Teaching, 1981.

Boyer, E. L., and Kaplan, M. *Educating for Survival.* New Rochelle, N.Y.: Change Magazine Press, 1977.

Boyer, E. L., and Levine, A. *A Quest for Common Learning.* Washington, D.C.: Carnegie Foundation for the Advancement of Teaching, 1981.

Branscomb, H., and others. *The Competent College Student.* Nashville: Tennessee Higher Education Commission, 1977.

Brooklyn College. *The Core Curriculum.* New York: City University of New York, 1981.

Bucknell University. Application to Project on General Education Models, sponsored by the Society for Values in Higher Education, Washington, D.C., 1978.

Cahn, S. M. "Rethinking Requirements." *College Board Review,* Winter 1981-82, pp. 11-13.

California Postsecondary Education Commission. *One World in Common: General Education in a Statewide, National, and Historical Context.* Sacramento: California Postsecondary Education Commission, 1981.

Cannon, W. W., and Roberts, C. V. "Across the Curriculum: The Communication Skills Program at Central College." Paper presented at conference of the American Association for Higher Education, Washington, D.C., March 1981.

Carnegie Foundation for the Advancement of Teaching. *Missions of the College Curriculum: A Contemporary Review with Suggestions.* San Francisco: Jossey-Bass, 1977.

Carnegie Foundation for the Advancement of Teaching. Unpublished data from surveys, 1980.

Casey, B. Personal communication. 18 Apr. 1979.

Chickering, A. W. *Education and Identity*. San Francisco: Jossey-Bass, 1969.

Chickering, A. W., and Associates. *The Modern American College: Responding to the New Realities of Diverse Students and a Changing Society*. San Francisco: Jossey-Bass, 1981.

Cleveland, H. "Forward to Basics." *Change*, May–June 1980, pp. 18–22.

Cleveland, H. "The Leadership of Followers, and Vice Versa." Presentation at the Conference on General Education, Pennsylvania State University, University Park, May 1982.

Cohen, A. M., and Brawer, F. B. "Reviving the Humanities: Data and Direction." In R. Yarrington (Ed.), *Strengthening the Humanities in Community Colleges*. Washington, D.C.: American Association of Community and Junior Colleges, 1980.

Columbia University. "Science: The Missing Link in General Education." *Columbia College Today*, n.d., pp. 19–20.

Commission on the Humanities. *The Humanities in American Life*. Berkeley, Calif.: University of California Press, 1980.

Committee for Corporate Support of Private Universities. *Corporate Support of Private Universities: An Attitude Survey of Top Executives*. New York: Research and Forecasts, Ruder & Finn, 1979.

Conrad, C. F., and Weyer, J. C. *Liberal Education in Transition*. ERIC-AAHE/Higher Education Research Report, no. 3. Washington, D.C.: American Association for Higher Education, 1980.

"The Core Curriculum: What It Means for Undergraduate Education." *Harvard Gazette*, 8 June 1978, p. 7.

Cousins, N. "Editorial: How to Make People Smaller than They Are." *Saturday Review*, Dec. 1978, p. 15.

Coyle, J. Presentation at annual conference of the Association for General and Liberal Studies, Pennsylvania State University, University Park, Nov. 1979.

Cross, K. P. *Beyond the Open Door: New Students to Higher Education*. San Francisco: Jossey-Bass, 1971.

Cross, K. P. "Learner-Centered Curricula." In D. W. Vermilye (Ed.), *Learner-Centered Reform: Current Issues in Higher Education 1975.* San Francisco: Jossey-Bass, 1975.

Crossley, R. "Reflections on Liberal Learning." Unpublished paper, St. Andrews Presbyterian College, 1979.

Davis, M. L. "Evaluation: Assessment, Judgment and Decision." In Project on General Education Models, *General Education: Issues and Resources.* Washington, D.C.: Association of American Colleges, 1980.

Dowd, D. D. "The Uses and Abuses of General Education." *Proceedings of the SUNY Inter-Campus Conference on General Education.* Utica, N.Y.: Community College General Education Association, Mohawk Valley Community College, 1980.

Ducharme, E. "Liberal Arts in Teacher Education: The Perennial Challenge." *Journal of Teacher Education,* May–June 1980, pp. 7–12.

Eckerd College. "Proposal for Revision of the Curriculum." Eckerd College, St. Petersburg, Fla., 1980.

Erikson, E. *Youth: Change and Challenge.* New York: Basic Books, 1963.

Erikson, E. *Identity: Youth and Crisis.* New York: Norton, 1968.

Feldman, K. A., and Newcomb, T. M. *The Impact of College on Students.* San Francisco: Jossey-Bass, 1969.

Feldman, R. "Project GEM and Revising the Basic Program at UNI." *The Innovator* [Center for Program Development, Northeastern Illinois University, Chicago], Jan.–Feb. 1979, p. 2.

"Foreign Language Requirement Reinstated for Frosh in 1982." *Stanford Observer,* May 1981, p. 1.

Frankel, C. "The Unhumanistic Humanities." In *Proceedings of the General Education Seminar.* New York: Columbia University, 1979.

Franklin and Marshall College. "Resolutions of the Faculty of Franklin and Marshall College." Franklin and Marshall College, 1980.

Franklin and Marshall College. "F & M Today." Franklin and Marshall College, 1981.

Friedman, E. A. "Professional Education and the Liberal Arts." Paper delivered at annual meeting of Association of American Colleges, Washington, D.C., Feb. 1979.

Froula, C., and Munich, A. "Women, Literature and the Humanities: A Reply to Carolyn Lougee." *Women's Studies Quarterly,* Summer 1981, pp. 14-15.

Gaff, J. G. *The Cluster College.* San Francisco: Jossey-Bass, 1970.

Gaff, J. G. *Toward Faculty Renewal: Advances in Faculty, Instructional, and Organizational Development.* San Francisco: Jossey-Bass, 1975.

Gaff, J. G. (Ed.). *New Directions for Higher Education: Institutional Renewal Through the Improvement of Teaching,* no. 24. San Francisco: Jossey-Bass, 1978.

Gaff, J. G., and Davis, M. L. "Student Views of General Education." *Liberal Education,* Summer 1981, pp. 112-123.

Gaff, S. S., Festa, C., and Gaff, J. G. *Professional Development: A Guide to Resources.* New Rochelle, N.Y.: Change Magazine, 1978.

Gamson, Z. Workshop session at Project on General Education Models summer conference, University of the Pacific, Stockton, Calif., June 1980.

Garvin, C. C. Remarks to the Council for Financial Aid to Education, Boston, May 1981.

General Education Committee, State University of New York at Buffalo. Application to the Project on General Education Models, sponsored by the Society for Values in Higher Education, Washington, D.C., 1978.

General Education Models Task Force. Report. Valparaiso University, Valparaiso, Ind., Oct. 1980.

Guardo, C. "A Critique of the General Education Movement." Paper presented at annual meeting of the Association of American Colleges, Boston, Jan. 1982.

Guroff, K. S. (Ed.). *Quality in Liberal Learning.* Washington, D.C.: Association of American Colleges, 1981.

Hand, C. Vice-President, University of the Pacific, personal letter, 11 Dec. 1979.

Harvard Committee. *General Education in a Free Society.* Cambridge, Mass.: Harvard University Press, 1945.

Harvard Committee. *Report on the Core Curriculum.* Cambridge, Mass.: Office of the Dean, Faculty of Arts and Sciences, Harvard University, 1978.

Harvard University. *Report on the Core Curriculum.* Cambridge, Mass.: Harvard University, 1979.

Heath, D. H. "Academic Predictors of Adult Maturity and Competence." *Journal of Higher Education,* 1977, pp. 613-632.

Hechinger, F. M., and Hechinger, G. *Growing Up in America.* New York: McGraw-Hill, 1975.

Hefferlin, J. L. *Dynamics of Educational Reform.* San Francisco: Jossey-Bass, 1969.

Hefferlin, J. L. "Hauling Academic Trunks." In U. Walker (Ed.), *Elements Involved in Academic Change.* Washington, D.C.: Association of American Colleges, 1972.

Hill, P. J. "Communities of Learners." Unpublished paper, State University of New York at Stony Brook, 1979.

Hill, P. J. "Medium and Message in General Education." *Liberal Education,* Summer 1981, pp. 129-145.

Holton, G. "Where Is Science Taking Us?" Jefferson Lecture in the Humanities, presented in Washington, D.C., May 1981.

Huber, C. E. "The Dynamics of Change: A Core Humanities Program." *Liberal Education,* May 1977, pp. 159-170.

Hutchins, R. M. *The Higher Learning in America.* New Haven, Conn.: Yale University Press, 1936.

Jacob, P. *Changing Values in College.* New York: Harper, 1957.

Jencks, C., and Riesman, D. *The Academic Revolution.* New York: Doubleday, 1968.

Joint Steering Committee on General Education. Report of the Joint Senate/Administration Steering Committee on General Education. University of California, Davis, May 1980.

Kaplan, M. (Ed.). *What Is an Educated Person?* New York: Praeger, 1980.

Katz, J. "Harvard's Report on the Core Curriculum." *AAHE Bulletin* [American Association for Higher Education], Sept. 1978, p. 5.

Kerr, C. *The Uses of the University.* New York: Harper & Row, 1966.

Kerr, C. "Foreword." In F. Rudolph, *Curriculum: A History of the American Undergraduate Course of Study Since 1636.* San Francisco: Jossey-Bass, 1977.

Klein, T. D., and Gaff, J. G. "Reforming General Education: A Survey." Washington, D.C.: Association of American Colleges, 1982.

Knox, A. *Adult Development and Learning: A Handbook on Individual Growth and Competence in the Adult Years.* San Francisco: Jossey-Bass, 1977.

Kramer, M. "In Defense of Distribution." *Change Magazine,* Nov.–Dec. 1981, pp. 26–31.

Leestma, R. "Global Education." *Forum for Liberal Education* [Association of American Colleges], Jan. 1979, pp. 1–3.

Leitert, E. "Toward a Balanced Curriculum." *Wheaton College Alumnae Magazine,* Spring 1981, pp. 1–7.

Levine, A. *Handbook on Undergraduate Curriculum: Prepared for the Carnegie Council on Policy Studies in Higher Education.* San Francisco: Jossey-Bass, 1978.

Levine, A. *When Dreams and Heros Died: A Portrait of Today's College Student.* San Francisco: Jossey-Bass, 1980a.

Levine, A. *Why Innovation Fails.* Albany: State University of New York Press, 1980b.

Levine, G. "Notes Toward a Humanist Anti-Discipline." *Federation Reports,* Nov. 1978, pp. 2–6.

Lockwood, T. O. "A Skeptical Look at the General Education Movement." *Forum for Liberal Education* [Association of American Colleges], Nov. 1978, p. 1.

Los Medanos College. "A Position Paper: Tier I Criteria and Procedures for Application." Los Medanos College, Pittsburg, Calif., Dec. 1981.

Lougee, C. C. "Women, History, and the Humanities: An Argument in Favor of the General Studies Curriculum." *Women's Studies Quarterly,* Spring 1981, pp. 4–7.

Lowell, A. L. *What a University President Has Learned.* New York: Macmillan, 1938.

McCabe, R. H. "Excellence Is for Everyone: Quality and the Open Door Community College." Presentation at the national conference of the American Association on Higher Education, Washington, D.C., Mar. 1982.

McClelland, D. C. "Testing for Competence Rather than for Intelligence." *American Psychologist,* 1973, pp. 1-14.

Maguire, J. D. "The Disadvantaged Student and the Undergraduate Curriculum at SUNY at Old Westbury." *Liberal Education,* Spring 1980, pp. 78-85.

Maher, T. M. "Congratulations, But . . ." *AAHE Bulletin* [American Association for Higher Education], Sept. 1978, pp. 3-8.

Maher, T. M. "General Education in the Land of the Body Snatchers." Paper presented at annual conference, Association for General and Liberal Studies. University of Dallas, Oct. 1980.

Maher, T. M. Personal letter to Dr. William Lavery, President, Virginia Polytechnic Institute and State University, 10 Feb. 1982.

Masat, F. E. *Computer Literacy in Higher Education.* ERIC-AAHE/Higher Education Research Report, no. 6. Washington, D.C.: American Association for Higher Education, 1981.

Matthews, J. T. "Decline in Education." *Washington Post,* 13 Oct. 1981, p. A-23.

Maxwell, M. *Improving Student Learning Skills: A Comprehensive Guide to Successful Practices and Programs for Increasing the Performance of Underprepared Students.* San Francisco: Jossey-Bass, 1979.

Mayhew, L. *General Education and the Meta-Theory of the Course.* Teaching Resources Center Monograph 10. Davis: University of California, 1980.

Merton, R. K. *Social Theory and Social Structure.* New York: Free Press, 1968.

Middleton, L. "Emphasis on Standards at Miami-Dade Leads to 8,000 Dismissals and Suspensions in 3 Years." *Chronicle of Higher Education,* 2 Feb. 1981, pp. 3-4.

Milton, O. *The Testing and Grading of Students.* New Rochelle, N.Y.: Change Magazine Press, 1976.

Muscatine, C. "University of California—'Strawberry Creek College.' " In *Resources for Change: A Guide to Projects 1977-78.* Fund for the Improvement of Postsecondary Education, Washington, D.C.: U.S. Government Printing Office, 1977.

National Assembly on Foreign Languages and International Studies. *Toward Education With a Global Perspective.* Washington, D.C.: Association of American Colleges, 1980.

National Research Council. *Science for Non-Specialists: The College Years.* Washington, D.C.: National Academy Press, 1982.

National Science Foundation and the Department of Education. *Science and Engineering: Education for the 1980's and Beyond.* Washington, D.C.: U.S. Government Printing Office, 1980.

Nelsen, W. C., and Siegel, M. E. *Effective Approaches to Faculty Development.* Washington, D.C.: Association of American Colleges, 1980.

Neusner, J. "To Weep with Achilles." *Chronicle of Higher Education,* 29 Jan. 1979, p. 40.

Newman, J. *The Idea of University.* New York: Longmans, Green, 1947. (Originally published 1873.)

Nichols, J. Remarks made at session on "Faculty Renewal: The Case for Interdisciplinary Approaches." National Conference of the American Association for Higher Education, Washington, D.C., Apr. 1979.

Northwestern University. *Liberal Education at Northwestern.* Evanston, Ill.: Northwestern University, College of Arts and Sciences, Office of the Dean, 1980.

Oregon State University. "Liberal Studies 100: Connections." Oregon State University, College of Liberal Arts, n.d.

Parlett, M., and Dearden, G. *Introduction to Illuminative Education.* Washington, D.C.: Council of Independent Small Colleges, 1977.

Perry, W. G., Jr. *Forms of Intellectual and Ethical Development in the College Years.* New York: Holt, Rinehart and Winston, 1970.

Peterson, R. E., and Associates. *Lifelong Learning in America: An Overview of Current Practices, Available Resources and Future Prospects.* San Francisco: Jossey-Bass, 1979.

Piaget, J. *The Moral Judgment of the Child.* New York: Free Press, 1965. (Originally published 1932.)

Pollack, R. "From Theory to Praxis." *Columbia College Today.* n.d., pp. 21-24.

President's Commission on Foreign Language and International Studies. *Strength Through Wisdom.* Washington, D.C.: U.S. Government Printing Office, 1979.

Project on General Education Models. *General Education: Issues and Resources.* Washington, D.C.: Association of American Colleges, 1980.

Radzialowski, T. "The Future of Ethnic Studies." *Forum for Liberal Education* [Association of American Colleges], Mar. 1981, pp. 1-3.

Redwine, J. A. "Teaching and Advising in General Education." In Project on General Education Models, *General Education: Issues and Resources.* Washington, D.C.: Association of American Colleges, 1980.

Reynolds, C. Comments in meeting of Project on General Education Models, Washington, D.C., Mar. 1981.

Riesman, D. *On Higher Education: The Academic Enterprise in an Era of Rising Student Consumerism.* San Francisco: Jossey-Bass, 1981.

Riley, G. "The Reform of General Education." *Liberal Education,* Fall 1980, pp. 298-306.

Rives, S. Memorandum to President Watkins. Illinois State University, 16 Jan. 1980.

Rochester Institute of Technology. "General Studies Curriculum Proposal." Rochester Institute of Technology, 1980.

Rosovsky, H. "An Educated Person." *New Yorker,* 4 Dec. 1978, pp. 40-43.

Rosovsky, H. Interview, *Washington Post,* 3 Sept. 1979, p. A-23.

Rudolph, F. *Curriculum: A History of the American Undergraduate Course of Study Since 1636.* San Francisco: Jossey-Bass, 1977.

Sadler, W. A., and Whimbey, A. "Teaching Cognitive Skills: An Objective for Higher Education." *National Forum,* Fall 1980, pp. 43-46.

Sandler, B. R. "Mainstreaming Women's Studies: A Guide for

Change." Grant proposal by Association of American Colleges, Washington, D.C., 1981.

Sanford, N. *Where Colleges Fail: A Study of the Student as a Person.* San Francisco: Jossey-Bass, 1967.

Schmidt, R., and Spanier, B. "Toward a Balanced Curriculum: Integrating the Study of Women into the Liberal Arts." Wheaton College, n.d.

Scriven, M. "Goal Free Evaluation." In E. House (Ed.), *School Evaluation: The Politics and Process.* Berkeley, Calif.: McCutchan, 1973.

Scully, M. "An Interview with David Riesman." *Chronicle of Higher Education,* 30 March 1981, pp. 19-20.

Seamans, R. C., Jr., and Hansen, K. F. "Engineering Education for the Future." *Technology Review,* Feb.-Mar. 1981, pp. 22-23.

Select Committee on the Curriculum. *Education at Amherst Reconsidered.* Amherst, Mass.: Amherst College, 1978.

Shoenberg, R. E. Personal communication, 11 Sept. 1980.

Spitzberg, I. J. "The Professoriate in General Education." *Academe,* December 1980, pp. 426-427.

State University of New York at Stony Brook. "A Learning Community in Social and Ethical Issues in the Life Sciences." State University of New York at Stony Brook, n.d.

Stephenson, J. B. "The Return to Order at Harvard." *AAHE Bulletin* [American Association for Higher Education], September 1978, p. 4.

Stufflebeam, D., and Associates. *Educational Evaluation and Decision Making.* Itasca, Ill.: Peacock, 1971.

Sullivan, M. Memorandum to the faculty, Rochester Institute of Technology, Oct. 18, 1980.

"Taking Foreign Languages Out of the Classroom." *Chronicle of Higher Education,* 22 Sept. 1980, p. 9.

Task Force on the Core Curriculum. *Report on the Core Curriculum.* Cambridge, Mass.: Harvard University, 1978.

Task Force on Implementation of General Education. Report. State University of New York at Buffalo, 1980.

Thomas, L. "The Art of Teaching Science." *New York Times Magazine,* 14 Mar. 1982, pp. 89-93.

Torgersen, P. E. "Engineering Education and the Second Obligation." *Engineering Education,* Nov. 1979, pp. 169-174.

Trillin, A. S., and Associates. *Teaching Basic Skills in College: A Guide to Objectives, Skills, Assessment, Course Content, Teaching Methods, Support Services, and Administration.* San Francisco: Jossey-Bass, 1980.

Trilling, L. "The Uncertain Future of the Humanistic Educational Ideal." In M. Kaplan (Ed.), *What Is an Educated Person?* New York: Praeger, 1980.

Tussman, J. *Experiment at Berkeley.* New York: Oxford University Press, 1969.

University Educational Policy Committee/General Education Models Task Force. Final Report. Northeastern Illinois University, Chicago, 1980.

University of Maryland. "University Studies." Curricular proposal approved by campus senate, University of Maryland, Apr. 19, 1979.

University of the Pacific. Application to participate in the Project on General Education Models, 1978.

University of Southern California. "Procedures and Guidelines for Submission of Courses for Approval for General Education Credit." University of Southern California, Los Angeles, 1980.

University Undergraduate Studies Committee. Proposals for Undergraduate Curriculum Revision. American University, Washington, D.C., 1980.

Unumb, D. "From Task Force to Director: Meditations on a Job Description." *GEM* [General Education Models] *Newsletter,* June 1981, pp. 6-7.

Van Haitsma, G. "A Liberal Arts Faculty Speaks Its Mind on General Education." *GEM Newsletter,* Mar. 1980, pp. 1-4.

Vander Meer, A. W., and Lyons, M. D. "Professional Fields and the Liberal Arts: 1958-78." *Educational Record,* Spring 1979, pp. 197-201.

Warren, J. R. *Sample Questions Assessing Academic Competencies.* Berkeley, Calif.: Educational Testing Service, 1982.

Wee, D. *On General Education: Guidelines for Reform.* New Haven, Conn.: Society for Values in Higher Education, 1981.

Wegener, C. *Liberal Education and the Modern University*. Chicago: University of Chicago Press, 1978.

Whitehead, A. N. *The Aims of Education*. New York: Macmillan, 1929.

Whitla, D. K. Discussion of the Harvard Plan at "Charting the Future of General Education," conference sponsored by the Association of American Colleges, Baltimore, Md., Apr. 1982.

"Why Higher Education Continues to Fail." *Journal of Chemical Education*, Feb. 1979, p. 69.

Wiener, H. "Administering Comprehensive Writing Programs Within Liberal Education." *Forum for Liberal Education*, Apr. 1981, pp. 1-2.

Wilson, J. H. "A Grand Illusion." *Women's Studies Quarterly*, Winter 1981, pp. 5-6.

Wilson, J. Q. "Harvard Core Curriculum: An Inside View." *Change*, Nov. 1978, pp. 40-43.

Wilson, R. C., and others. *College Professors and Their Impact on Students*. New York: Wiley, 1975.

Winkler, K. J. "Decline of History Blamed on Tendency of Scholars to Write for Each Other." *Chronicle of Higher Education*, 21 Apr. 1980a, p. 10.

Winkler, K. J. "Wanted: A History That Pulls Things Together." *Chronicle of Higher Education*, 7 July 1980b, p. 3.

Winkler, K. J. "With a 'Judicious' Eye on the Past, Historians Consider the State of Their Art." *Chronicle of Higher Education*, 22 Sept. 1980c, pp. 17-18.

Winkler, K. J. "World History Contests with 'Western Civ.' as Colleges Debate Role of Survey Courses." *Chronicle of Higher Education*, 27 Jan. 1982, p. 7.

Winter, D. G. "Defining and Measuring the Competencies of a Liberal Education." *Current Issues in Higher Education*, no. 5. Washington, D.C.: American Association for Higher Education, 1979.

Winter, D. G., McClelland, D. C., and Stewart, A. J. *A New Case for the Liberal Arts: Assessing Institutional Goals and Student Development*. San Francisco: Jossey-Bass, 1981.

Wittig, S. Personal communication, 6 June 1981.

Youngblood, D. " 'U' Business College to Expand Student's Liberal Arts Training." *Minneapolis Star Tribune*, 1981, p. A-24.

Index

A

Academic disciplines, and general education, 32-42

Academic regulations, and curricular organization, 83-84

Accreditation, and professional education, 28, 176

Administration: by chief academic officer, 135-136; by committees, 138-140; by departments, 136-137; by directors, 140-142; of general education, 135-142; by separate college, 137-138

Adults, as students, 16, 50

Affect, in global perspective, 92, 93-94

Albion College, 213

Allentown College, 218

Alverno College, agenda focus at, 174

American Association of University Professors, 115

American College Testing Program, 161

American Historical Association, 40

American University, 209, 221; distinctiveness of, 70; internships at, 118; University Undergraduate Studies Committee of, 118, 233

Amherst College, xii, 212; freshman experience at, 86-87; Select Committee on the Curriculum at, 86, 232

Antioch College, 217, 221; cooperative learning at, 118-119; global perspective at, 98; restructuring

of, 170; women and minorities at, 98
Appalachian State University, 216
Aquinas, T., 48
Aquinas College, 213
Aristotle, 48
Arizona State University, women's studies and, 98
Arkansas at Monticello, University of, 208
Armstrong, F. H., 71, 221
Arons, A. B., 38, 221
Ashby, E., 64, 221
Association of American Colleges (AAC), xiv, xix, 45, 120; survey by, 78, 79, 80, 81, 82, 87, 103, 116-117, 148, 197-206
Assumption College, 212
Astin, A., 149, 221
Atlantic Christian College, 216

B

Babson College, 212
Bach, J. S., 80
Bailey, S. K., xii, 4, 10-11, 63, 221
Bailyn, B., 40
Baker University, 211
Baltimore, Community College of, 212
Barat College, 210
Bard College, 215; and idealist philosophy, 3
Barrows, T. S., 92, 161, 222
Bartell, E., xix
Bay Area Writing Program, 89
Beaver College, 218; writing at, 89
Beck, R. E., 45-46, 222
Beethoven, L., 80
Belknap, R., 178, 222
Bell, D., 63, 164, 222
Bell & Howell Educational Group, 210
Bell System, liberal arts majors in, 45-46
Bennington College, and progressivism, 4

Berea College, 211
Bergquist, W. H., 121, 222
Bernstein, A., 34, 222
Berry, D., 108, 222
Bethel College, 213
Bethune-Cookman College, 209
Bird, C., 147, 222
Birmingham Southern College, 208
Birnbaum, N., 41, 222
Blackburn, R., 9, 222
Blake, H., xviii
Blake, J. H., 49-50, 222
Bloom, B. S., 90, 222
Bloomfield College, 214
Bonham, G., 97, 222
Boston University, 212
Botstein, L., 3, 223
Bowen, H. R., 149-150, 223
Bowling Green State University, 217
Boyer, E. L., xii, 1, 5, 11, 32, 68, 81, 163, 174, 193, 223
Branscomb, H., 60-61, 223
Brawer, F. B., 34-35, 224
Bridgeport, University of, 209
Brigham Young University, 219; competency approach at, 119
Brooklyn College, 215, 223; global perspective at, 93
Brown University, language not required at, 95
Bucknell University, 223; and general education and specialization, 63-64; in Project GEM, xiii, 218
Bunting, C., xix
Bush Foundation, 145
Business community, and general education, 45-46

C

Cahn, S. M., 66, 223
California: community colleges in, 192; secondary school topics in, 19
California at Berkeley, University of: enclaves at, 166; evaluation

of Strawberry Creek College at, 156; writing at, 18, 89
California at Davis, University of, 208; Joint Steering Committee on General Education of, 65, 227; and writing skills, 65
California at Los Angeles, University of, values at, 101
California at Riverside, University of, 208; comparative analyses at, 97
California at Santa Cruz, University of, 208: core curriculum at, 11; minority students at, 49
California Lutheran College, 208; faculty development at, 71, 168; integrative curriculum at, 104-105
California Postsecondary Education Commission, 192, 223
California State University and Colleges, 208
Cannon, W. W., 89, 223-224
Carleton College, 213
Carnegie Council for Policy Studies in Higher Education, 6, 10
Carnegie Foundation for the Advancement of Teaching, xii, 1, 9, 170, 223
Carnegie-Mellon University, 218; evaluation at, 155-156
Carroll College (Montana), 214
Carroll College (Wisconsin), in Project GEM, xiii, 220
Case Western Reserve University, 217
Casey, B., 224
Casper College, 220
Catonsville Community College: amount of general education at, 79; interdisciplinary studies at, 80; in Project GEM, xiii, 212
Cedar Valley College, 219
Centenary College of Louisiana, 212
Central College, skills at, 89
Central Florida, University of, 209
Central State University, 217

Central Wesleyan College, 218
Centre College, 211
Chapman College, 208
Chase, A., 56
Chemeketa Community College, 217
Chicago, University of: curriculum at, 77; and essentialism, 5; general education at, 17; and integration of knowledge, 176; language requirement at, 95; leadership at, 166, 170
Chickering, A. W., xii, 90, 149, 224
Churchill, W., 180
Citadel Military College of South Carolina, 218
City College of Chicago, 210
Clark, J. L., 92, 161, 222
Clark College, 210
Clayton Junior College, 210
Cleveland, H., 42, 96, 224
Clinton, R., xviii, 171
Cohen, A. M., 34-35, 224
Colgate University, 215
College impact, research on, 149-154
College Outcome Measures Project (COMP), 161
Colorado at Boulder, University of, 209
Colorado College, 209
Colorado School of Mines, 209
Colorado State Board for Community Colleges and Occupational Education, and external criterion for evaluation, 156
Columbia Christian College, 217
Columbia University: faculty development at, 71; general education at, xii, 17, 164; language requirement at, 95; sciences at, 37, 224; teaching companies at, 178; values at, 100
Commission on the Humanities, 2, 33, 224
Committee for Corporate Support of Private Universities, 45, 224
Committees for general education:

composition of, 139-140; tasks of, 138-139
Community colleges: amount of general education in, 78-79; general education in, 17; humanities in, 34-35; and reform, 192; standards in, 51
Connecticut, secondary school topics in, 19
Conrad, C. F., xii, xix, 224
Core curriculum, as general education organization, 10-11
Cornell University, 215; language requirement at, 95
Council of Independent Colleges, 158, 230
Council of Writing Program Administrators, 88
Courses: criteria for, 110-114, 129-134; and faculty development, 114-115; for general education, 108-115; issues of, 110-112; metatheories on, 109-110; for nonmajors, 112; practices related to, 114-115; writing in, 112-113
Cousins, N., 46-47, 224
Coyle, J., 26-27, 224-225
Cross, K. P., xviii, 15, 60, 224
Crossley, R., 70, 225
Culhane, B., xviii
Curie, M., 80
Curricular reform: critics of, 182-183; faculty approval for, 180-185; faculty development contrasted with, 123-124; implementation of, 163-186; preparation for, 166-168; procedures for, 171-174; program planning for, 177-180; strategies for, 164-166; support for, 171-172; task definition in, 169-170; task force for, 171; and understanding general education, 174-177
Curriculum: and academic regulations, 83-84; amount of general education in, 77-79; approaches

to, 60-62; coherence of, 67; concept of, 59; content of, 84-106; courses, teaching, and faculty development related to, 107-134; freshman experience in, 85-87; global perspective in, 92-97; integration of, 103-106; length of general education in, 81-82; organization of, 76-84; patterns in, 76-106; philosophy of, 59-75; review of existing, 167-168; skills in, 50-51, 87-92; as social contract, x; standards in, 82-83; structure of, 79-81; tenets of philosophy of, 62-73; values in, 99-102; women's and minorities' perspectives in, 97-99
Curtis, M., xix

D

Dakota Wesleyan University, 218
Dallas County Community College District, 219
Darwin, C., 80
David Lipscomb College, 219; values at, 102
Davidson College, 216
Davis, M. L., xviii, 52, 155, 156, 178, 225, 226
Davis and Elkins College, 220
Dayton, University of, 217
Daytona Beach Community College, 209
Dearden, G., 157, 230
Degas, E., 80
Dennison University, comparative analyses at, 97
Denver, Community College of: amount of general education at, 79; both-and thinking at, 178-179; faculty involvement at, 173; in Project GEM, xiii, 209
DePaul University, 210
DePauw University, 210, faculty development at, 125; skills at, 89-90

Dewey, J., 4, 62

Directors, for general education, 140-142

Disciplines, academic, and general education, 32-42

Distribution requirements: as general education organization, 10; ineffectiveness of, 76-77

Doane College, 214

Dominican College (California), 208

Dominican College (New York), 215

Dorrill, W., 185

Dowd, D. D., 19, 225

Drake University, 211

Drew University, 214

Ducharme, E., 225

Duke University, 216

Dutchess Community College, 215

E

Earlham College, 210

East Carolina University, 216

East Texas State University, 219

Eastern Connecticut State College, 209

Eastern Mennonite College, 220

Eastern Michigan College, 213

Eastern Montana College, 214

Eckerd College, 209, 225; faculty involvement at, 173; values at, 102

Educational Testing Service, 160-161

Einstein, A., 80

Eisenhower College, 215

Electives, as general education organization, 11

Elon College, 216

Empire State College: and electives, 11; as new institution, 170

Erie Community College, 215

Erikson, E., 90, 225

Eskow, S., 94

Essentialism, and general education, 4-5, 7

Evaluation: approaches to, 154-158; on college impact, 149-154; decision-oriented, 156; by external criterion, 156; formative 147; of general education, 146-162; for general education courses, 119-120; goal-based, 155; goal-free, 155-156; illuminative, 157; instruments for, 158-161; issues in, 157-158; and pilot testing, 158; and political support, 148; portrayal, 156-157; rationale for, 147-148; summative, 148

Evansville, University of, 211

Evergreen State College, as new institution, 170

Exxon Corporation, 45

Exxon Education Foundation, xiii, xiv, xix, 145

F

Faculty: approval of, for curricular reform, 180-185; culture of, 13-14, 23-24; educating, for curricular reform, 168, 183; recruiting of, 72-73, 184-185

Faculty development: accomplishments of, 121-122; and courses, 114-115; examples of, 124-125; and general education, xv, 71, 120-128; general education reform contrasted with, 123-124; goal of, 123

Fairlie, H., 56

Feldman, K. A., 149, 150, 151, 225

Feldman, R., xviii-xix, 164-165, 225

Festa, C., 121, 226

Finance: and funding agencies, 145; for general education, 142-146; by reallocation, 144-145

Fitchburg State College, 212

Flaming Rainbow University, 217

Florida, faculty development in, 114

Florida, University of, 210; values at, 101

Florida Agricultural and Mechanical University: faculty development at, 114; implementation at, 184; in Project GEM, xiii, 209; skills at, 90

Fordham University, 215

Fort Hays State University, 211

Foster, M., xix

Franck, B., xviii

Frankel, C., 34, 225

Franklin and Marshall College, 218, 225; course criteria at, 129-134

Franklin Pierce College, 214

Frascella, W., xix

Freshmen, curriculum for, 85-87

Freud, S., 42, 48, 80

Friedman, E. A., 26, 226

Frostburg State College, 212

Froula, C., 48-49, 226

Fund for the Improvement of Postsecondary Education (FIPSE), xii, xiii, xix, 145

G

Gaff, D., xix

Gaff, J. G., 52, 121, 178, 198, 226, 228

Gaff, S. S., 121, 226

Galileo, G., 38

Gamson, Z., 147, 226

Gardner-Webb College, 216; and religious curriculum, 70

Garvin, C. C., 45, 226

General education: and academic disciplines, 32-42; accomplishments in, 189-191; administration of, 135-142; administrative responsibility for, 24-25; amount of, 8-9, 77-79; attention to, ix-x, 1-2; case example of development of, 73-75; and common

learning, 67-68; concept of, 7-8; conditions fostering goals of, 152-154; constraints on, 71-72; controversy over, 1-58; costs of, 142-143; current progress of, 187-196; curricular philosophy of, 59-75; economies of, 143-144; evaluation of, 146-162; and faculty development, xv, 71, 120-128; finance for, 142-146; future of, 191-192, 195-196; and graduate training, 69; Harvard Plan for, 53-58; and historical trends, 11-13, 193-194; ideal of, 2-8; implementation of, 163-186; innovations in, 47-51; and institutional character, 69-70; institutional directory for, 207-220; institutional view of, 20-25; issues in, 1-29; length of, 81-82; need for, xvii; optimism about, 194-196; organization of, 9-11; philosophies of, 3-7; practices in, 59-162; and priorities in knowledge, 65; professional education related to, 25-29, 64-65; program operation for, 21; rationale for, 21-22; recent scholarship in, 70-71; and required subjects, 66; responsibility for, 68-69; and societal changes, 18-20; specialization related to, 63-64; staffing for, 72-73, 184-185; standards for, 66-67; student attitudes toward, 51-53; support for, 135-162; tarnishing of, 8-20; and undergraduate education, xv; understanding, 174-177; utility of, 44-47; viewpoints on, 30-53; vocational value of, 27-28

George Mason University, 220

Gettysburg College, 218

Global perspective, curriculum for, 92-97

Goethe, J. W., 80

Gonzaga University, writing at, 90

Goshen College, global perspective at, 94
Governors State University, 210
Graceland College, 211
Graduate Record Examination, 159
Graduate training, and general education, 69
Grinnell College, 211
Guardo, C., 191, 226
Guroff, K. S., 120, 226
Gustavus Adolphus College, 213
Gwynedd-Mercy College, 218

H

Hand, C., xix, 88, 226
Hansen, K. F., 28, 232
Hartford, University of, 209
Harvard Committee, ix, x, 18, 31-32, 226-227
Harvard University, xii, 17-18, 213, 227; criticism of core program at, 53-58; discussion sections at, 114; funding at, 145; general education structure at, 79; language requirement at, 95; new and old courses at, 113; and professional education, 26; requirements at, 66, 179; Task Force on the Core Curriculum of, 1, 54, 232; time spent by, 172, 180
Heath, D. H., 158, 227
Hechinger, F. M., xii, 179, 223, 227
Hechinger, G., 179, 227
Hefferlin, J. L., xix, 136, 170, 227
Hendrix College, 208
Hill, P. J., 67, 103-104, 227
Hiram College, 217
Hobart and William Smith Colleges, 215; integrative curriculum at, 106
Holton, G., 36, 227
Holy Cross, College of the, 212
Hood College, 212
Houston, University of, 219

Huber, C. E., 126-127, 227
Humanities: in curriculum, 84; general education role of, 33-36
Hutchins, R. M., 4-5, 6, 26, 62, 64, 87, 166, 170, 227

I

Idealism: and general education, 3, 6-7; practical, 62-73
Illinois Central College, 210; reasoning skills at, 91
Illinois State University, 210; academic regulations at, 83
Indiana State University, 210
Indiana University at South Bend, in Project GEM, xiii, 210
Indiana University of Pennsylvania, 218
Institutions: character of, and general education, 69-70; differentiation of, x, 16-18; directory of, 207-220; general education view of, 20-25; mission of, 167
Intellectual Flexibility in Analysis of Argument, 160
Inter-American University of Puerto Rico, 218
Interdisciplinary studies: and curricular structure, 80-81; general education role of, 42-44
Iona College, 215
Iowa Wesleyan College, 211

J

Jacob, P., 149, 150-151, 227
James Madison University, 220
Jamestown College, 217
Jencks, C., 13, 227
John Brown University, 208
Johnson, C., xix
Johnson, R., xix
Johnson C. Smith University, 216
Johnson County Community Col-

lege, 211; global perspective at, 96

Joyce, J., 80

K

Kalamazoo College, global perspective at, 94
Kansas Wesleyan College, 211
Kaplan, M., 1, 5, 68, 174, 223, 227
Katz, J., xviii, 57, 227
Kean College of New Jersey, 214
Keene State College, 214
Kendall, P., xviii
Kentucky, University of, 212
Kenyon College, 217
Kerr, C., xii, 5-6, 59, 227-228
Keuka, College, 215
Klein, S. F., 92, 161, 222
Klein, T. D., xiv, 198, 228
Knowledge: in global perspective, 92, 93; priorities of, 65
Knox, A., 16, 228
Kramer, M., 81, 228
Kuhns, R., 178, 222

L

La Guardia Community College, 215
Lafayette College, 218
Lake County, College of, 210
Lakeland College, 220
Language, in global perspective, 92, 94-95
Leestma, R., 92, 228
Leitert, E., 99, 228
Levine, A., xii, xviii, xix, 5, 10, 11, 35, 44, 81, 163, 165-166, 193, 223, 228
Levine, G., 228
Lewis and Clark College, 217
Liberal arts, in curriculum, 84
Lilly, D., 27
Lindquist, J., xviii

Literacy, and general education, 31-32
Livingston, R., 63
Lockwood, T. O., 170, 228
Lord Fairfax Community College, 220
Loretto Heights College, 209; Project Transition at, 85-86
Los Medanos College, 208; course criteria at, 110-111, 228
Lougee, C. C., 47-48, 228
Louisville, University of, 212
Lowell, A. L., 179-180, 228
Loyola University, 212
Lynchburg College, 220
Lynn, K., 56
Lyons, M. D., 25, 44, 233

M

Macalester College, 213
McCabe, R. H., 50-51, 82, 228
McClelland, D. C., 158, 159, 229, 234
McNeill, W., 40-41
Maguire, J. D., xviii, 67, 229
Maher, T. M., 8, 10, 56, 119, 141-142, 229
Marian College, 211
Marian College of Fond Du Lac, 220
Maricopa Community College, 208
Marion College, 211
Marist College, 215
Mars Hill College, agenda focus at, 174
Marx, G., 56-57
Marx, K., 80
Mary Washington College, 220
Marycrest College, 211
Maryland at College Park, University of, 212, 233; experiential learning at, 118; integrative curriculum at, 105
Marymount Manhattan College, 215

Maryville College, 219
Maryville State College, 217
Masat, F. E., 39, 229
Massachusetts, University of, 213
Massachusetts Institute of Technology: language not required at, 95; and professional education, 26; School of Engineering of, 28
Matthews, J. T., 31, 229
Maxwell, M., 88, 229
Mayhew, L., 63, 108-110, 229
Mellon Foundation, 145
Mercer County Community College, 214
Mercer University, 210
Mercy College of Detroit, 213
Meredith College, 216
Merton, R. K., xvi, 61, 229
Metropolitan State College, 209
Meyers, P., xix
Miami-Dade Community College, 209; amount of general education at, 79; standards at, 51, 82-83
Michigan, secondary school topics in, 19
Michigan, University of, 213; Residential College at, 103, 165
Michigan State University, 213; University College at, 11, 138
Middlesex County College, 214
Middleton, L., 82, 229
Milliken University, 210
Milton, O., 158, 229
Minnesota, University of, College of Business Administration at, 27-28
Minority students: curricular perspective of, 97-99; and general education, 49-50; and humanities, 34; as new students, 16; and social sciences, 42
Mission, institutional, and curricular reform, 167
Mississippi Industrial College, 214
Mohawk Valley Community College, 215

Monmouth College, 214
Montana College of Mineral Science and Technology, 214
Montana State University, 214
Monterey Peninsula College, 208
Montevallo, University of, 208
Montgomery College, 212
Moorhead State College, 213
Morris, R., 40
Morris College, 218
Moskowitz, H., xix
Mount Marty College, 218
Mount St. Joseph, College of, 217
Munich, A., 48-49, 226
Murray State University, 212
Muscatine, C., 166, 229

N

National Assembly on Foreign Languages and International Studies, 93, 230
National Endowment for the Humanities, 145
National Project IV: Examining the Varieties of Liberal Education, xii
National Research Council, 36, 230
National Science Foundation, 2, 230
Nazareth College, 213
Nebraska at Lincoln, University of, 214; writing in courses at, 83, 112-113
Nelsen, W. C., 121, 230
Neusner, J., 35-36, 230
New York, secondary school topics in, 19
Newcomb, T. M., 149, 150, 151, 225
Newcomb College, values at, 102
Newman, J., 3, 230
Newton, I., 38
Niagara County Community College, 215

Nichols, J., 71, 230
North Carolina at Asheville, University of, 216
North Carolina at Chapel Hill, University of, 216
North Carolina at Charlotte, University of, 217
North Carolina at Wilmington, University of, 217
North Dakota, University of, 217
North Dakota State University, 217
North Florida Junior College, 209
North Texas State University, 219
Northeastern Illinois University: and constraints, 71-72; faculty approval at, 181; general education director at, 140-141; in Project GEM, xiii, 210; qualities desired at, 175; responsibility for general education at, 68; and standards, 66-67; University Educational Policy Committee/ General Education Models Task Force of, 67, 68, 72, 233
Northeastern University, 213
Northern Colorado, University of, 209
Northwest Area Foundation, 145
Northwest Community College, 220
Northwest Nazarene College, 210
Northwestern College, 211
Northwestern University, 210, 230; structure of general education at, 80
Notre Dame College of Ohio, 217
Notre Dame of Maryland, College of, 212

O

Oakland City College, 211
Oakland University, 213
O'Connell, B., 56
O'Connell, W., xxi
Ohio Dominican University, 217

Ohio State University, languages at, 95-96
Ohio University, 217; implementation at, 185
Ohio Wesleyan University, 217
Olivet College, 213
Oregon State University: freshman experience at, 85, 117, 230; progress report at, 171; in Project GEM, xiii, 217; teaching at, 117
Organization of American Historians, 40, 98

P

Pacific, University of the: faculty approval at, 183, 184; guidelines at, 73-75; in Project GEM, xiii, 208, 233; skills at, 88
Pacific Christian College, 208
Pacific Lutheran University, 220; faculty development at, 126-127; integrative curriculum at, 103
Parlett, M., 157, 230
Payton, R., xix
Pembroke State University, 216
Pennsylvania, University of, 218; language requirement at, 95
Pennsylvania State University, 218; School of Business at, 26-27
Perry, W. G., Jr., 90, 230
Peters, J., xix
Peterson, R. E., 230-231
Phillips, S. R., 121, 222
Philosophy: of curriculum, 59-75; of general education, 3-7
Piaget, J., 90, 230
Pittsburg State University, 211
Pollack, R., 37, 231
Portland State University, 217
Practical idealism, tenets of, 62-73
Pragmatism, and general education, 5-6, 7
President's Commission on Foreign

Language and International Studies, 1-2, 231
Princeton University, language requirement at, 95
Professional and Organizational Development (POD) Network in Higher Education, 121
Professional education: and accreditation, 28, 176; general education related to, 25-29, 64-65
Progressivism, and general education, 4, 7
Project on General Education Models (GEM), xii, xiii-xiv, xiii, 231; applicants to, 20-25; resource guide of, 18, 177; survey by, 178; task forces for, 169, 171
Project on Quality Undergraduate Education, 158, 185
Project on Redefining the Meaning and Purpose of Baccalaureate Degrees, xix
Puerto Rico, University of, 218
Puget Sound, University of, 220
Purdue University Calumet, 211

Q

Quality in Liberal Learning Project, 120
Quehl, G., 121, 222

R

Radzialowski, T., 98, 231
Ramapo College, global perspective at, 93
Redwine, J. A., 116, 231
Reform. See Curricular reform
Reidel, M., xix
Reynolds, C., xviii, 231
Rhode Island, University of, 218; skills at, 91
Richard Bland College of the College of William and Mary, 220

Ricks College, 210
Rider College, 214
Riesman, D., 6, 13, 227, 231
Riley, G., xviii, 60, 231
Riley, P. P., xix
Rives, S., 83-84, 231
Roberts, C. V., 89, 223-224
Rochester Institute of Technology, 231; amount of general education at, 78; curriculum review at, 168; integrative curriculum at, 104; in Project GEM, xv, 215; staffing at, 73
Rockland Community College, global perspective at, 94, 96
Rockmont College, 209
Rosovsky, H., 55, 58, 231
Rudolph, F., xii, 12-13, 231
Russell Sage College, 215
Rutgers University, 214

S

Sadler, W. A., 90-91, 231
St. Andrews Presbyterian College, 216; case study at, 117-118; core curriculum of, 70; and institutional character, 69-70; new and old courses at, 113
Saint Anselm's College, 214
Saint Francis, College of, 210
St. John's College, general education at, 17
St. John's University, 213
Saint Joseph College (Connecticut), 209
Saint Joseph's College (Indiana), 211; faculty development at, 71; interdisciplinary studies at, 81; values at, 102
St. Mary College, 211
St. Mary's Dominican College, 212
St. Meinrad Archabbey, 211
St. Olaf College, 213; global perspective at, 93; Paracollege at, 103, 179

St. Teresa, College of, 213
San Diego, University of, 208
San Diego State University, 208
Sandler, B. R., 99, 231
Sanford, N., 75, 232
Santa Clara, University of, 209
Santa Fe Community College, 209
Sarah Lawrence College, and progressivism, 4
Schilling, D., 97-98
Schmidt, R., 99, 232
Scholastic Aptitude Test, 159
Schramm, D., 168
Sciences, general education role of, 36-39
Scriven, M., 155, 232
Scully, M., 6, 232
Seamans, R. C., Jr., 28, 232
Seton Hall University, 215
Shaw College at Detroit, 213
Shoenberg, R. E., 105, 232
Siegel, M. E., 121, 230
Siena Heights College, 213
Simmons College, 213
Simpson College, 211
Sinte Gleska College, 218
Skane, D., xix
Skills programs, and general education, 50-51, 87-92
Sloan Foundation, 39
Smith, D., xviii
Smith, J., 176
Snow, C. P., 24
Social sciences, general education role of, 39-42
Society, changes in, 18-20
Society for Values in Higher Education, xiii, xviii, xix
Somerset County College, 215
Sonoma State University, Hutchins School of Liberal Studies at, 103
Southeastern Massachusetts University, 213
Southern California, University of, 209; course criteria at, 112, 114, 233; general education commit-
tee at, 139-140; structure of general education at, 79
Southern Illinois University, 210; partisanship avoided at, 179
Southern Louisiana, University of, 212
Southern Maine, University of, 212
Southern Utah State University, 219
Southwest State University, 214
Southwest Texas State University, 219
Spanier, B., 99, 232
Specialization: general education related to, 63-64; and sciences, 37; trends in, 12-13
Spelman College, 210; mission of, 167
Spitzberg, I. J., 115, 142, 232
Springfield Technical Community College, 213
Standards: in curriculum, 82-83; for general education, 66-67
Stanford University, 208; language requirement at, 95; and women, 47-48
State University of New York (SUNY) Agricultural and Technical College of Alfred, 216
SUNY at Binghamton, 215
SUNY at Stony Brook, 216, 232; integrative curriculum at, 103-104; learning communities at, 67, 100-101, 104, 179; values at, 100-101
SUNY College at Brockport: faculty approval at, 181; freshman experience at, 85, 114; in Project GEM, xiii, 216; structure of general education at, 80; values at, 101-102
SUNY College at Buffalo, 216; General Education Committee of, 176, 226; reallocation at, 144-145; specialization at, 176; Task Force on Implementation of General Education of, 144, 232

SUNY College at Fredonia, 216
SUNY College at New Paltz, 216
SUNY College at Old Westbury, 216; integrated electives at, 67, 104
SUNY College at Oswego, 216
SUNY College at Plattsburgh, 216
SUNY College at Potsdam, 216
Stephens College, 214
Stephenson, J. B., 56-57, 232
Stevenson, A., 26
Stewart, A. J., 159, 234
Stewart, D., xviii
Strayer, R., xix, 80
Students: adult, 16, 50; attitudes of, toward general education, 51-53; college impact on, 149-154; minority, 16, 34, 42, 49-50, 97-99; new, 14-16, 22-23; women, 16, 34, 42, 48-49, 86, 97-99
Stufflebeam, D., 156, 232
Sullivan, M., xix, 73, 232
Survey courses, and faculty culture, 14
Sweeney, R., xix
Syracuse University, 216; clusters of courses at, 179; faculty development at, 114-115, 125; science at, 39

T

Tacoma Community College, 220
Taylor University, 211
Teaching, for general education, 115-120
Tennessee at Chattanooga, University of, 219
Tennessee at Knoxville, University of: ethnic and women's studies at, 97-98; faculty approval at, 168, 183
Tennessee at Martin, University of, 219
Tennessee Higher Education Commission, 60-61

Test of Thematic Analysis, 159-160
Texas A & M University, 219
Texas at Arlington, University of, 219
Texas Tech University, 219
Theories: and metatheories, 109-110; of middle range, xvi, 61
Thiel College, 218
Thomas, L., 38-39, 154, 232
Thomas College, 212
Torgersen, P. E., 28, 29, 233
Touro College, 216
Towson State University, 212
Toynbee, A., 80
Trillin, A. S., 233
Trilling, L., 115, 233
Trinity College, 219
Tufts University, 213
Tulane University, 212
Tussman, J., 166, 233

U

U.S. Department of Education, 2, 230
Unumb, D., 140-141, 233
Utah State University, 219
Utilitarianism, and general education, 44-47

V

Valencia Community College, 210; interdisciplinary studies at, 103
Valley City State College, 217
Valparaiso University: amount of general education at, 78; course criteria at, 111-112; General Education Models Task Force at, 226; professional education at, 175-176; in Project GEM, xiii, 211; series of reports at, 173
Values, in curriculum, 99-102
Vanderbilt University, 219
Van Eyck, J., 80

Van Haitsma, G., xix, 178, 233
Vander Meer, A. W., 25, 44, 233
Vassar College, 216
Vermont, University of, 219
Virginia, University of, 220
Virginia Commonwealth University, 220
Virginia Polytechnic Institute and State University, 220; and professional education, 28

W

Wagner College, 216
Wanton, E., xix, 184
Warner Pacific College, 218
Warren, J. R., 160, 233
Wartburg College, 211
Washington, University of, 220
Washington and Lee University, 220
Washington State University, 220
Watson, W., xix
Weber State College, 219
Webern, A., 80
Wee, D., xii, xviii, 100, 233
Wegener, C., 12, 234
West Virginia, University of, 220
Western Carolina University, 217
Western Illinois University, 210
Western International University, 208
Western Michigan University, 213; College of General Studies at, 137
Western State College of Colorado, 209
Western Wyoming College, 220
Westmar College, 211
Weyer, J. C., xii, 224
Wheaton College, women's studies at, 99

Whimbey, A., 90-91, 231
Whitehead, A. N., 4, 234
Whitla, D. K., 57, 234
Wichita State University, 211
Widener College, 218
Wiener, H., 88, 234
William and Mary, College of, 219
William Jewel College, 214
William Patterson College of New Jersey, 214
Wilson, J. H., 49, 234
Wilson, J. Q., 55-56, 180, 234
Wilson, R. C., 151, 234
Winkler, K. J., 40-41, 98, 234
Winter, D. G., 159, 234
Winthrop College, 218
Wisconsin, University of, Integrated Liberal Studies at, 165
Wisconsin-Green Bay, University of, faculty development at, 71
Wisconsin-Parkside, University of, 220
Wisconsin-Platteville, University of, 220
Wittig, S., xviii, 102, 235
Women: curricular perspective of, 97-99; and humanities, 34; as new students, 16; reentry of, 86; and social sciences, 42; studies for, in core curriculum, 48-49

Y

Yale University, language requirement at, 95
Yankton College, 219
York College of Pennsylvania, 218
Youngblood, D., 27, 235
Yount, R., xviii